Mastering
Accounting skills

Palgrave Master Series

Accounting
Accounting Skills
Advanced English Language
Advanced Pure Mathematics
Arabic
Basic Management
Biology
British Politics
Business Communication
Business Environment
C Programming
C++ Programming
Chemistry
COBOL Programming
Communication
Computing
Counselling Skills
Counselling Theory
Customer Relations
Database Design
Delphi Programming
Desktop Publishing
e-Business
Economic and Social History
Economics
Electrical Engineering
Electronics
Employee Development
English Grammar
English Language
English Literature
Fashion Buying and Merchandising
    Management
Fashion Marketing
Fashion Styling
Financial Management
Geography
Global Information Systems
Globalization of Business

Human Resource Management
International Trade
Internet
Java
Language of Literature
Management Skills
Marketing Management
Mathematics
Microsoft Office
Microsoft Windows, Novell NetWare and
    UNIX
Modern British History
Modern European History
Modern United States History
Modern World History
Networks
Novels of Jane Austen
Organisational Behaviour
Pascal and Delphi Programming
Philosophy
Psychology
Physics
Poetry
Practical Criticism
Psychology
Public Relations
Shakespeare
Social Welfare
Sociology
Spanish
Statistics
Strategic Management
Systems Analysis and Design
Team Leadership
Theology
Twentieth-Century Russian History
Visual Basic
World Religions

www.palgravemasterseries.com

Palgrave Master Series

Series Standing Order ISBN 0-333-69343-4
(outside North America only)

You can receive future titles in this series as they are published by placing a standing order. Please contact your bookseller or, in case of difficulty, write to us at the address below with your name and address, the title of the series and the ISBN quoted above.

Customer Services Department, Macmillan Distribution Ltd
Houndmills, Basingstoke, Hampshire RG21 6XS, England

Mastering
Accounting skills
Third Edition

Margaret Nicholson

First edition 1989
Second edition 2000
Third edition 2006

Published by
PALGRAVE MACMILLAN
Houndmills, Basingstoke, Hampshire RG21 6XS and
175 Fifth Avenue, New York, N.Y. 10010
Companies and representatives throughout the world

PALGRAVE MACMILLAN is the global academic imprint of the Palgrave Macmillan
division of St. Martin's Press, LLC and of Palgrave Macmillan Ltd. Macmillan® is a
registered trademark in the United States, United Kingdom and other countries.
Palgrave is a registered trademark in the European Union and other countries.

ISBN–13: 978–1–4039–9270–3
ISBN–10: 1–4039–9270–3

This book is printed on paper suitable for recycling and made from fully managed and
sustained forest sources.

A catalogue record for this book is available from the British Library.

10   9   8   7   6   5   4   3   2
15   14   13   12   11   10   09   08   07

Printed and bound in China

■ ⩔ Contents

100510498

657

Nic

Acknowledgement

Sincere thanks are due to my husband David for his help and support.

■ ▼ Introduction

This third edition of *Mastering Accounting Skills* has been fully revised and now aims to cover the latest developments in the assessment requirements of the manual units for OCR (Oxford, Cambridge and RSA) Level 1 Certificate in Bookkeeping and Levels 2 and 3 Certificates in Accounting. It also provides the underpinning knowledge for London Chamber of Commerce and Industry and Pitman examination boards as well as those preparing for a range of professional examinations in accounting.

Mastering Accounting Skills is designed for complete beginners with no prior knowledge or experience. Features of the text are straightforward explanations combined with illustrated examples to help you gain a real understanding of the subject. There are many practical assignments for you to complete together with help on how to approach them. At the end of each chapter there is a section headed *'Points to Remember'* – these will enable you to focus on the main topics.

An answer section is provided at the back of the book giving solutions to all the assignments – answers for some assignments are fully displayed in each chapter. You will be able to see if you have drawn up your accounts in the correct way as well as checking your figures.

MARGARET NICHOLSON

■ Ⅴ ▮ Assets, liabilities and capital

Starting a business

There are many different types of businesses. A good way of classifying them is according to how they are owned. Among the most numerous are those of *sole traders*, where one person owns the business. Sole traders are the easiest form of business to set up, and the owner is known as the *proprietor*. The owner has personal control over the decisions, provides all of the money and resources to run the business, and receives all of the profits. Other types of businesses include partnerships, limited companies, co-operatives and public corporations.

Those people who decide to start a business feel that they have some useful product or service to offer and believe they can make money from their business dealings. Typical examples of sole traders are: small retail shops, farms, cafés, hairdressers, plumbers, electricians and building firms.

Keeping records

We all need to have some idea of our own financial position to ensure that our bills are paid on time. Keeping orderly records is of vital importance to the smooth running of any business, otherwise it would be impossible to know whether the business was successful. If records are kept properly, it should be possible to find out quickly the firm's financial position at any time.

Bookkeeping or *accounting* is the name given to the work of keeping the financial records of a business, and special accounting terms are used to describe things.

Assets, liabilities and capital

What are assets?

Assets are the possessions of a business and include such items as: land, property and buildings, plant and machinery, motor vehicles, office furniture, office equipment, stocks of goods, money in cash, money in the bank account, money owing by debtors. People who owe a firm money are called *debtors*. (Customers who have bought goods on credit are called debtors until they have paid their accounts.) Anything that a business owns or is owed is called an *asset*.

What are liabilities?

Liabilities consist of money owing for goods bought on credit, loans made to a firm, and for expenses such as gas, electricity, rates, rent, telephone. People who are owed money by a firm are called *creditors*. (People who have supplied goods or services on credit are creditors until their accounts have been paid.) Anything that a business owes is called a *liability*.

What is capital?

It is important to understand correctly the meaning of *capital* in relation to accounting. The total resources supplied by the owner of a business are known as capital. *Capital is a liability*. This may seem strange at first, but you must remember that you are keeping the books of the business and *not* the owner's personal books.

For legal reasons, business dealings must be kept entirely separate from the financial activities of the owner. Starting a new business is rather like creating a new person who has a completely different identity, so it is considered to be lending money to another person. Capital is probably best described as a 'loan' to the new person. When the owner puts his/her money or some other asset into the firm he/she becomes a creditor of the business. Capital represents the amount 'loaned' to the business by the owner.

Assignments

1.1 In your notebook make two headings like this:
   Assets   *Liabilities*
   Now place each of the following items under the correct heading.
   ● Motor van
   ● Creditors
   ● Cash at bank
   ● Office equipment
   ● Stock of goods

1.2 Now place each of the following items under the correct heading – Assets or Liabilities
   ● Premises
   ● Debtors
   ● Creditors
   ● Motor vehicle
   ● Office furniture

- Capital
- Cash in hand

1.3 A firm has the following assets and liabilities. What is the total of its assets?

	£
Capital	22,250
Debtors	5,825
Cash at bank	1,500
Creditors	2,450
Office equipment	8,425
Stock of goods	9,250

1.4 A firm has the following assets and liabilities. What is the total of its liabilities?

	£
Capital	17,500
Office furniture	1,750
Motor van	6,450
Creditors	3,000
Stock of goods	3,230
Machinery	4,900
Cash at bank	420
Debtors	3,750

1.5 A firm has the following assets and liabilities. What is the total of its assets?

	£
Fixtures and fittings	10,200
Office equipment	2,275
Capital	19,200
Stock of goods	1,750
Creditors	1,800
Debtors	2,825
Cash at bank	3,950

The accounting equation

Accounting is based on a very simple idea called the *accounting equation*, which sounds difficult, but in fact it is easy to understand. In any business the value of assets always equals the value of capital and liabilities. The formula is:

$$\textbf{Assets} = \textbf{Capital} + \textbf{Liabilities}$$

If we know the value of two items in this equation it is always possible to calculate the third item, for example:

$$\text{assets less liabilities} = \text{capital} \text{ or}$$
$$\text{assets less capital} = \text{liabilities} \text{ or}$$
$$\text{capital plus liabilities} = \text{assets}$$

Practise the equation by completing the following tasks.

1.6 Complete the table by calculating and filling in the missing figures.

	Assets	Liabilities	Capital
(a)	42,000	17,300	?
(b)	87,500	?	61,000
(c)	?	19,950	39,800
(d)	71,450	22,750	?
(e)	64,500	?	39,500

1.7 Complete the table by calculating and filling in the missing figures.

	Assets	Liabilities	Capital
(a)	51,500	19,700	?
(b)	?	27,500	64,700
(c)	57,750	?	38,800
(d)	63,330	14,500	?
(e)	?	17,850	63,150

1.8 Complete the table by calculating and filling in the missing figures.

	Assets	Liabilities	Capital
(a)	65,000	?	32,250
(b)	?	16,750	27,900
(c)	78,350	18,900	?
(d)	?	12,750	18,350
(e)	45,000	?	20,200

1.9 Complete the table by calculating and filling in the missing figures.

	Assets	Liabilities	Capital
(a)	47,200	18,250	?
(b)	51,500	?	16,450
(c)	?	27,800	28,900
(d)	31,150	17,250	?
(e)	48,750	?	26,650

The balance sheet in action

The accounting equation is shown on a *balance sheet*. Now we are going to look at how it changes once a business starts operating. The actual assets and liabilities will alter, as illustrated in the following examples, but the formula will always hold true no matter how many transactions are entered into.

A balance sheet is always drawn up at a specific date. For this example, David Nicholson commenced business on 1 January 20-6 with £25,000, which he placed in a bank account for the business. His balance sheet looked like this:

Balance sheet as at 1 January 20-6

Assets	£	Liabilities	£
Cash at bank	25,000	Capital	25,000
	25,000		25,000

Each time a transaction is made it will affect the balance sheet. On 7 January, David Nicholson completes his first transaction: he decides to buy a motor vehicle costing £5,000 and pays for it out of his business bank account. After this transaction his capital remains at £25,000 but the assets change. The money in the bank will be reduced to £20,000 and there will be another asset, a motor vehicle. His balance sheet still balances, but now looks like this:

Balance sheet as at 7 January 20-6

Assets	£	Liabilities	£
Cash at bank	20,000	Capital	25,000
Motor vehicle	5,000		
	25,000		25,000

At this point David Nicholson decides to buy a stock of goods that he eventually hopes to re-sell. On 12 January 20-6 he buys some goods costing £600 and agrees to pay for them in one month's time. This transaction will create the liability of a creditor (a person to whom money is owed for goods or services is known as a *creditor*), and there will be another asset, a stock of goods. His balance sheet still balances, but now looks like this:

Balance sheet as at 12 January 20-6

Assets	£	Liabilities	£
Cash at bank	20,000	Capital	25,000
Motor vehicle	5,000	Creditor	600
Stock of goods	600		
	25,600		25,600

On 16 January 20-6 goods that had cost £100 were sold to D. Davey, who agreed to pay for the goods in one month's time. This transaction creates a

new asset of a *debtor* (a person who owes the firm money is known as a *debtor*) and the stock of goods will be reduced. This balance sheet still balances, but now looks like this:

Balance sheet as at 16 January 20-6

Assets	£	Liabilities	£
Cash at bank	20,000	Capital	25,000
Motor vehicle	5,000	Creditor	600
Stock of goods	500		
Debtor	100		
	25,600		25,600

Now see if you can keep track of the changes resulting from a series of transactions by completing the following tasks.

1.10
On 21 January, David Nicholson decides to buy some office equipment costing £1,500 and pays by cheque. Draw up his balance sheet to show the effect of this transaction.

1.11
On 31 January, David Nicholson buys further goods on credit costing £1,800 and manages to persuade a business associate, A. Goodson, to lend him £5,000, which is placed in the business bank account. Draw up a balance sheet as at 31 January 20-6 to show the effect of these transactions.

Points to remember

- For legal reasons, the financial dealings of a business must be kept completely separate from those of the owner of the business.
- The total amount of resources supplied by the owner of the business is known as *capital*. It represents the amount *loaned* to the business by the owner, and is a liability of the business.
- Anything that a business owns or is owed is an *asset*.
- Anything that a business owes is a *liability*.
- In accounting language the name *debtor* is given to a person who owes the firm money.
- In accounting language people who are owed money by a firm are called *creditors*.
- A balance sheet shows the financial position of a business at a particular point in time.

Assignment

1.12

William Dyson sets up a new business with the following assets and liabilities: premises £7,000; stock of goods £3,250; motor vehicle £5,750; creditors £2,200; debtors £3,950; loan from D. James £5,000; office equipment £1,750; machinery £2,700; cash at bank £5,850.

You are required to calculate the amount of William Dyson's capital and draw up his balance sheet as at 31 December 20-8.

▪ ✓ 2 Double entry accounts

We have already seen that every transaction affects two items on a balance sheet. If there were only a few transactions each day we could draw up a balance sheet after each transaction, but if there were numerous daily transactions it would become impossible to draw a balance sheet after each one.

In business, *accounts* tell the story of what is happening. Entering this information in the various accounts is called *bookkeeping*. The main book used to record these transactions is known as the *ledger*. At one time all ledgers were heavy, bound volumes but today loose-leaf paper, ledger cards and computer-based systems are also used. Whatever system is used to record transactions, the principles and methods are basically the same.

The *double entry* system of bookkeeping is the basis of all financial accounting. To gain a clear understanding of how the system works we must put what we learn into practice. Learning how to operate the double entry system is not nearly as difficult as many people would have you believe, but you will need to practice by 'doing' it.

Record keeping

All businesses, however small, need some form of accounting because they must keep records of all their financial dealings. They need to know how much money they spend and how much they receive.

There are some rules you will need to learn to ensure that your records are kept accurately and that the information can be found quickly when it is needed.

Business transactions

Any type of business deal is a *transaction*. If you go into a shop to buy a packet of mints, this is a business transaction. Two things happen: the shopkeeper *receives* the money and *gives* you the mints.

In every business transaction there are always two parties involved – one is the *receiver* and the other is the *giver*. It is these two aspects of every transaction that form the basis of the double entry system of bookkeeping.

Double entry system

The most important rule to remember is that in every transaction *two* things happen, and this will affect *two* accounts.

Every transaction involves a debit entry in one account and a credit entry in another account.

This means that every transaction must be recorded in two accounts: one account will be *debited* because it *receives* value, and the other will be *credited* because it has *given* value.

The words *debit* and *credit* can be a little confusing to begin with. Debit originates from the Latin and means *value received*. Credit also originates from the Latin and means *value given*. If you always think, *what value is received* and then *what value is given* you will find it quite straightforward.

The double entry system of accounting records every transaction twice. Two separate accounts are involved in every transaction: one account recording the receiving aspect (debit entry) and the other account recording the giving or paying aspect (credit entry).

Debit the account that receives goods, services or money
Credit the account that gives goods, services or money

Shortened, the rule to remember is:

Debit the receiver.
Credit the giver.

Whether they are hand-written or computerised, the ledger contains accounts of each asset and liability of the business and for the capital of the owner. A separate account is kept for every item in which a business deals.

You need to appreciate that cash and cheques are different and are kept in separate accounts. Cash consists of notes and coins, but cheques cannot be spent like money as they need to be paid into a bank. The Cash Account is used to record cash received and paid out by the firm (notes and coins). The Bank Account is used to record cheques received and paid out by the firm.

To help you grasp the basic idea, look at the illustration of some typical business transactions showing which accounts are involved in each transaction.

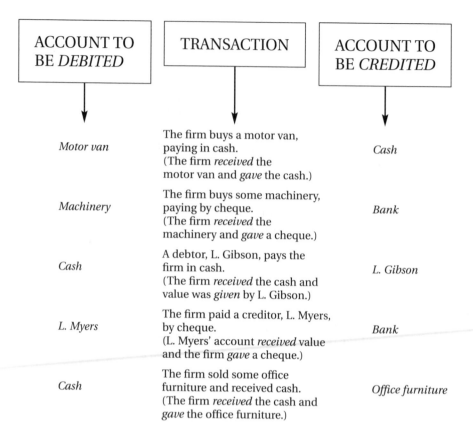

ACCOUNT TO BE *DEBITED*	TRANSACTION	ACCOUNT TO BE *CREDITED*
Motor van	The firm buys a motor van, paying in cash. (The firm *received* the motor van and *gave* the cash.)	Cash
Machinery	The firm buys some machinery, paying by cheque. (The firm *received* the machinery and *gave* a cheque.)	Bank
Cash	A debtor, L. Gibson, pays the firm in cash. (The firm *received* the cash and value was *given* by L. Gibson.)	L. Gibson
L. Myers	The firm paid a creditor, L. Myers, by cheque. (L. Myers' account *received* value and the firm *gave* a cheque.)	Bank
Cash	The firm sold some office furniture and received cash. (The firm *received* the cash and *gave* the office furniture.)	Office furniture

2.1

Look at the following typical business transactions and work out which accounts are involved in each transaction. In every case, think what has happened and decide which account has received value (the account to be debited) and which account has given value (the account to be credited).

Complete the blank spaces by inserting the name of the account to be debited and the name of the account to be credited.

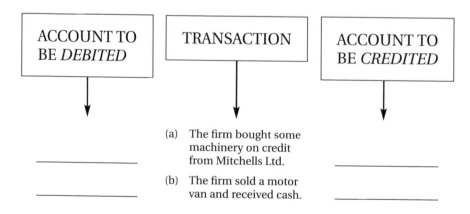

ACCOUNT TO BE *DEBITED*	TRANSACTION	ACCOUNT TO BE *CREDITED*
_____	(a) The firm bought some machinery on credit from Mitchells Ltd.	_____
_____	(b) The firm sold a motor van and received cash.	_____

_____	(c) The firm paid a creditor, M. Fieldhouse, by cheque.	_____
_____	(d) A loan was received from D. Nelson in cash.	_____
_____	(e) The firm bought some office equipment, paying by cheque.	_____
_____	(f) A debtor, B. Dixon, paid the firm in cash.	_____

2.2

Look at the following typical business transactions and work out which accounts are involved in each transaction. In every case, think what has happened and decide which account has received value (the account to be debited) and which account has given value (the account to be credited).

Complete the blank spaces by inserting the name of the account to be debited and the name of the account to be credited.

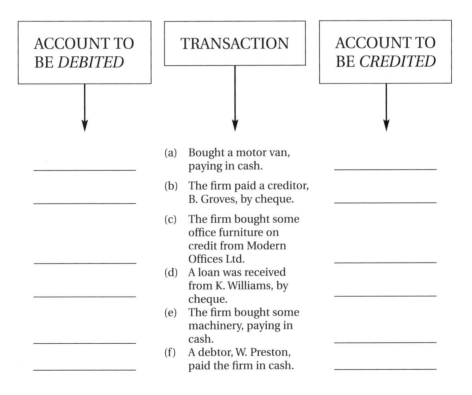

ACCOUNT TO BE *DEBITED*	TRANSACTION	ACCOUNT TO BE *CREDITED*
_____	(a) Bought a motor van, paying in cash.	_____
_____	(b) The firm paid a creditor, B. Groves, by cheque.	_____
_____	(c) The firm bought some office furniture on credit from Modern Offices Ltd.	_____
_____	(d) A loan was received from K. Williams, by cheque.	_____
_____	(e) The firm bought some machinery, paying in cash.	_____
_____	(f) A debtor, W. Preston, paid the firm in cash.	_____

The ledger

All the accounts of a business are kept in a book called a ledger. Years ago the bookkeeper kept the books of account on a ledge, so the ledger was 'the book lying on the ledge'. There was another book called the Journal, or day book, but the ledger was, and still is, the main book of account.

The *ledger* is a book of ruled pages, all ruled exactly the same. An *account* is a page in a ledger. The ledger page is divided into two halves; think of it as having a wall down the centre of the page separating the two halves. The left-hand side of the page is called the *debit side*, and the right-hand side of the page is called the *credit side*. The name of the account is written across the top of the page, in the centre.

Each account is kept on a separate page in the ledger and two accounts would *never* appear on the same page. However, when you are doing your assignments it would be a great waste of paper to show every account on a separate page. So it is usual for students to put several accounts on each page, leaving a few lines of space between each account. Ledger paper and books can be purchased from most good stationers and you will need to get a supply. This is how ledger paper is ruled.

Debit side   Credit side

					Name of Account				
Date	Particulars	Folio	£	p	Date	Particulars	Folio	£	p

The double entry system of bookkeeping is based on the fact that every transaction has two parts; this is why two entries are made in the ledger for each transaction.

Entries are made in the ledger by setting up various accounts. A debit entry is made in the account *receiving value* and a credit entry in the account *giving value*.

Elaine Mellor has decided to start her own business. On 1 March she started the business with £5,000 in cash. This is the first transaction of the new business.

The business *receives* £5,000 in cash, so the debit entry is made in the cash account, like this

DR   **Cash Account**   **CR**

	£	
1 Mar	5,000	

The credit entry will be in the capital account because the owner has *given* £5,000 to the new business. Think of the capital account as the owner's personal account in the new business. It shows how much the owner has given to the business.

DR	Capital Account		CR
			£
	1 Mar		5,000

The date and the amount of money will be the same in both accounts, but the particulars column is completed by cross-reference; it shows the name of the corresponding account involved in the transaction. It may sound a little confusing at first but as you will see it is very helpful.

In real life each account is on a separate page, so when the particulars column is completed by cross-reference it always shows where the corresponding entry has been made.

The word *capital* appears in the cash account like this:

DR	Cash Account		CR
	£		
1 Mar Capital	5,000		

The word *cash* appears in the capital account, like this:

DR	Capital Account		CR
			£
	1 Mar Cash		5,000

On 5 March, the firm buys a motor van costing £4,500 on credit from Crossways Garage. The firm *receives* the motor van, so the debit entry is made in the motor van account, like this:

DR	Motor Van Account		CR
	£		
5 Mar Crossways Garage	4,500		

The credit entry will be in Crossways Garage Account because they have *given* value. The account would look like this:

DR   **Crossways Garage Account**   **CR**

		£
	5 Mar Motor van	4,500

On 18 March, Elaine Mellor goes to an auction and buys some machinery for the business costing £350, and pays in cash. The firm receives the machinery, so the debit entry is made in the machinery account, like this:

DR   **Machinery Account**   **CR**

	£	
18 Mar Cash	350	

The credit entry would be in the cash account because the firm has paid out cash. The cash account would now look like this:

DR   **Cash Account**   **CR**

	£		£
1 Mar Capital	5,000	18 Mar Machinery	350

On 24 March, Elaine Mellor buys some office furniture costing £200, paying in cash. The firm receives the office furniture, so the debit entry is made in the office furniture account, like this:

DR   **Office Furniture Account**   **CR**

	£	
24 Mar Cash	200	

The credit entry would be in the cash account because the firm has paid out cash. The cash account would now look like this:

DR   **Cash Account**   **CR**

	£		£
1 Mar Capital	5,000	18 Mar Machinery	350
		24 Mar Office furniture	200

On 30 March the firm receives a loan of £2,000 in cash from John King. The firm receives the money in cash, so the debit entry is made in the cash account. The cash account would now look like this:

DR		Cash Account			CR
		£			£
1 Mar	Capital	5,000	18 Mar	Machinery	350
30 Mar	John King (Loan)	2,000	24 Mar	Office furniture	200

The credit entry would be in John King's loan account because he has given value to the firm.

DR	John King (Loan) Account		CR
			£
	30 Mar	Cash	2,000

Points to remember

- In every business transaction *two* things happen. Some form of value is *received* and some form of value is *given*. The double entry system of accounting means that every transaction *must* be entered *twice* in the ledger, a debit entry in one account and a credit entry in another account.
- The date of the transaction and the amount of money will be the same in both accounts; the particulars column is completed by cross-reference. It always names the account where the corresponding entry is made.
- A cash account is used to keep a record of *cash*; that is, notes and coins received and paid out by the firm.
- A bank account is used to keep a record of *cheques* received and paid out by the firm.

Assignments

Now use your ledger to work through the following assignments.

2.3

K. Chippendale started a new business on 1 May. In your ledger write up the double entry accounts needed to record the following transactions:

May 1 Started a new business with £2,000 in cash
  3 Bought a motor van costing £950 on credit from Crossways Garage
  12 Bought office furniture costing £500, paying in cash
  24 Received a loan of £500 in cash from L. Gibson
  30 Paid Crossways Garage £950 in cash

2.4

S. Curtis started a new business on 1 April. In your ledger write up the double entry accounts needed to record the following transactions:

Apr 1 Started business with £5,000 in a business bank account
  4 Bought office furniture costing £450 on credit from Design Centre
  10 Bought motor van costing £1,500, paying by cheque
  20 Received a loan of £2,000 by cheque from D. Lester
  23 Bought machinery costing £500, paying by cheque
  29 Paid Design Centre £450 by cheque

2.5

J. Patel started a new business on 1 June. In your ledger write up the double entry accounts needed to record the following transactions:

Jun 1 Started a new business with £7,000 in cash
  3 Opened a bank account for the business and paid £6,500 of the cash into the bank account
  6 Bought a motor van costing £1,950, paying by cheque
  9 Bought office furniture costing £500 on credit from Elite Supplies
  14 Received a loan of £1,000 in cash from P. Wilson
  20 Returned some of the office furniture costing £150 to Elite Supplies because it was faulty
  23 Bought machinery costing £750, paying by cheque
  30 Paid Elite Supplies the amount owing to them £350 by cheque

2.6

M. Sanchez started a new business on 1 October. In your ledger write up the double entry accounts needed to record the following transactions:

Oct 1 Started business by placing £5,000 in a business bank account
  3 Bought office equipment costing £750 on credit from Systems Ltd
  5 Took £250 out of the bank and put it in the cash till
  10 Bought motor van costing £1,750, paying by cheque

12   Received a loan of £2,000 by cheque from S. Ramsden

15   Returned some of the office equipment costing £56 to Systems Ltd because it was faulty

20   Bought some machinery costing £250, paying by cheque

23   Bought some shop fittings costing £175, paying in cash

26   Paid Systems Ltd the amount owing to them, £694, by cheque

31   Sold some of the shop fittings because they were unsuitable and received £60 in cash

■ ☑ **3** Purchases and purchase returns

The usual aim of a business is to make a profit. So far we have examined the double entry accounts for the assets, liabilities and the capital of a business. All other transactions of the business must be recorded in a similar way.

Many businesses are involved in buying and selling, so we must now look at the accounts needed when a firm buys goods. The firm will not be selling goods at the same price as it buys them because it hopes to make a profit. This is why the words *purchases* and *purchase returns* have a special meaning in accounting. There has to be a separate account for *purchases* and a separate account for *purchase returns*.

When a firm buys goods for resale they are called *purchases*, and when goods are returned to a supplier they are called *purchase returns*. It is essential that the purchases and the purchase returns of a business are kept completely separate and are not confused with each other.

Business transactions may be carried out either for cash or on a credit basis. In many businesses, most of the purchases will be made on a credit basis, with the goods being received immediately but payment being made at a later date. Credit transactions will need personal accounts.

Purchase of goods on credit

When a firm buys goods on credit, the supplier will send a document to the buyer showing full details of the goods, prices and any trade discount. This document is known as a *purchase invoice* and is the original document that provides the financial information that will subsequently be recorded in the ledger accounts.

You will find that invoices differ in appearance, each business having its own individual design. For convenience, invoices are frequently prepared in sets, with each copy being used for a specific purpose. This enables a firm to properly organise the sending of the goods and ensures that they can confirm the goods have been received safely. The exact number of copies of the invoice will vary from one firm to another, but the supplier will keep at least one copy for his own records. Extra copies may be used as:

- Advice Notes   These are sent to the customer before the goods are despatched. Their purpose is to notify customers that the goods are on the way, they state the method of transport and when the goods are expected to arrive.
- Delivery Notes   These are sent with the goods to enable the customer to check immediately that all the items listed have been received.

Trade discount

Trade discount is a reduction, usually quoted as a percentage of the selling price, given by a supplier to trading customers. For example, Office Solutions sells a wide range of office supplies to two different kinds of customers:

- firms and businesses who regularly buy from them; and
- direct to the general public.

Trade discount is simply a way of calculating prices. You do not need to worry about trade discount, as it is *never* entered in any account. When writing up the accounts, you will record the figure *after* any trade discount has been deducted.

Value Added Tax (VAT)

Value Added Tax, usually known as VAT, is a tax charged on the supply of most goods and services. The percentage rate is set by the government and is changed from time to time, usually on Budget Day. It is the responsibility of the firm making the sale to charge and collect VAT from the customer. The government authority that deals with VAT is HM Revenue & Customs Department. Most goods and services are subject to VAT, but there are some exceptions:

- Some services and certain classes of goods are completely exempt from VAT. Examples of these are food and children's clothes.
- Some classes of goods are not taxed and are said to be *zero rated*. In effect, this means that, at the present time, these goods or services are not subject to VAT. However, changes may take place in the future and VAT could then be applicable.
- There are some traders or providers of services whose taxable turnover is under a certain amount. This figure is referred to as the *taxable threshold*. The taxable threshold limit is usually reviewed and increased each year. Firms with a turnover of less than the threshold limit do not have to register for VAT. However, firms who are not registered for VAT

cannot charge VAT to their customers, nor can they recover the amount of VAT paid on their own purchases.

Firms whose turnover is above the threshold limit must by law register for VAT and are given a VAT registration number, which you will see printed on invoices. Firms charging VAT will receive the VAT amount from their customers and must eventually pay it to the government. For this reason it is essential to keep accurate records of VAT.

This is an illustration of a typical invoice received from a supplier:

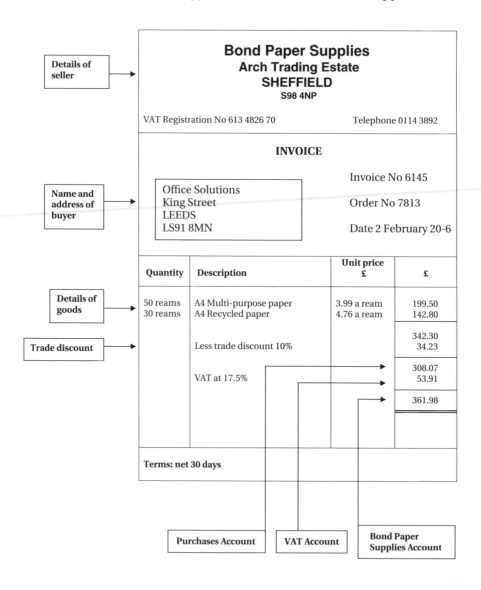

When invoices are received from suppliers they should always be checked to ensure that they are both genuine and accurate.

When a firm buys goods for resale, they are called *purchases*. They are bought with the intention of being resold at a profit. The purchases account keeps a record of all goods bought for resale.

As we have already seen, the double entry system involves two entries being made in accounts for each transaction. When VAT is charged on invoices it means that three entries will need to be made in the accounts for each invoice; however, despite this, it is still called the double entry system. Always remember, the debit entries will always equal the credit entries. VAT must always be recorded in its own separate account.

We shall use the purchase invoice on page 20 to illustrate the procedure. The firm will *receive* the goods, so the first debit entry will be in the purchases account, where a record of all the purchases of goods is kept, like this:

DR	Purchases Account		DR
20-6	£		
Feb 2 Bond Paper	308.07		
Supplies			

The second debit entry will be in the Value Added Tax account, for the amount of the VAT charged on the invoice, like this:

DR	Value Added Tax Account		CR
	£		
Feb 2 Bond Paper	53.91		
Supplies			

The credit entry of the value *given*, is recorded in the account of the person who has supplied the goods (in this example Bond Paper Supplies). Their account is credited with the *total* amount of the invoice, including VAT, like this:

DR	**Bond Paper Supplies Account**		CR
			£
	Feb 2	Purchases	361.98

Personal accounts are always posted with the total value of each invoice, including VAT, as this is the amount the firm will have to pay to the supplier. The Value Added Tax account fits easily into the double entry system; it is just another account we have to deal with.

Cash purchases

When goods are bought and payment is made immediately, either in cash or by cheque, these are called *cash purchases*. The firm will receive the goods, so the debit entry will be in the Purchases Account, where a record of all the purchases of goods is kept. When payment is made immediately, either in cash or by cheque, the credit entry, the value given, would be entered in the cash account or the bank account.

Credit notes

In any business where goods are bought it is likely that some will need to be returned. Goods are returned for many reasons: it may be that the goods supplied were the wrong size or colour, they may be faulty, or they may have been damaged in transit. Whatever the reason, when goods are returned, the necessary entries must be made in the accounts. When goods are returned, a *credit note* is issued. A credit note is a type of refund document, which reduces the amount owed by the buyer. A credit note is made out by the seller showing full details of the goods returned, the prices and any trade discount. The top copy is sent to the customer, and the seller keeps copies of all credit notes for his/her own records. It is the original document that provides the financial information that will subsequently be recorded in the ledger accounts.

This is an illustration of a typical credit note:

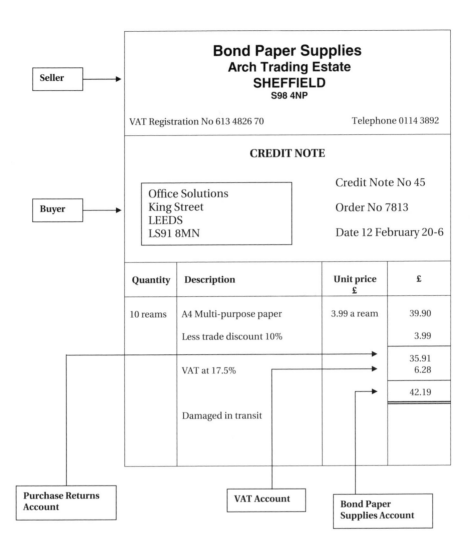

Seller

Buyer

Bond Paper Supplies
Arch Trading Estate
SHEFFIELD
S98 4NP

VAT Registration No 613 4826 70   Telephone 0114 3892

CREDIT NOTE

Office Solutions
King Street
LEEDS
LS91 8MN

Credit Note No 45

Order No 7813

Date 12 February 20-6

Quantity	Description	Unit price £	£
10 reams	A4 Multi-purpose paper	3.99 a ream	39.90
	Less trade discount 10%		3.99
			35.91
	VAT at 17.5%		6.28
			42.19
	Damaged in transit		

Purchase Returns Account

VAT Account

Bond Paper Supplies Account

This credit note has been sent by Bond Paper Supplies to Office Solutions because some of the paper was damaged in transit. Now look at the original invoice on page 20 and work out the cost of ten reams of paper.

Because trade discount was allowed on the original invoice it *must* now be deducted on the credit note for the items returned. It is vital to understand this important principle. When goods are sold less a trade discount it reduces the price of the goods: if it is not deducted on a credit note the customer will receive a higher price for the returned goods than was first paid.

When a firm returns goods to a supplier they are called *purchase returns*. As the name suggests, they were purchases that have now been returned to the supplier. Purchase returns are kept in a separate account, which enables the business to keep a check on the level of returns to suppliers.

When VAT is charged on a credit note it means that three entries will need to be made in the accounts for each credit note. Remember that VAT must always be recorded in its own separate account. Now we shall record this credit note in the accounts. The original purchases have been inserted so that the entries you need to consider are meaningful; it would be unrealistic to show returns if we had not purchased goods in the first place. The firm will *receive* the value of the credit note, and this will reduce the amount owed, so the debit entry will be in Bond Paper Supplies' account for the full amount, like this:

DR	Bond Paper Supplies Account		CR
	£		£
Feb 12 Purchase returns	42.19	Feb 2 Purchases	361.98

The credit entries will be made in the purchase returns account and the VAT account. The entry in the purchase returns account will be for the amount of the goods returned *excluding VAT*, like this:

DR	Purchase Returns Account		CR
			£
		Feb 12 Bond Paper Supplies	35.91

The entry in the Value Added Tax account will be for the amount of VAT, like this:

DR	Value Added Tax Account		CR
	£		£
Feb 2 Bond Paper Supplies	53.91	Feb 12 Bond Paper Supplies	6.28

Points to remember

- In accounting, *purchases* are goods bought with the intention of being resold. An example of this could be an electrical business, where the firm would buy toasters and kettles. If a firm buys something else, such as an office desk, this would not be regarded as purchases because the office desk was bought to be used in the business. Office furniture would have its own separate account because it is an asset of the business and not for resale.
- When entering the transactions in the accounts, *never* write the word 'goods' in any account. The description of the transaction will usually call the items 'goods', but if goods are bought the word 'purchases' should be written in the personal account of the supplier; and 'purchases' should appear in the cash account or the bank account for 'cash purchases'.
- Similarly when goods are returned to a supplier, never write the word 'goods'; if goods are returned the words 'purchase returns' should be written in the personal account of the supplier. The supplier's name should be written in the Purchase Returns and VAT accounts.

Worked example

Style Plus is a local boutique. Below are some of the transactions for the month of March. Consider each transaction carefully, then write up in your ledger the accounts needed to record the following transactions.

Mar 3   Bought goods on credit from Marcus Singer costing £150.00 plus VAT £26.25, total invoice £176.25

      12   Bought goods on credit from James Davine costing £380.80 plus VAT £66.64, total invoice £447.44

      14   Goods returned to Marcus Singer costing £30.00 plus VAT £5.25, a credit note for £35.25 is received

      18   Bought goods on credit from E. Stockwell costing £250.35 plus VAT £43.81, total invoice £294.16

      24   Goods returned to James Davine for £72.80 plus VAT £12.74, a credit note for £85.54 is received

Solution

These transactions have now been recorded in the double entry accounts. Compare the entries with those in your ledger.

DR   **Purchases Account**   **CR**

			£	
Mar	3	Marcus Singer	150.00	
	12	James Davine	380.80	
	18	E. Stockwell	250.35	

DR   **Value Added Tax Account**   **CR**

			£				£
Mar	3	Marcus Singer	26.25	Mar 14		Marcus Singer	5.25
	12	James Davine	66.64	Mar 24		James Davine	12.74
	18	E. Stockwell	43.81				

DR   **Marcus Singer Account**   **CR**

		£			£
Mar 14	Purchase returns	35.25	Mar 3	Purchases	176.25

DR   **James Davine Account**   **CR**

		£			£
Mar 24	Purchase returns	85.54	Mar 12	Purchases	447.44

DR   **Purchase Returns Account**   **CR**

					£
		Mar 14		Marcus Singer	30.00
			24	James Davine	72.80

DR   **E. Stockwell Account**   **CR**

				£
		Mar 18	Purchases	294.16

Assignments

Now use your ledger to work through the following assignments.

3.1
J. Singh started a new business on 1 May. In your ledger write up the double entry accounts needed to record the following transactions:

May 1 Started a new business with £5,000 in cash
2 Bought goods on credit from G. Moore costing £258.00 plus VAT £45.15, total invoice £303.15
4 Paid £3,000 of the cash into a bank account for the business
8 Bought goods on credit from Kilroy Ingram costing £175.20 plus VAT £30.66, total invoice £205.86
15 Goods returned to G. Moore for £62.40 plus VAT £10.92, a credit note for £73.32 is received
20 Bought goods on credit from Kilroy Ingram costing £204.76 plus VAT £35.83, total invoice £240.59
24 Paid G. Moore £229.83 by cheque
28 Goods returned to Kilroy Ingram for £58.76 plus VAT £10.28, a credit note for £69.04 is received
30 Paid Kilroy Ingram £100.00 in cash

3.2
S. Munro started a new business on 1 July. In your ledger write up the double entry accounts needed to record the following transactions:

Jul 1 Started a new business with £8,000 in a business bank account
2 Bought goods on credit from M. Clifton costing £362.40 plus VAT £63.42, total invoice £425.82
5 Withdrew £500 cash from the bank for use in the business.
8 Bought goods on credit from E. Mason costing £273.50 plus VAT £47.86, total invoice £321.36
14 Goods returned to M. Clifton for £68.40 plus VAT £11.97, a credit note for £80.37 is received
19 Bought goods on credit from E. Mason costing £420.76 plus VAT £73.63, total invoice £494.39
25 Paid M. Clifton £250 in cash
27 Goods returned to E. Mason for £58.30 plus VAT £10.20, a credit note for £68.50 is received
31 Paid E. Mason £747.25 by cheque

3.3
C. Gulliver started a new business on 1 September. In your ledger write up the double entry accounts needed to record the following transactions:

Sep 1 Started a new business with £7,000 in cash
3 Bought goods on credit from G. Stewart costing £386.76 plus VAT £67.68, total invoice £454.44

5 Paid £5,500 of the cash into a bank account for the business

10 Bought goods on credit from W. Rycroft for £294.24 plus VAT £51.49, total invoice £345.73

15 Goods returned to G. Stewart for £62.80 plus VAT £10.99, a credit note for £73.79 is received

18 Bought goods on credit from F. Armitage costing £196.58 plus VAT £34.40, total invoice £230.98

24 Paid G. Stewart £380.65 by cheque

26 Goods returned to W. Rycroft for £54.76 plus VAT £9.58, a credit note for £64.34 is received

30 Paid F. Armitage £50.00 in cash

3.4

M. Gonzalas started a new business on 1 October. In your ledger write up the double entry accounts needed to record the following transactions:

Oct 1 Started a new business with £9,000 in a business bank account

2 Bought goods on credit from Tee-Jay Products costing £392.75 plus VAT £68.73, total invoice £461.48

4 Withdrew £750 cash from the bank for business use

8 Bought goods on credit from Demland Supplies costing £268.92 plus VAT £47.06, total invoice £315.98

12 Bought goods on credit from W. Jackson costing £302.99 plus VAT £53.02, total invoice £356.01

16 Goods returned to Demland Supplies for £48.00 plus VAT £8.40, a credit note for £56.40 is received

20 Paid Tee-Jay Products £150.00 in cash

23 Bought goods on credit from W. Jackson costing £374.80 plus VAT £65.59, total invoice £440.39

26 Returned goods to W. Jackson for £56.00 plus VAT £9.80, a credit note for £65.80 is received

31 Paid Tee-Jay Products £311.48 by cheque

■ ⌄ **4** Sales and sales returns

Sales of goods on credit

Most businesses are involved in both buying and selling, so we must now look at the accounts needed when a firm sells goods.

The firm will not be selling goods at the same price as it buys them, because it hopes to make a profit. This is why the words *sales* and *sales returns* have a special meaning in accounting. There has to be a separate account for *sales* and a separate account for *sales returns*.

When a firm sells goods they are called *sales*. It is essential that the sales and the *sales returns* of a business are kept completely separate and are not confused with each other. Business transactions may be carried out either for cash or on a credit basis. In many businesses, most of the sales will be made on a credit basis, which means that the goods are received immediately but payment is made at a later date. Credit transactions will need personal accounts.

When a firm sells goods on credit it will send a document to the customer showing full details of the goods, prices and any trade discount. This document is known as a *sales invoice*. It is the original document that provides the financial information that will subsequently be recorded in the ledger accounts.

In practice, you will find that invoices differ in appearance, each business having its own individual design. For convenience, invoices are frequently prepared in sets, with each copy being used for a specific purpose. This enables a firm to properly organise the sending of the goods and ensures that they can confirm the goods have been received safely. The exact number of copies will vary from one firm to another, but the firm will keep at least one copy for its own records.

Here is an illustration of a typical sales invoice sent to a customer:

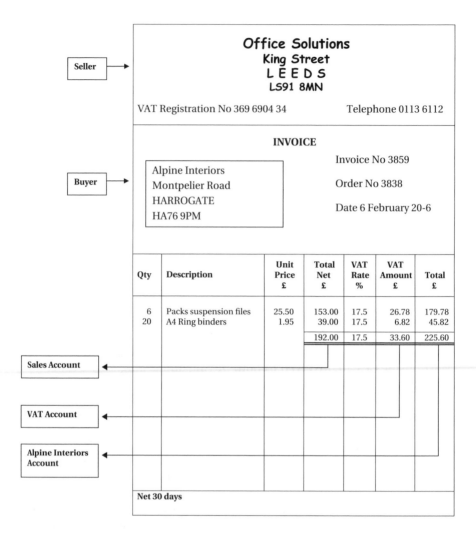

Seller

Buyer

Office Solutions
King Street
L E E D S
LS91 8MN

VAT Registration No 369 6904 34   Telephone 0113 6112

INVOICE

Alpine Interiors
Montpelier Road
HARROGATE
HA76 9PM

Invoice No 3859

Order No 3838

Date 6 February 20-6

Qty	Description	Unit Price £	Total Net £	VAT Rate %	VAT Amount £	Total £
6	Packs suspension files	25.50	153.00	17.5	26.78	179.78
20	A4 Ring binders	1.95	39.00	17.5	6.82	45.82
			192.00	17.5	33.60	225.60

Sales Account

VAT Account

Alpine Interiors Account

Net 30 days

We can now look at the accounts to show how credit sales transactions are recorded in the double entry accounts. When VAT is charged on invoices, this means that there are three entries in the accounts for each invoice, but despite this, it is still called the double entry system.

Remember that the debit entries will always equal the credit entries, and VAT must always be recorded in its own separate account. We shall use this sales invoice to illustrate the procedure. The customer, Alpine Interiors, will *receive* the goods, so the debit entry will be in the Alpine Interiors account for the total amount, like this:

DR   **Alpine Interiors Account**   **CR**

	£	
Feb 6 Sales	225.60	

The first credit entry will be in the sales account, where a record of all the sales of goods is kept for the actual amount of the sale, like this:

DR	Sales Account	CR
		£
	Feb 6 Alpine Interiors	192.00

The second credit entry will be in the Value Added Tax account, like this:

DR	Value Added Tax Account	CR
		£
	Feb 6 Alpine Interiors	33.60

Cash sales

When goods are sold and payment is received immediately, either in cash or by cheque, these are called *cash sales*. The firm will *receive* the money, so the debit entry will be in the cash account, if cash is received; or in the bank account if a cheque is received.

The credit entry would be in the sales account, where a record of all sales of goods is kept.

Credit notes

In any business where goods are bought it is likely that some will need to be returned. Goods are returned for many reasons: it may be that the goods supplied were the wrong size or colour, they may be faulty, or they may have been damaged in transit. Whatever the reason, when goods are returned, the necessary entries must be made in the accounts. When goods are returned, a *credit note* is issued. A credit note is a type of refund document which reduces the amount owed by the buyer. A credit note is made out by the seller showing full details of the goods returned, the prices and any trade discount. The top copy is sent to the customer, and the seller keeps copies of all credit notes for his/her own records. It is the original document that provides the financial information that will subsequently be recorded in the ledger accounts.

This is an illustration of a typical credit note:

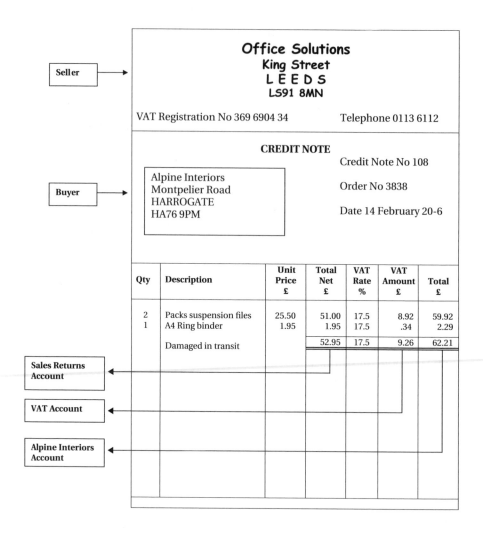

Seller

Office Solutions
King Street
L E E D S
LS91 8MN

VAT Registration No 369 6904 34   Telephone 0113 6112

CREDIT NOTE

Credit Note No 108

Buyer

Alpine Interiors
Montpelier Road
HARROGATE
HA76 9PM

Order No 3838

Date 14 February 20-6

Qty	Description	Unit Price £	Total Net £	VAT Rate %	VAT Amount £	Total £
2	Packs suspension files	25.50	51.00	17.5	8.92	59.92
1	A4 Ring binder	1.95	1.95	17.5	.34	2.29
	Damaged in transit		52.95	17.5	9.26	62.21

Sales Returns Account

VAT Account

Alpine Interiors Account

After a sale has been made, any goods returned to the firm by its customers must be recorded in the accounts. When a customer returns goods they are called *sales returns*. As the name suggests, they were sales that have now been returned by the customer. Sales returns are kept in a separate account, which enables the business to keep a check on the level of returns from its customers.

When VAT is charged on a credit note it means that three entries will need to be made in the accounts for each credit note. Remember that VAT must always be recorded in its own separate account. Now we shall record this credit note in the accounts. The original sales have been inserted so that the entries you need to consider are meaningful; it would be unrealistic to show returns if we had not sold the goods in the first place. The firm will *receive* the goods, so the first debit entry will be in the sales returns account, where a record of all goods returned to the firm is kept, like this:

DR **Sales Returns Account** **CR**

	£		
Feb 14 Alpine Interiors	52.95		

The second debit entry will be in the Value Added Tax account, like this:

DR **Value Added Tax Account** **CR**

	£		£
Feb 14 Alpine Interiors	9.26	Feb 6 Alpine Interiors	33.60

The credit entry is recorded in the account of the person who has returned the goods, in this example Alpine Interiors, like this:

DR **Alpine Interiors Account** **CR**

	£		£
Feb 6 Sales	225.60	Feb 14 Sales returns	62.21

Points to remember

- In accounting, sales are the goods in which the firm normally deals, such as an electrical business selling radios and television sets; these goods are bought with the intention of being sold. If a firm sells something else, such as a motor vehicle, this would not be regarded as sales, because the motor vehicle was bought to be used in the business. A motor vehicle would have its own separate account because it is an asset of the business and not for resale.
- When entering transactions in the double entry accounts, *never* write the word 'goods' in any account. The description of the transaction will usually call the items goods; but if goods are sold the word *sales* should be written in the personal account of the customer.
- Similarly, when a customer returns goods the words *sales returns* should appear in the customer's account.

Worked example

Vigilant Alarms sells security equipment. Below are some of their transactions for the month of January. In your ledger write up the accounts needed to record the following transactions.

Jan 4 Sold goods on credit to Brooklands priced at £250.80 plus VAT £43.89, total invoice £294.69.

10 Sold goods on credit to Sureguard Systems priced at £496.25 plus VAT £86.84, total invoice £583.09.

15 Goods returned by Brooklands for £38.75 plus VAT £6.78, a credit note for £45.53 is issued.

20 Sold goods on credit to Mark Swift priced at £104.92 plus VAT £18.36, total invoice £123.28.

24 Goods returned by Sureguard Systems for £58.70 plus VAT £10.27, a credit note for £68.97 is issued.

Now compare the entries in your ledger with the following worked solution.

DR	Brooklands Account			CR
	£	£		
Jan 4 Sales	294.69	Jan 15 Sales returns		45.53

DR	Sales Account			CR
				£
		Jan 4 Brooklands		250.80
		10 Sureguard Systems		496.25
		20 Mark Swift		104.92

DR	Value Added Tax Account			CR
	£			£
Jan 15 Brooklands	6.78	Jan 4 Brooklands		43.89
24 Sureguard Systems	10.27	10 Sureguard Systems		86.84
		20 Mark Swift		18.36

DR	Sureguard Systems Account			CR
	£			£
Jan 10 Sales	583.09	Jan 24 Sales returns		68.97

DR	Sales Returns Account		CR
	£		
Jan 15 Brooklands	38.75		
24 Sureguard Systems	58.70		

DR	Mark Swift Account	CR
	£	
Jan 20 Sales	123.28	

Assignments

Now use your ledger to work through the following assignments.

4.1

Dean Sayer started a new business on 1 May. In your ledger write up the accounts needed to record the following transactions.

May 1   Started business with £7,000 in cash

      3   Sold goods on credit to K. Bradshaw priced at £300.80 plus VAT £52.64, total invoice £353.44

      6   Paid £5,000 of the cash into a bank account for the business

   10   Sold goods on credit to V. Reedman priced at £192.40 plus VAT £33.67, total invoice £226.07

   15   Goods returned by K. Bradshaw for £48.00 plus VAT £8.40, a credit note for £56.40 is issued

   20   Sold goods to James Seymore priced at £286.20 plus VAT £50.08, total invoice £336.28

   26   Received £226.07 in cash from V. Reedman

   28   Goods returned by James Seymore for £35.56 plus VAT £6.22, a credit note for £41.78 is issued

4.2

M. Daswani started a new business on 1 June. In your ledger write up the accounts needed to record the following transactions.

Jun 1 Started business with £10,000 in a business bank account
     2 Sold goods on credit to T. Ross priced at £369.20 plus VAT £64.61, total invoice £433.81
     4 Sold goods on credit to Aztec Sportswear priced at £604.00 plus VAT £105.70, total invoice £709.70
     8 Withdrew £850.00 cash from the bank and put it in the cash till for use in the business
    14 Goods returned by T. Ross for £48.30 plus VAT £8.45, a credit note for £56.75 is issued
    18 Sold goods on credit to Classic Casuals priced at £530.40 plus VAT £92.82, total invoice £623.22
    24 Goods returned by Aztec Sportswear for £75.38 plus VAT £13.19, a credit note for £88.57 is issued
    28 Received £377.06 by cheque from T. Ross

4.3

Thomas Wagner started a new business on 1 July. In your ledger write up the accounts needed to record the following transactions.

Jul 1 Started business with £8,000 in cash
     3 Sold goods on credit to Oakwood Stores priced at £295.26 plus VAT £51.67, total invoice £346.93
     7 Paid £7,500 of the cash into a bank account for the business
    10 Sold goods on credit to M. Shah priced at £408.70 plus VAT £71.52, total invoice £480.22
    14 Sold goods on credit to J. Courtway priced at £197.50 plus VAT £34.56, total invoice £232.06
    18 Goods returned by Oakwood Stores for £36.25 plus VAT £6.34, a credit note for £42.59 is issued
    24 Received £250.00 in cash from M. Shah
    30 Goods returned by J. Courtway for £28.75 plus VAT £5.03, a credit note for £33.78 is issued

4.4

Joseph McKenzie started a new business on 1 August. In your ledger write up the accounts needed to record the following transactions.

Aug 1 Started business with £7,000 in a business bank account
     3 Sold goods on credit to Montague Giles priced at £250.64 plus VAT £43.86, total invoice £294.50
     8 Withdrew £750.00 cash from the bank and put it in the cash till for use in the business
    12 Sold goods on credit to D. Towers priced at £402.80 plus VAT £70.49, total invoice £473.29
    15 Sold goods on credit to Buywise priced at £268.24 plus VAT £46.94, total invoice £315.18

20 Goods returned by D. Towers for £35.60 plus VAT £6.23, a credit note for £41.83 is issued

24 Sold goods on credit to Montague Giles priced at £390.52 plus VAT £68.34, total invoice £458.86

26 Goods returned by Buywise for £48.75 plus VAT £8.53, a credit note for £57.28 is issued

31 Received £294.50 by cheque from Montague Giles

■ Ⅴ **5** The double entry system for expenses

Expenses

There will always be some expenses incurred when running a business. All firms will have to make payments for expenses such as telephone, gas, electricity, rent, rates, wages, motor expenses and so on. If a business kept only one account called an *expenses account* this would only give the overall total of all the expenses. Because a business needs to know exactly how much is spent on each individual expense, separate ledger accounts are opened for each type of expense. Every transaction must be recorded in the double entry accounts, one account will be debited and another account will be credited. When VAT is involved there will be three entries to be made.

A typical example would be: on 8 March the firm paid wages of £550 in cash. The firm's employees *receive* the wages, so the debit entry will be in the wages account, where a record of all payments for wages is kept, like this:

Wages Account

	£	
Mar 8 Cash	550	

The credit entry, the value *given*, is recorded in the cash account like this,

Cash Account

		£
	Mar 8 Wages	550

Another example of an expense account could be motor expenses; these usually include items such as petrol, oil, servicing and repairs.

On 21 March the firm paid motor expenses of £76.00 plus VAT of £13.30, a total of £89.30 by cheque. The first debit entry will be in the motor expenses account, where a record of all payments for motor expenses is kept, like this:

Motor Expenses Account

	£		
Mar 21 Bank	76.00		

The second debit entry is recorded in the Value Added Tax account, like this:

Value Added Tax Account

	£		
Mar 21 Bank	13.30		

The credit entry, the value given, is recorded in the bank account like this:

Bank Account

		£
	Mar 21 Motor expenses	89.30

The proprietor's drawings account

Sometimes, the proprietor, who is the owner of the business, will want to take money or goods out of the business for his/her private use. Whether cash or goods is taken, these withdrawals are known in bookkeeping as *drawings*.

We have already seen that the owner's original investment in the business is recorded in the capital account. This is a very important account, and in order to prevent numerous entries being made in it, any withdrawals from the business by the owner are recorded in a drawings account. At the end of the financial year the total of the drawings account will be transferred to the capital account. Drawings are recorded in the double entry accounts as illustrated in the following examples.

A typical example would be, on 8 March, the proprietor takes £100 cash out of the business for personal use. The debit entry will be in the drawings account, where a record of all money or goods taken by the owner is kept, like this:

Drawings Account

	£		
Mar 8　Cash	100		

The credit entry (the value given) is recorded in the cash account like this:

Cash Account

			£
		Mar 8　Drawings	100

Another example would be: on 17 March the proprietor takes £60 of goods out of the business for his/her own use. The debit entry will be in the drawings account, where a record of all money or goods taken by the owner is kept, like this:

Drawings Account

	£		
Mar 8　　Cash	100		
Mar 17　Purchases	60		

The credit entry (the value given) is recorded in the purchases account, like this:

Purchases Account

			£
		Mar 17　Drawings	60

Revenue received accounts

While all businesses will have to pay for various expenses to enable them to operate, some will also *receive income* for the services they provide to others. This is *revenue* (money) that is received by the business. Special attention is required when dealing with *revenue received accounts*. An example of this could be if a firm occupied a large building with three floors and decided to sublet one complete floor, as renting this part of the building to another firm would provide a useful income. To avoid confusion with the rent account, which is an expense, a separate account is opened for rent received. This is illustrated in the following example:

A retailer lets the flat above his shop for £245 a month. The rent is received by cheque on the first of each month from the sub-tenant. Consider the twofold effect: the money is received by cheque, so a debit entry is made in the bank account, like this:

Bank Account

	£		
Mar 1 Rent received	245		

The credit entry is recorded in the rent received account, like this:

Rent Received Account

			£
	Mar 1 Bank		245

Another example of revenue received would be *commission received*. One firm may provide a service for another and charge a commission. On 8 March, £60 cash is received for commission earned by the firm. Consider the twofold effect: the money is received in cash, so a debit entry is made in the cash account, like this:

Cash Account

	£		
Mar 8 Commission received	60		

The credit entry is recorded in the commission received account, like this:

Commission Received Account

			£
	Mar 8 Cash		60

Points to remember

- Various expenses are incurred in running a business; each type of expense is kept in a *separate account*. This is to enable the business to see exactly how much is spent on each individual expense.
- All withdrawals from a business by the owner for his/her *private use*, are recorded in a drawings account.
- *Revenue* (money) *received* transactions always require careful consideration: a debit entry is made in the bank or cash account, and a credit entry in the revenue received account.

Assignments

5.1

For each of the following transactions, complete the blank spaces by inserting the name of the account to be debited and the name of the account to be credited. (For the moment we shall concentrate on the debit and credit aspects of each transaction and ignore VAT.)

(a) Paid motor expenses in cash.
Debit _____ Account   Credit _____ Account

(b) Paid rent by cheque.
Debit _____ Account   Credit _____ Account

(c) Proprietor took cash out of the business for own private use.
Debit _____ Account   Credit _____ Account

(d) Paid rates by cheque.
Debit _____ Account   Credit _____ Account

(e) Received commission in cash.
Debit _____ Account   Credit _____ Account

(f) Paid insurance by cheque.
Debit _____ Account   Credit _____ Account

5.2

For each of the following transactions, complete the blank spaces by inserting the name of the account to be debited and the name of the account to be credited. (For the moment we shall concentrate on the debit and credit aspects of each transaction and ignore VAT.)

(a) Bought goods paying in cash.
Debit _____ Account   Credit _____ Account

(b) Received rent by cheque.
Debit _____ Account   Credit _____ Account

(c) Paid motor expenses by cheque.
Debit _____ Account   Credit _____ Account

(d) Sold goods on credit to J. Kendall.

Debit _____ Account   Credit _____ Account

(e) Bought motor van on credit from Leaders Garages.

Debit _____ Account   Credit _____ Account

(f) Paid wages in cash.

Debit _____ Account   Credit _____ Account

5.3

For each of the following transactions, complete the blank spaces by inserting the name of the account to be debited and the name of the account to be credited. (For the moment we shall concentrate on the debit and credit aspects of each transaction and ignore VAT.)

(a) Paid electricity bill by cheque.

Debit _____ Account   Credit _____ Account

(b) Sold goods and received cash.

Debit _____ Account   Credit _____ Account

(c) Received commission by cheque.

Debit _____ Account   Credit _____ Account

(d) Goods are returned to the firm by J. Kilburn.

Debit _____ Account   Credit _____ Account

(e) Bought office furniture, paying by cheque.

Debit _____ Account   Credit _____ Account

(f) Proprietor took cash out of the business for personal use.

Debit _____ Account   Credit _____ Account

5.4

For each of the following transactions complete the blank spaces by inserting the name of the account to be debited and the name of the account to be credited. (For the moment we shall concentrate on the debit and credit aspects of each transaction and ignore VAT.)

(a) Goods are returned to R. Bright.

Debit _____ Account   Credit _____ Account

(b) Paid rates by cheque.

Debit _____ Account   Credit _____ Account

(c) Sold goods on credit to K. Williams.

Debit _____ Account   Credit _____ Account

(d) Proprietor took goods for his own use.

Debit _____ Account   Credit _____ Account

(e) Goods are returned to the firm by K. Williams.

Debit _____ Account   Credit _____ Account

(f) Received a refund of rates in cash.

Debit _____ Account   Credit _____ Account

Now use your ledger to work through the following assignments.

5.5

A. Oldridge started a new business on 1 May 20-7. In your ledger write up the double entry accounts needed to record the following transactions:

May 1   Started business with £5,000 in a business bank account

2   Bought goods on credit from J. Richardson costing £750.00 plus VAT £131.25, total invoice £881.25

4   Withdrew £500 cash from the bank and placed it in the cash till for use in the business

6   Returned goods to J. Richardson for £40.00 plus VAT £7.00; a credit note for £47.00 is received

7   Proprietor took £100.00 cash for personal use

11   Sold goods on credit to K. Stead priced at £150.00 plus VAT £26.25, total invoice £176.25

12   Paid rent £275.50 by cheque

14   K. Stead returned goods priced at £24.00 plus VAT £4.20; a credit note for £28.20 is issued

15   Paid motor expenses (£148.60, VAT £26.00), total £174.60 in cash

16   Received rent for premises sublet, £230.00 by cheque

19   Bought goods on credit from S. Ramsden costing £720.80 plus VAT £126.14, total invoice £846.94

22   Paid wages £150 in cash

24   Received £148.05 by cheque from K. Stead

26   Sold goods on credit to T. Barnett priced at £122.00 plus VAT £21.35, total invoice £143.35

27   Returned goods to S. Ramsden for £68.94 plus VAT £12.06; a credit note for £81.00 is received

30   Proprietor took £150 by cheque for his private use

5.6

Keith Wilson started a new business on 1 June 20-7. In your ledger write up the double entry accounts needed to record the following transactions:

Jun 1   Started business with £10,000 in cash

2   Bought goods on credit from Kruger Imports costing £502.54 plus VAT £87.94, total invoice £590.48

3   Paid rent of £250.00 in cash

6   Paid £9,000 of the cash into a business bank account

8   Sold goods on credit to J. Stevens priced at £250.92 plus VAT £43.91, total invoice £294.83

10   Bought goods on credit from A. Dawson costing £329.50 plus VAT £57.66, total invoice £387.16

12   Keith Wilson took £175 cash for his own use

14   Goods returned by J. Stevens priced at £25.90 plus VAT £4.53; a credit note for £30.43 is issued

16   Returned goods to Kruger Imports costing £38.52 plus VAT £6.74; a credit note for £45.26 is received

18   Paid rates by cheque £150.00

20   Bought goods on credit from A. Dawson costing £650.70 plus VAT £113.87, total invoice £764.57

23   Sold goods on credit to G. Blackman priced at £495.60 plus VAT £86.73, total invoice £582.33

26   Keith Wilson took £120 by cheque for personal use

28   Received £264.40 from J. Stevens by cheque

29   Goods returned by G. Blackman priced at £58.00 plus VAT £10.15; a credit note for £68.15 is issued

30   Paid Kruger Imports £250.00 by cheque

5.7

Denise Shelley started a new business on 1 August 20-7. In your ledger write up the double entry accounts needed to record the following transactions:

Aug 1   Started business with £5,000 in a business bank account

2   Bought goods on credit from Smith & Weston costing £359.20 plus VAT £62.86, invoice total £422.06

5   Sold goods on credit to H. Gibson priced at £280.69 plus VAT £49.12, total invoice £329.81

7   Returned goods to Smith & Weston costing £38.75 plus VAT £6.78; a credit note for £45.53 is received

10   Withdrew £300 cash from the bank and placed it in the cash till for use in the business

12   Denise Shelley took £150 by cheque for her private use

15   Paid rent of £280 in cash

19   Goods returned by H. Gibson priced at £40.00 plus VAT £7.00; a credit note for £47.00 is issued

21   Received part of the amount owing from H. Gibson, £200 in cash.

22   Paid wages in cash £175

23   Bought goods on credit from Dale Supplies costing £620.54 plus VAT £108.59, total invoice £729.13

24   Sold goods on credit to J. Youngman £278.54 plus VAT £48.74, total invoice £327.28

27   Goods returned to Dale Supplies costing £57.50 plus VAT £10.06; a credit note for £67.56 is received

28   Received rent of £50 in cash for part of premises sublet

31   Paid Smith & Weston £250.00 by cheque

5.8

Thomas Garside started a new business on 1 October 20-8. In your ledger write up the double entry accounts needed to record the following transactions:

Oct 1   Started business with £7,000 in the business bank account

2   Bought goods on credit from T. Richie costing £750.00 plus VAT £131.25, total invoice £881.25

3   Withdrew £750.00 cash from the bank and placed it in the cash till for use in the business
5   Sold goods on credit to D. Jenkins priced at £295.50 plus VAT £51.71, total invoice £347.21
7   Paid rent of £195 in cash
10 Goods returned to T. Richie costing £62.54 plus VAT £10.94; a credit note for £73.48 is received
12 Received commission of £75 by cheque
14 Bought goods on credit from R. Kemp costing £267.96 plus VAT £46.89, total invoice £314.85
15 Goods returned by D. Jenkins priced at £38.92 plus VAT £6.81; a credit note for £45.73 is issued
18 Sold goods on credit to J. Patel priced at £150.00 plus VAT £26.25, total invoice £176.25
20 Paid wages, £250 in cash
22 Bought goods on credit from R. Kemp costing £360.80 plus VAT £63.14, total invoice £423.94
24 Paid T. Richie £807.77 by cheque
26 Returned goods to R. Kemp costing £55.90 plus VAT £9.78; a credit note for £65.68 is received
27 Sold goods on credit to D. Jenkins £130.70 plus VAT £22.87, total invoice £153.57
28 Commission received in cash £165.00
29 Received a cheque for £301.48 from D. Jenkins
30 Thomas Garside took £150 in cash for his personal use
31 Paid wages, £275.50 in cash

■ ✗ **6** Balancing accounts

The term *balance* is the word used in accounting to describe the difference between the two sides of an account. It is the most important figure in any account because it tells the value of that account.

We shall now look at the method used to calculate the balance at a given time. Accounts can be balanced at any time, but in most firms they are *balanced* at the end of each month. This is how it is done:

1 Add up the side of the account that is greatest in value.
2 Add up the other side of the account.
3 Deduct the smaller total from the larger total: the difference between the two sides is the *'balance'*.
4 Now enter the balance on the side that is smallest in value. This is described as the *balance c/d*, which means that the balance is to be carried down.
5 Enter the totals on both sides of the account, making sure that the two totals are level and parallel with each other. As the difference between the two sides has been added to the smaller side, both sides will now be equal.
6 The *balance* is then brought down, to the opposite side of the account.

To illustrate the process, let us look at a typical cash account:

Cash Account

		£				£
Mar 1 Sales		350	Mar	2	Motor expenses	35
				4	Rent	65
				15	Drawings	100

Cash received is entered at the debit side of the account; cash paid out is entered at the credit side.

	£
The debit side is greatest in value; it totals	350
The credit side totals	200
the difference between the two sides is the *balance*	150
(this represents the amount of cash that remains)	

This is how the cash account will look after it has been balanced:

Cash Account

	£			£
Mar 1 Sales	350	Mar 2 Motor expenses		35
		4 Rent		65
		15 Drawings		100
		31 Balance c/d		150
	350			350
Apr 1 Balance b/d	150			

Most firms balance their accounts at the end of each month, so the balance to be *carried down*, abbreviated as *c/d* is written in the account on the last day of the current month. The balance is then *brought down (b/d)* on the first day of the next month. These two balancing entries are a *double entry*. Remember, if there is a balance c/d there will always be a balance b/d.

When the balance is brought down to the debit side of an account, it is described as a *'debit balance'*. When the balance is brought down to the credit side of an account, it is described as a *'credit balance'*.

Balancing debtors' accounts

Every firm will need to know how much is owed by its customers for goods supplied. We can now look at a customer's account for transactions during April 20-6.

B. Senior Account

	£			£
Apr 3 Sales	235	Apr 10 Sales returns		46
15 Sales	350	28 Bank		189
25 Sales	145			

To balance this account, the same principles apply. First total the side which is greatest in value:

	£
the debit side is greatest in value; it totals	730
the credit side totals	235
the difference between the two sides is the *balance*	495

(this represents the amount owed by B. Senior)

This is how B. Senior's account will look after it has been balanced:

B. Senior Account

		£			£
Apr 3	Sales	235	Apr 10	Sales returns	46
15	Sales	350	28	Bank	189
25	Sales	145	30	Balance c/d	495
		730			730
May 1	Balance b/d	495			

We now look at G. Palmer's account:

G. Palmer Account

		£			£
Apr 2	Sales	120	Apr 26	Bank	280
8	Sales	160			

This customer owed the firm nothing at the end of April 20-6 because his account was paid in full, both sides are equal so there is no balance, but the account still needs to be totalled, making sure that the totals are parallel with each other, like this:

G. Palmer Account

		£			£
Apr 2	Sales	120	Apr 26	Bank	280
8	Sales	160			
		280			280

If accounts contain only one entry *do not* enter a total. A double line ruled under each side will mean that the entry is its own total. The balance is written in and brought down like this:

H. Malik Account

		£			£
Apr 18	Sales	250	Apr 30	Balance c/d	250
May 1	Balance b/d	250			

Balancing creditors' accounts

Firms need to know regularly how much they owe to their suppliers. Exactly the same principles will apply when balances are brought down to the credit side. We now look at a supplier's account for transactions during April 20-6.

F. Reedman Account

		£				£
Apr 12	Purchase returns	25	Apr	7	Purchases	625
29	Bank	600		18	Purchases	300

To find the balance on this account, first total the side that is greatest in value:

	£
the credit side is greatest in value; it totals	925
the debit side totals	625
the difference between the two sides is the *balance*	300

(this represents the amount owed to F. Reedman)

This is how F. Reedman's account will look after it has been balanced:

F. Reedman Account

			£				£
Apr	12	Purchase returns	25	Apr	7	Purchases	625
	29	Bank	600		18	Purchases	300
	30	Balance c/d	300				
			925				925
				May	1	Balance b/d	300

If an account contains only one entry on each side and they are equal to each other, totals are not entered and a double line is ruled under each side, like this:

T. Gordon Account

	£				£
Apr 28 Bank	250	Apr	5	Purchases	250

So far, we have assumed that there were no balances on any of the accounts at the beginning of the month. In practice, most accounts will have an opening balance at the beginning of each month (if you have a bank account you will be familiar with the first line on your bank statement saying 'balance brought forward'). The same is true for a business – unless it is a new business there will be balances on the accounts. The opening balance on an account is the value of that account at that date.

If opening balances are given, they need to be entered into the accounts, on the correct side, *before* recording any transactions. Opening balances are always shown under the relevant headings of *debit* and *credit*, usually abbreviated to *DR* and *CR*. They are described as the '*balance brought down*', generally shortened to '*balance b/d*'. The procedure is:

Open an account for each of the balances given (debit balances are entered on the debit side, credit balances entered on the credit side), enter the date, balance b/d and the amount stated.

For example, the first three opening balances on 1 February 20-6 for Assignment 6.3 (see page 53) are:

	DR	CR
Keswick Timber		513.76
Premier Imports		394.82
Decking Centre	896.84	

These opening balances will be entered in the accounts like this:

Keswick Timber Account

		20-6		£
		1 Feb	Balance b/d	513.76

Premier Imports Account

		20-6		£
		1 Feb	Balance b/d	394.82

Decking Centre Account

20-6		£	
1 Feb	Balance b/d	896.84	

Separating the accounts into three main ledgers

So far we have been thinking of the ledger as one book containing all the accounts. However, even in a relatively small business it would be very difficult to keep all the accounts in one ledger, and this would mean that only one person would be able to use the ledger at any given time. It is therefore necessary to divide the ledger into smaller units to enable the work of recording transactions to be shared and carried out more efficiently. The names of the new ledgers are a good indication of the accounts they contain. The first stage involves removing *debtors'* and *creditors'* accounts, which will now be kept in their own separate ledgers.

Purchase ledger

This ledger contains all the suppliers' personal accounts. Goods purchased on credit are bought from suppliers, who then become *creditors*.

Sales ledger

This ledger contains all the customers' personal accounts. Sales on credit are made to customers, who then become *debtors*.

Nominal ledger

All other accounts are kept in the nominal ledger, which is also known as the *General Ledger*.

Points to remember

- The *balance* of an account is the difference between the two sides. It is the most significant figure in any account because it describes the value of that account. When the balance is brought down to the debit side, it is called a *debit balance*. When the balance is brought down to the credit side, it is called a *credit balance*. Accounts can be balanced at any time, but generally they are balanced at the end of each month.
- Balancing accounts uses more lines on the page, so make sure your accounts are positioned several lines apart to avoid a 'jumbled' appearance.
- If opening balances are given, they need to be entered into the accounts, on the correct side, *before* recording any transactions.
- The *sales ledger* contains all the customers' accounts (debtors).
- The *purchase ledger* contains all the suppliers' accounts (creditors).
- The *nominal ledger* (or *general ledger*) contains all other accounts.

Assignments

6.1

Complete the blank spaces by inserting the name of the ledger in which the following accounts would appear. The first one is completed as an example.

(a) D. Wilson customer's account   *Sales ledger*
(b) Purchase returns account   _____ ledger
(c) Motor expenses account   _____ ledger
(d) Motor vehicles account   _____ ledger
(e) Smith & Pearson supplier's account   _____ ledger
(f) Sales account   _____ ledger

6.2

Complete the blank spaces by inserting the name of the ledger in which the following accounts would appear:

(a) Machinery account   _____ ledger
(b) B. Senior customer's account   _____ ledger
(c) Purchases account   _____ ledger
(d) Office furniture account   _____ ledger
(e) Newstylax supplier's account   _____ ledger
(f) Purchase returns account   _____ ledger

6.3

You are responsible for keeping the purchase, sales and nominal ledgers of Oaklands Fencing. Open ledger accounts and enter the following balances as at 1 February 20-6:

	DR	CR
Keswick Timber		513.76
Premier Imports		394.82
Decking Centre	896.84	
Morris Parks	675.20	
Bank	5,979.76	
Furniture & fittings	7,520.58	
Purchases	3,050.92	
Purchase returns		419.64
Sales		12,576.18
Sales returns	306.70	
Capital		3,942.62
Value Added Tax		582.98

In your ledger write up the double entry accounts to record the following transactions for the month of February 20-6:

Feb 3 Purchased goods on credit from Premier Imports costing £409.26 plus VAT £71.62, total invoice £480.88

5 Purchased goods on credit from Keswick Timber costing £375.90 plus VAT £65.78, total invoice £441.68

10 Goods returned to Premier Imports costing £38.52 plus VAT £6.74; a credit note for £45.26 is received

12 Paid Keswick Timber £276.80 by cheque

15 Paid Premier Imports £207.42 by cheque

16 Sold goods on credit to Morris Parks priced at £394.98 plus VAT £69.12, total invoice £464.10

20 Sold goods on credit to Decking Centre priced at £502.54 plus VAT £87.94, total invoice £590.48

22 Goods returned by Morris Parks priced at £43.68 plus VAT £7.64; a credit note for £51.32 is issued

24 Paid HM Revenue & Customs £582.98 (VAT) by cheque

26 Received £620.42 by cheque from Decking Centre

27 Received £476.58 by cheque from Morris Parks

6.4

You are responsible for keeping the purchase, sales and nominal ledgers of Moorland Textiles. Open ledger accounts and enter the following balances as at 1 November 20-6:

	DR	CR
Giles Murray		369.20
Four Star Supplies		502.84
Escape Hotels	703.92	
Myers Group	850.38	
Bank	6,729.76	
Machinery	9,650.50	
Purchases	2,804.40	
Purchase returns		305.90
Sales		10,748.32
Sales returns	267.04	
Capital		8,587.00
Value Added Tax		492.74

In your ledger write up the double entry accounts to record the following transactions for the month of November 20-6. At the end of the month balance all the accounts.

Nov 2 Purchased goods on credit from Four Star Supplies costing £306.93 plus VAT £53.71, total invoice £360.64

7 Purchased goods on credit from Giles Murray costing £524.70 plus VAT £91.82, total invoice £616.52

10 Goods returned to Four Star Supplies costing £32.70 plus VAT £5.72; a credit note for £38.42 is received

12   Bought a new photocopier for use in the business (machinery £588.00, VAT £102.90), cheque total £690.90
15   Paid Four Star Supplies £251.42 by cheque
16   Paid Giles Murray £184.60 by cheque
18   Sold goods on credit to Myers Group priced at £560.70 plus VAT £98.12, total invoice £658.82
20   Sold goods on credit to Escape Hotels priced at £704.36 plus VAT £123.26, total invoice £827.62
26   Goods returned by Myers Group priced at £40.80 plus VAT £7.14; a credit note for £47.94 is issued
28   Received £352.96 by cheque from Escape Hotels
30   Received £426.50 by cheque from Myers Group

6.5

You are responsible for keeping the purchase, sales and nominal ledgers of David Williams. Open ledger accounts and enter the following balances as at 1 May 20-6:

	DR	CR
D. Morris		296.74
R. Johnson		402.90
Lewis Morgan	560.50	
G. Howard	738.42	
Bank	7,250.96	
Purchases	2,984.02	
Purchase returns		309.62
Sales		9,650.38
Sales returns	272.60	
Capital		7,618.90
Equipment	6,950.50	
Value Added Tax		478.46

In your ledger write up the double entry accounts to record the following transactions for the month of May 20-6. At the end of the month balance all the accounts.

May 2   Purchased goods on credit from D. Morris costing £395.60 plus VAT £69.23, total invoice £464.83
      8   Purchased goods on credit from R. Johnson costing £208.36 plus VAT £36.46, total invoice £244.82
     12   Goods returned to D. Morris costing £40.70 plus VAT £7.12, a credit note for £47.82 is received
     15   Goods returned to R. Johnson costing £28.76 plus VAT £5.03; a credit note for £33.79 is received
     16   Bought a new printer for use in the business (equipment £152.77, VAT £26.73), cheque total £179.50
     18   Paid D. Morris £296.74 by cheque
     20   Paid R. Johnson £402.90 by cheque

21 Sold goods on credit to Lewis Morgan priced at £384.59 plus VAT £67.30, total invoice £451.89

23 Sold goods on credit to G. Howard priced at £506.30 plus VAT £88.60, total invoice £594.90

28 Goods returned by Lewis Morgan priced at £34.18 plus VAT £5.98; a credit note for £40.16 is issued

29 Received £369.20 by cheque from G. Howard

31 Received £280.30 by cheque from Lewis Morgan

■ ⌄ **7** The trial balance

A *trial balance* is a simple way of checking that all entries made in the ledger have been completed correctly. When transactions are entered in the ledger accounts, every debit entry will have a corresponding credit entry; therefore, in principle the debit balances should equal the credit balances. To check that the debit balances do in fact equal the credit balances a *trial balance* is prepared.

A *trial balance* is a list of *balances* only, arranged in two columns according to whether they are *debit balances* or *credit balances*. When there is a debit balance on an account, the balance is entered in the debit column; when there is a credit balance on an account, the balance is entered in the credit column. *Accounts that do not have a balance are not entered.* When all the balances are entered, the two columns are totalled and they should agree. When they do agree, it is a good indication that the transactions have been entered correctly in the ledger accounts.

A trial balance is usually drawn up at the end of each month, its purpose being to test the arithmetical accuracy of the bookkeeping. Although useful as a means of checking the accuracy of transactions recorded in the ledger, the agreement of a trial balance does not prove that errors have not been made. It has limitations as there are some errors it will not reveal; these are considered in Unit 24.

A trial balance is always taken on a *specific date* and this date should be clearly written as part of the heading. A trial balance is not an account and should not be placed in the ledger; journal paper is ruled with two columns on the right-hand side and is generally used for preparing a trial balance.

Take care when listing your balances in a trial balance, because things can go wrong. You can make mistakes by entering a balance in the wrong column or copy the figures incorrectly, or you can miss out an entry completely.

We can now draw up a trial balance by listing all the balances remaining on the accounts for Oaklands Fencing that you tackled in Assignment 6.3.

Trial balance as at 28 February 20-6

	DR	CR
Keswick Timber		678.64
Premier Imports		623.02
Decking Centre	866.90	
Morris Parks	611.40	
Bank	6,009.56	
Furniture & Fittings	7,520.58	
Purchases	3,836.08	
Purchase returns		458.16
Sales		13,473.70
Sales returns	350.38	
Capital		3,942.62
Value Added Tax		18.76
	19,194.90	19,194.90

When all the balances are entered, the two columns are totalled, and they *should agree.*

Points to remember

- A *trial balance* is always drawn up at a *specific date*, and this date should be clearly written as part of the heading.
- If your *trial balance totals* do not agree, the following procedure will very often reveal the errors.
- Re-check the addition of the totals to make sure that the error is not just a simple matter of addition.
- Check the balances to make sure they have been entered into the correct column: has a debit balance in the ledger been incorrectly entered in the credit column of the trial balance, or vice versa?
- Check for transposition of figures: a very common mistake is for figures to be transposed (written down in the wrong order); for example, a balance of £275 written in the trial balance as £257.
- Check that you have calculated the balances on each account accurately.
- Errors can occur that are not revealed by a trial balance. These types of errors are covered in Unit 24, which deals with errors not affecting trial balance agreement.

Assignments

7.1

Prepare a trial balance as at 30 November 20-6 using the balances remaining on the accounts for Moorland Textiles (see Assignment 6.4).

7.2

Prepare a trial balance as at 31 May 20-6 by listing the balances remaining on the accounts for David Williams (see Assignment 6.5).

7.3

You are responsible for keeping the purchase, sales and nominal ledgers of Nikas Sportswear. Open ledger accounts and enter the following opening balances as at 1 February 20-7:

	DR	CR
Airedale Fabrics		376.94
Hollywell Mills		290.46
E. Kemp		485.30
Activity Centre	730.04	
Spot Sport	898.92	
Bank	4,372.86	
Capital		8,270.64
Equipment	9,650.80	
Purchases	2,095.48	
Purchase returns		256.30
Sales		8,704.62
Sales returns	202.34	
Sundry expenses	839.56	
Value Added Tax		405.74

In your ledger write up the double entry accounts to record the following transactions for the month of February 20-7. At the end of the month, balance all the accounts and extract a trial balance.

Purchases on credit		Goods £	VAT £	Total £
2 Feb	E. Kemp	208.53	36.49	245.02
8 Feb	Airedale Fabrics	252.80	44.24	297.04
12 Feb	Hollywell Mills	325.38	56.94	382.32
18 Feb	Airedale Fabrics	274.50	48.04	322.54
20 Feb	E. Kemp	196.46	34.38	230.84
24 Feb	Hollywell Mills	305.24	53.42	358.66

Purchase returns		Goods £	VAT £	Total £
15 Feb	Airedale Fabrics	43.68	7.64	51.32
18 Feb	E. Kemp	50.20	8.78	58.98

Sales on credit		Goods	VAT	Total
		£	£	£
3 Feb	Spot Sport	409.36	71.64	481.00
6 Feb	Activity Centre	714.50	125.04	839.54
19 Feb	Spot Sport	520.90	91.16	612.06
27 Feb	Activity Centre	639.20	111.86	751.06

Sales returns		Goods	VAT	Total
		£	£	£
14 Feb	Activity Centre	65.38	11.44	76.82
15 Feb	Spot Sport	57.86	10.12	67.98

Payments made by cheque

			£
5 Feb	Offtex	(*Equipment £109.99 VAT £19.25*)	129.24
8 Feb	Y. D. Council	(*Rates – Sundry expenses*)	274.80
19 Feb	E. Kemp	(*Creditor*)	368.52
20 Feb	Airedale Fabrics	(*Creditor*)	295.38
24 Feb	Hollywell Mills	(*Creditor*)	170.96
26 Feb	HM Revenue & Customs	(*VAT*)	405.74

Payments received by cheque

		£
16 Feb	Spot Sport	650.28
18 Feb	Activity Centre	590.40

7.4

You are responsible for keeping the purchase, sales and nominal ledgers of Paramont Designs. Open ledger accounts and enter the following opening balances as at 1 May 20-7:

	DR	CR
Linkwell Bros		574.94
Springfields		1,408.30
Moonstones	1,527.68	
Owen & Robins	2,434.72	
Vandervilles	1,860.36	
Bank		1,039.58
Capital		5,231.54
General expenses	792.42	
Machinery	12,095.90	
Purchases	9,363.34	
Purchase returns		306.24
Sales		19,053.62
Sales returns	290.58	
Value Added Tax		750.78

In your ledger write up the double entry accounts to record the following transactions for the month of May 20-7. At the end of the month, balance all the accounts and extract a trial balance.

Purchases on credit		Goods £	VAT £	Total £
4 May	Springfields	490.50	85.84	576.34
10 May	Linkwell Bros	304.68	53.32	358.00
19 May	Springfields	372.46	65.18	437.64
24 May	Linkwell Bros	501.92	87.84	589.76

Purchase returns		Goods £	VAT £	Total £
12 May	Springfields	38.74	6.78	45.52
20 May	Linkwell Bros	43.56	7.62	51.18

Sales on credit		Goods £	VAT £	Total £
3 May	Owen Robins	408.36	71.46	479.82
5 May	Moonstones	296.70	51.92	348.62
8 May	Vandervilles	501.48	87.76	589.24
12 May	Moonstones	320.24	56.04	376.28
19 May	Owen & Robins	680.60	119.10	799.70
26 May	Vandervilles	475.56	83.22	558.78

Sales returns		Goods £	VAT £	Total £
11 May	Moonstones	50.30	8.80	59.10
14 May	Owen & Robins	48.94	8.56	57.50

Payments made by cheque

			£
2 May	Freshcool	*(General expenses £67.66 VAT £11.84)*	79.50
10 May	Epsonex	*(Printer, Machinery £238.21 VAT £41.69)*	279.90
15 May	Springfields	*(Creditor)*	820.68
28 May	Linkwell Bros	*(Creditor)*	1,471.52
29 May	SKS (UK)	*(General expenses £81.70 VAT £14.30)*	96.00
30 May	HM Revenue & Customs	*(VAT)*	750.78

Payments received by cheque

		£
16 May	Vandervilles	1,530.26
20 May	Moonstones	1,065.34

7.5

You are responsible for keeping the purchase, sales and nominal ledgers of Focus Lighting. Open ledger accounts and enter the following opening balances as at 1 November 20-7:

	DR	CR
Court Fabrics		514.68
Walkers Ltd		396.70
Yorkshire Supplies		450.24
Aladdin Lamps	826.92	
Supreme Deco	647.80	
Bank	4,605.26	
Capital		11,667.50
Fixtures & fittings	16,580.50	
Purchases	7,992.94	
Purchase returns		583.72
Sales		18,024.36
Sales returns	406.68	
Sundry expenses	1,389.90	
Value Added Tax		812.80

In your ledger write up the double entry accounts to record the following transactions for the month of November 20-7. At the end of the month, balance all the accounts and extract a trial balance.

Purchases on credit		Goods	VAT	Total
		£	£	£
2 Nov	Yorkshire Supplies	290.58	50.85	341.43
4 Nov	Court Fabrics	302.96	53.02	355.98
8 Nov	Yorkshire Supplies	215.30	37.68	252.98
14 Nov	Walkers Ltd	124.74	21.83	146.57
20 Nov	Court Fabrics	368.80	64.54	433.34
25 Nov	Walkers Ltd	176.26	30.84	207.10

Purchase returns		Goods	VAT	Total
		£	£	£
12 Nov	Court Fabrics	47.95	8.39	56.34
14 Nov	Yorkshire Supplies	38.23	6.69	44.92

Sales on credit		Goods	VAT	Total
		£	£	£
3 Nov	Supreme Deco	450.80	78.89	529.69
5 Nov	Aladdin Lamps	394.28	69.00	463.28
10 Nov	Supreme Deco	536.56	93.90	630.46
18 Nov	Aladdin Lamps	372.34	65.16	437.50

Sales returns		Goods	VAT	Total
		£	£	£
10 Nov	Supreme Deco	42.80	7.49	50.29
15 Nov	Aladdin Lamps	34.26	5.99	40.25

Payments made by cheque

			£
2 Nov	T. McKay	*(Fixtures & fittings £595.32, VAT £104.18)*	699.50
7 Nov	Teleco	*(Sundry expenses £208.74, VAT £36.53)*	245.27
14 Nov	Court Fabrics	*(Creditor)*	395.84
18 Nov	Yorkshire Supplies	*(Creditor)*	999.73
20 Nov	Fordhams	*(Fixtures & fittings £166.38, VAT £29.12)*	195.50
26 Nov	Walkers Ltd	*(Creditor)*	278.46

Payments received by cheque

		£
17 Nov	Aladdin Lamps	680.38
21 Nov	Supreme Deco	459.76

■ ☑ **8** Analysed petty cash book and the imprest system

All organisations regularly incur small items of expenditure. *Petty cash* is the name given to money that can be used to pay for *small cash purchases*. The word 'petty' means small. For example, if someone was asked to buy a new plant for the Reception area, the money spent would be repaid out of petty cash. A receipt should be obtained for all transactions involving cash. Petty cash is often used to pay for small items of expense such as stationery, postage stamps, refreshments, petrol and travelling expenses such as taxi, bus and train fares. Small items of expense like these are usually recorded in the *petty cash book*, which is designed specifically for this purpose. The rules for entering petty cash transactions are the same as for any other cash account; that is, debit receipts of cash and credit payments.

In an office, the person responsible for petty cash is known as the *petty cashier*. That person will be provided with a sum of money known as a '*float*'. The petty cashier is responsible for this money, making payments to members of staff to repay them for expenses incurred on behalf of the organisation, keeping records of payments made and amounts received, and balancing the petty cash book at regular intervals. This person will usually carry out these duties alongside their other work.

The business will decide on the maximum value for any transaction that can be paid out of petty cash; this is generally about £25.00.

Petty cash vouchers

Whenever anyone needs to claim money out of petty cash they must fill in a *petty cash voucher* showing exactly what the payment was for. Members of staff are usually expected to obtain receipts for items purchased, which are then attached to the petty cash vouchers. Each completed voucher is then signed by the person receiving the money, to verify that the petty cashier has paid the amount claimed. Vouchers are dated and numbered in the order they are received, each voucher being given the next highest number.

Here is an illustration of a typical petty cash voucher:

	Folio	48	
PETTY CASH VOUCHER	Date	_2 Feb 20-6_	

For what required	AMOUNT	
	£	p
Milk	8	52
	8	52

Signature	D Mason
Passed by	M Nicholson

Rules for dealing with cash

- Cash is valuable. When you are receiving or paying out cash *always* count it carefully.
- Petty cash should only be paid out in return for a completed voucher accompanied by a receipt.
- Never leave cash unattended for even a few minutes.
- Always keep cash in a lockable box and store it in a safe place.
- Be careful with keys.

The imprest system

Under the *imprest system* of keeping petty cash, an agreed sum of money is given to the petty cashier as a *float*; this is known as the *imprest*. It is used to make petty cash payments over a period of time, which could be a week or a month. At the end of the designated period, the petty cash book is totalled and balanced, and the petty cashier is repaid the amount required to bring the float back to its starting level. Each new period begins with the imprest at the original level. This is known as *restoring the imprest*.

For example, if the petty cashier started the month with £100, and during the month paid out £85.50, there should be £14.50 left in the petty cash box at the end of the period. This £14.50 is known as the *balance*. A senior member of staff would check that the amount of cash remaining (the balance) agrees with the amount shown in the petty cash book, the petty cashier would then receive £85.50, which would restore the petty cash to the original amount of £100. Each new period starts with the *full amount* of the imprest.

	£ p
Imprest (float) at start of week was	100.00
Total paid out during the week was	85.50
Balance of cash at end of week	14.50

A petty cashier should check the contents of the petty cash box regularly.

This is done by counting the cash in the petty cash box, then adding together the amounts shown on the vouchers. The total cash in the petty cash box, plus the total of the vouchers, should equal the amount of the float (imprest) at any time during the period.

Now test yourself on these important points by completing this assignment.

8.1

(a)   The imprest (float) to start the month was £150.00. You have petty cash vouchers to the value of £135.20. How much should be in your petty cash box?

(b)   The imprest at the start of the month was £175.00. If £164.30 is spent during the month, how much will you receive at the end of the month?

(c)   To start the month, the imprest was £200.00. Your petty cash box now contains: 4 × £5 notes, 2 × £1 coins, 5 × 50p coins, 1 × 10p coin, 3 × 2p coins and 4 × 1p coins. How much has been spent during the month?

(d)   The imprest to start the month was £230.00. You have petty cash vouchers to the value of £179.25. How much should be left in your petty cash box?

(e)   You have petty cash vouchers to the value of £142.45. Your petty cash box contains: 4 × £1 coins, 3 × 50p coins, 6 × 20p coins, 7 × 10p coins and 3 × 5p coins. How much was the imprest?

Receipts

Sometimes the petty cashier may receive money from a member of staff. This could be for the purchase of postage stamps, use of the firm's telephone or perhaps personal use of the photocopier. When this happens, the petty cashier completes a receipt in duplicate. The top copy is given to the person paying for the item, and the petty cashier uses the copy to enter the details into the petty cash book. This is an illustration of a typical receipt:

```
┌─────────────────────────────────────────────┐
│  5 February 20-6                No    20      │
│                                               │
│  Received                                     │
│         from    R Patel                       │
│                                               │
│  The sum of   Two pounds and eighty           │
│                                               │
│               pence (for postage stamps)      │
│                                               │
│  Cheque    ┌──────┬──────┐                    │
│            │      │      │                    │
│  Cash      │  2   │  80  │   M Nicholson      │
│            └──────┴──────┘                    │
│                                               │
│               WITH THANKS                     │
└─────────────────────────────────────────────┘
```

The petty cashier will enter the receipt of £2.80 in cash into the petty cash book in the column headed *Receipts*.

Value Added Tax (VAT)

Most of the goods and services we buy in shops and from companies are subject to Value Added Tax. This is generally abbreviated and known as VAT. It is a type of sales tax that is charged as a percentage and added to the price of certain goods and services, as we saw in Unit 3.

Some petty cash payments may be subject to VAT, and when they are, the amount of VAT should be shown on the petty cash voucher. This is because firms that are registered for VAT can reclaim the amount of VAT paid on business expenses from HM Revenue & Customs. Firms who wish to reclaim VAT must keep a separate VAT column in their petty cash book to enter amounts of VAT.

When petty cash expenses are subject to VAT, the amount of VAT is shown separately on the voucher, like this:

| PETTY CASH VOUCHER | Folio | 49 |
| | Date | 9 Feb 20-6 |

For what required	AMOUNT £	p
Envelopes	4	25
VAT		74
	4	99

Signature   E Bailey

Passed by   M Nicholson

Analysis columns

In the analysed petty cash book, the types of expenditure that occur most frequently will be given an analysis column of their own. The word *analysis* means breaking up into smaller parts, so various items of expense can be arranged under a suitable column heading. It is then possible to see how much is being spent on particular items. Obviously, the number of analysis columns used will depend on what each business finds useful. When payments are subject to VAT, the amount of VAT *must* be shown separately and entered in the VAT column.

At the end of the period, all the analysis columns are totalled to show the amount spent under each heading.

Various types of payment are made through petty cash, but generally they will fit under one of the following analysis column headings:

VAT	Postage	Stationery	Refreshments	Sundry expenses	Ledger

Most firms use a *Sundry expenses* column for items that will not easily fit under any of the other column headings.

One of the columns is usually chosen as a *Ledger* column. This is only used for items paid out of petty cash which need posting to a ledger other than the general ledger; for example, when a creditor is paid out of petty cash.

At the end of the period, the total of each individual analysis column will be posted to the ledger account for that expense. For example, the stationery paid for out of petty cash will be posted to the stationery account in the general ledger.

Filling in the petty cash book

Each new period begins with the amount of the balance brought down from the previous month. This is entered in the *Receipts* column. The receipts column is the *debit* side of the petty cash book. This is followed by the entry to record the money received to restore the (float) imprest.

- In this example the imprest amount is £100. There was a balance brought down from the previous month of £15.50, so cash received to restore the imprest is £84.50. To illustrate the process, let us look at a typical petty cash book showing the balance b/d and the cash provided to restore the imprest.

Petty cash book

Receipts £ p	Date	Details	Voucher number	Total payments £ p	VAT £ p	Postage £ p	Stationery £ p	Refreshments £ p	Sundry expenses £ p	Ledger £ p
15.50	1 Feb	Balance b/d								
84.50	1 Feb	Cash								

All entries are made in date order.

- The total payments column is the credit side of the petty cash book.
- Details of the item(s) purchased are always stated on the petty cash voucher and these must be entered correctly in the details column.
- The total amount spent is first entered in the *Total payments* column and then the relevant amounts are entered in the analysis columns.
- Money received is entered only in the *Receipts* column, followed by the date, and the details column is completed with the name of the person from whom the money is received and the reason. Receipts are *never* entered in the total payments or analysis columns.

Now we can see two petty cash vouchers and a receipt entered in the petty cash book.

		Folio	48		
PETTY CASH VOUCHER		Date	2 Feb 20-6		

PETTY CASH VOUCHER Folio 48 Date 2 Feb 20-6

For what required	AMOUNT £	p
Milk	8	52
	8	52

Signature _D Mason_

Passed by _M Nicholson_

---

5 February 20-6 No 20

Received from _R Patel_

The sum of _Two pounds and eighty pence (for postage stamps)_

Cheque			
Cash	2	80	_M Nicholson_

WITH THANKS

PETTY CASH VOUCHER Folio 49 Date 9 Feb 20-6

For what required	AMOUNT £	p
Envelopes	4	25
VAT		74
	4	99

Signature _E Bailey_

Passed by _M Nicholson_

Petty cash book

Receipts £ p	Date	Details	Voucher number	Total payments £ p	VAT £ p	Postage £ p	Stationery £ p	Refreshments £ p	Sundry expenses £ p	Ledger £ p
15.50	1 Feb	Balance b/d								
84.50	1 Feb	Cash								
	2 Feb	Milk	48	8.52				8.52		
2.80	5 Feb	R Patel (postage)	20							
	9 Feb	Envelopes	49	4.99	.74		4.25			

Balancing the petty cash book

When all the payments and receipts during the period (usually a month) have been entered, all the columns are totalled separately.

The total of all the analysis columns should *always* equal the addition of the *total payments* column. This method of checking is known as *cross casting* and will usually reveal any mistakes, either in the addition of the columns or if an item has been entered in the total payments column but not extended into one of the analysis columns.

This is the procedure to balance the petty cash book:

- Add up the total payments column and all the analysis columns.
- Cross cast the analysis columns; this figure should equal the total payments.
- Calculate the balance by deducting the amount of the total payments from the total of the receipts column.
- This amount is entered as the balance to carry down, generally abbreviated to *balance c/d* (this is the amount of cash in hand).
- Enter the totals, in the *Receipts* column and *Total payments* column, make sure the two totals are written on the same line, parallel with each other.
- The balance is then brought down into the *Receipts* column to start the next period.

When a senior member of staff has checked the petty cash book, the amount of the difference between the balance b/d and the imprest (float) is then handed to the petty cashier to restore the imprest to the original amount.

To illustrate this process, we now look at the completed petty cash book, balanced for the month of February 20-6.

Petty cash book

Receipts £ p	Date	Details	Voucher number	Total payments £ p	VAT £ p	Postage £ p	Stationery £ p	Refreshments £ p	Sundry expenses £ p	Ledger £ p
15.50	1 Feb	Balance b/d								
84.50	1 Feb	Cash								
	2 Feb	Milk	48	8.52				8.52		
2.80	5 Feb	R. Patel (Postage)	20							
	9 Feb	Envelopes	49	4.99	.74		4.25			
	12 Feb	Registered post	50	5.75		5.75				
	16 Feb	Torch and batteries	51	9.99	1.49				8.50	
	18 Feb	G. King (Creditor PL 24)	52	8.62						8.62
	20 Feb	Coffee and stamps	53	9.85		5.60		4.25		
	21 Feb	Parcel tape and string	54	12.83	1.91		10.92			
3.72	23 Feb	S. Roberts (use of telephone)	21							
	24 Feb	Petrol for van	55	24.08	3.58				20.50	
	26 Feb	Adel Newsagents (PL 30)	56	7.42						7.42
	28 Feb			92.05	7.72	11.35	15.17	12.77	29.00	16.04
		Balance c/d		14.47						
106.52				106.52						
14.47	1 Mar	Balance b/d								

To calculate the amount required to restore the imprest we deduct the balance b/d (this is the cash that remains) from the amount of the imprest. In this example, the imprest is £100.00 less £14.47, so £85.53 is required. A cheque would be made out for this amount.

We can now look at an illustration of a *cheque* and *counterfoil* ready to be completed for the amount to restore the imprest.

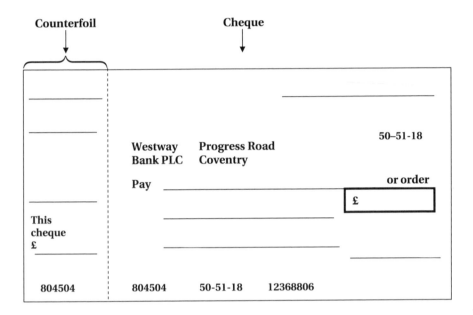

We need to complete the cheque by filling in the following details:

- Write the date (in this example *28 February 20-6*).
- On the line starting 'Pay', write *Cash*.
- Write the amount of the cheque (*£85.53*) in the box.
- Write the amount in words: *Eighty-five pounds and fifty-three pence.*

We then complete the counterfoil by filling in the following details:

- Write the date, which will be abbreviated since there is very little space (*28 Feb 20-6*).
- On the next line write the reason for the cheque, *Restore imprest.*
- On the next line write the purpose of the cheque, *Petty cash.*
- Write the amount of the cheque for references purposes (*£85.53*).

When you have filled in all the details on this cheque compare it with the illustration of the completed cheque:

```
28 Feb 20-6                                    28 February 20-6
                                                          50–51-18
Restore
imprest          Westway      Progress Road
                 Bank PLC     Coventry
─────────
Petty cash       Pay   Cash                              or order
─────────                                          ┌──────────────┐
                       Eighty-five pounds and      │  £ 85.53     │
This                                               └──────────────┘
cheque                 fifty-three pence
£ 85.53          ─────────────────────────────
─────────
                                                   ──────────────
   804504        804504      50-51-18    12368806
```

At the end of the period, each individual analysis column *total* will be posted to the relevant ledger account for that expense.

8.2

Look carefully at the illustration of the completed petty cash book for the month of February 20-6 on page 72 and answer the following questions:

(a) What is the amount of the imprest?
(b) How much was spent on stationery during the month?
(c) Was there any petty cash left at the end of the month? If so, how much?
(d) What was the total of all the analysis columns?
(e) How much was needed to restore the imprest on 1 February?
(f) What was the total amount spent during the month?
(g) How much was received in cash from receipt number 21.
(h) How much is needed to restore the imprest on 1 March?

Points to remember

- The rules for entering *petty cash* transactions are the same as for any other cash account; that is, *debit receipts of cash* and *credit payments*. Only the receipts column represents the debit side of the petty cash book.
- Always enter details of the items purchased and names from the receipts. Voucher numbers are placed alongside each entry. When petty cash payments are subject to VAT, the amount of *VAT must be shown separately* in the petty cash book.
- Total all the columns.
- The totals of the combined analysis columns should *always* agree with the addition of the total payments column, this is called *cross casting* and will usually locate any errors.
- *To find the balance of petty cash in hand*, deduct the total payments from the total of the receipts column.
- *To calculate the amount to restore the (float) imprest*, deduct the balance b/d at the end of the month from the amount of the imprest.
- At the end of the month, the total of each analysis column is posted to the relevant expense account in the nominal ledger.

Assignments

8.3

Pudsey Electronics operates an analytical petty cash book using the imprest system with analysis columns for: VAT, Postage, Stationery, Refreshments, Sundry expenses and Ledger. On 1 September 20-7 there was an opening balance of £38.42.

As the petty cashier, you are required to perform the following tasks:

(a) Enter the opening balance into the petty cash book.
(b) Enter the correct amount of cash that has been collected from the bank to restore the imprest to £200.00.
(c) Enter the details of the petty cash vouchers and receipts that have been sorted into date order into the petty cash book.
(d) Total and cross cast the petty cash book.
(e) Balance the petty cash book as at 30 September 20-7 and bring down the balance ready for 1 October 20-7.
(f) Prepare the cheque for the petty cash reimbursement for signing by the Director, and date the cheque 30 September 20-7.

PETTY CASH VOUCHER	Folio	38	
	Date	2 Sept 20-7	

For what required	AMOUNT £	p
Kettle	15	75
Tea and coffee	8	75
VAT	2	75
	27	25

Signature   K Smith

Passed by   M Dyson

PETTY CASH VOUCHER	Folio	39	
	Date	6 Sept 20-7	

For what required	AMOUNT £	p
Envelopes	5	72
Batteries	4	25
VAT	1	74
	11	71

Signature   A Schofield

Passed by   M Dyson

---

7 Sept 20-7   No   101

Received
From   J Martinez

The sum of Six pounds and seventy

eight pence (use of telephone)

Cheque		
Cash	6	78	M Dyson

WITH THANKS

PETTY CASH VOUCHER	Folio	40	
	Date	10 Sept 20-7	

For what required	AMOUNT £	p
Postage stamps	13	50
Parcel post	8	68
	22	18

Signature   B Dixon

Passed by   M Dyson

PETTY CASH VOUCHER	Folio	41	
	Date	12 Sept 20-7	

For what required	AMOUNT £	p
Petrol (includes £2.75 VAT)	18	50
	18	50

Signature   T Moore

Passed by   M Dyson

PETTY CASH VOUCHER	Folio	42	
	Date	15 Sept 20-7	

For what required	AMOUNT £	p
Milk		95
Tea bags	2	59
	3	54

Signature   K Smith

Passed by   M Dyson

		AMOUNT	
	Folio	43	
PETTY CASH VOUCHER	Date	15 Sept 20-7	
For what required		£	p
Special delivery parcel		16	80
		16	80
Signature	B Dixon		
Passed by	M Dyson		

19 Sept 20-7	No	102

Received
From _____ M Readings _____

The sum of _____ Seven pounds and fifty _____
_____ pence (use of photocopier) _____

Cheque			M Dyson
Cash	7	50	

WITH THANKS

		AMOUNT	
	Folio	44	
PETTY CASH VOUCHER	Date	24 Sept 20-7	
For what required		£	p
G Van Owen (Creditor PL 14)		20	98
		20	98
Signature	G Van Owen		
Passed by	M Dyson		

		AMOUNT	
	Folio	45	
PETTY CASH VOUCHER	Date	24 Sept 20-7	
For what required		£	p
Eight beakers		14	60
Marker pens		5	52
VAT		3	52
		23	64
Signature	E Bailey		
Passed by	M Dyson		

		AMOUNT	
	Folio	46	
PETTY CASH VOUCHER	Date	26 Sept 20-7	
For what required		£	p
Printer ribbon		6	38
Parcel post		14	20
VAT		1	12
		21	70
Signature	K Smith		
Passed by	M Dyson		

		AMOUNT	
	Folio	47	
PETTY CASH VOUCHER	Date	27 Sept 20-7	
For what required		£	p
D Chippendale (Creditor PL 19)		18	26
		18	26
Signature	D Chippendale		
Passed by	M Dyson		

```
  _____                                              _____

  _____                                              50–51-18
                        Westway      Progress Road
                        Bank PLC     Coventry

                        Pay  _____  or order
                                                              ┌──────────────┐
  _____                                                    │ £            │
  This                       _____         └──────────────┘
  cheque
  £                          _____
  _____

    804504                   804504      50-51-18    12368806
```

8.4

Mark Alexander is a sole trader who operates an analytical petty cash book using the imprest system, with analysis columns for VAT, Postage, Stationery, Refreshments, Sundry Expenses and Ledger. The imprest of £230.00 is restored at the beginning of each month.

As petty cashier, you are required to enter the following transactions for the month of October 20-7. Total and balance the petty cash book at the end of the month and bring down the balance for 1 November 20-7. State the amount required to restore the imprest on 1 November 20-7.

Oct 1   Opening balance of £42.76
     1   Enter correct amount of cash to restore the imprest to £230
     3   Paid for wall clock £13.58 plus VAT £2.37, voucher number 32
     5   Paid for stamps £8.40 and coffee £4.98, voucher number 33
     7   Paid for envelopes £2.75, box files £5.20, plus VAT £1.39, voucher number 34
     9   Received £12.50 from S. Groves (use of car park), receipt number 72
    12   Paid for dusters and polish £4.58 plus VAT 80p, voucher number 35
    14   Paid for registered post £10.75, voucher number 36
    14   Paid a creditor M. Datar (PL 26) £19.20 voucher number 37
    16   Paid for stapler and staples £6.38 plus VAT £1.12, voucher number 38
    19   Paid for tea bags and sugar £5.02, voucher number 39
    21   Received £2.80 from W. Bradshaw for postage stamps, receipt number 73
    23   Paid for seat covers for van £17.01 plus VAT £2.98, voucher number 40
    25   Paid a creditor J. Spencer (PL 32) £23.62, voucher number 41

28 Paid for computer cleaning kit £6.20 plus VAT £1.08, voucher number 42

29 Paid for parcel post £4.76, parcel tape £2.95 plus VAT 52p, voucher number 43

8.5

Hazar Khan operates an analytical petty cash book using the imprest system, with analysis columns for VAT, Postage, Stationery, Refreshments, Sundry expenses and Ledger. The imprest of £180.00 is restored at the beginning of each month.

As petty cashier you are required to enter the following transactions for the month of September 20-8. Total and balance the petty cash book at the end of the month and bring down the balance for 1 October 20-8. State the amount required to restore the imprest on 1 October 20-8.

Sep 1 Opening balance of £26.98

1 Enter correct amount of cash to restore the imprest to £180.00

2 Paid for adhesive labels £4.21 plus VAT 74p, voucher number 69

3 Paid milkman £7.58, voucher number 70

6 Paid a creditor M. Bianco (PL 15) £19.76, voucher number 71

8 Paid for registered parcel £12.38, voucher number 72

10 Received £15.50 from J. Rycroft (use of car park), receipt number 24

13 Paid for petrol and oil £19.72 plus VAT £3.45, voucher number 73

16 Paid for A4 paper £3.99 plus VAT 70p, and postage stamps £11.20, voucher number 74

18 Paid a creditor T. Millar (PL 34) £21.50, voucher number 75

20 Paid for sponge and tea towels £5.53 plus VAT 97p, voucher number 76

23 Paid for coffee £5.39, teabags £3.42, sugar 65p, voucher number 77

25 Received £7.84 from S. Templar (use of telephone), receipt number 25

26 Paid for two box files £5.96 plus VAT £1.04, voucher number 78

28 Paid for parcel post £4.80, petrol £18.50 plus VAT £3.24, voucher number 79

29 Paid for cakes and biscuits £5.25, voucher number 80

8.6

Michelle Singleton operates an analytical petty cash book using the imprest system, with analysis columns for VAT, Postage, Stationery, Refreshments, Sundry expenses and Ledger. The imprest of £220.00 is restored at the beginning of each month.

As petty cashier, you are required to enter the following transactions for the month of October 20-8. Total and balance the petty cash book at the end of the month and bring down the balance for 1 November 20-8. State the amount required to restore the imprest on 1 November 20-8.

Oct 1 Opening balance of £35.62
     1 Enter correct amount of cash to restore the imprest to £220.00
     2 Paid for scissors £4.94, string £2.76 plus VAT £1.35, voucher number 94
     4 Paid a creditor R. Kellerman (PL 24) £24.38, voucher number 95
     5 Paid for biscuits £1.59, coffee £4.95, voucher number 96
     8 Paid for postage stamps £11.20, parcel post £4.95, voucher number 97
    11 Received £5.76 from T. Myers (use of telephone), receipt number 32
    14 Paid for electric kettle £15.75 plus VAT £2.75, voucher number 98
    16 Paid for fax machine paper £5.32 plus VAT 93p, voucher number 99
    18 Paid a creditor W. Quinn (PL 15) £21.62, voucher number 100
    20 Paid for registered parcel £18.76, voucher number 101
    21 Paid for teabags £4.70, sugar 68p, voucher number 102
    24 Paid for torch and batteries £9.84 plus VAT £1.72, voucher number 103
    25 Paid for computer labels £6.20 plus VAT £1.08, voucher number 104
    28 Received £15.50 from S. Ripley (use of car park), receipt number 33
    29 Paid for parcel post £9.82, milkman £7.36, voucher number 105

8.7
Robert Groves operates an analytical petty cash book using the imprest system, with analysis columns for VAT, Postage, Stationery, Refreshments, Sundry expenses and Ledger. The imprest of £200.00 is restored at the beginning of each month.

As petty cashier, you are required to enter the following transactions for the month of September 20-9. Total and balance the petty cash book at the end of the month and bring down the balance for 1 October 20-9. State the amount required to restore the imprest on 1 October 20-9.

Sep 1 Opening balance of £47.98
     1 Enter correct amount of cash to restore the imprest to £200.00
     3 Paid for stamps £9.80, tea bags £4.25, voucher number 72
     5 Paid for petrol and oil £21.60 plus VAT £3.78, voucher number 73
     8 Received £5.76 from I. Hassan (use of photocopier), receipt number 28
     9 Paid for envelopes £4.52 plus VAT 79p, voucher number 74
    12 Paid a creditor V. Stanton (PL 30) £23.90, voucher number 75
    14 Paid for parcel post £17.62, coffee £4.85, voucher number 76
    17 Paid for soap and paper towels £6.76 plus VAT £1.18, voucher number 77
    18 Received £17.50 from E. Bailey (use of car park), receipt number 29

21 Paid for wrapping paper £6.99, string £2.69 plus VAT £1.69, voucher number 78

23 Paid a creditor L. King (PL 34) £14.05, voucher number 79

24 Paid for registered post £16.24, biscuits £4.36, voucher number 80

26 Paid for car mats for van £16.60 plus VAT £2.90, voucher number 81

27 Paid for computer labels £7.83 plus VAT £1.37, voucher number 82

29 Paid milkman £8.35, postage stamps £6.80, voucher number 83

8.8

Thomas Wagner operates an analytical petty cash book using the imprest system, with analysis columns for VAT, Postage, Stationery, Refreshments, Sundry expenses and Ledger. The imprest of £190.00 is restored at the beginning of each month.

As petty cashier, you are required to enter the following transactions for the month of October 20-9. Total and balance the petty cash book at the end of the month and bring down the balance for 1 November 20-9. State the amount required to restore the imprest on 1 November 20-9.

Oct 1 Opening balance of £24.78

1 Enter correct amount of cash to restore the imprest to £190.00

3 Paid for marker pens £3.99 plus VAT 70p, voucher number 105

5 Paid a creditor T. Noble (PL 18) £16.94, voucher number 106

8 Paid for parcel post £5.20, coffee £4.69, voucher number 107

12 Paid for clock and batteries £12.65 plus VAT £2.21, voucher number 108

14 Paid for bubble wrap and string £7.90 plus VAT £1.38, voucher number 109

16 Received £5.94 from S. Rhodes (use of fax machine), receipt number 34

17 Paid for registered post £9.62, biscuits £2.04, voucher number 110

20 Paid a creditor B. Malik (PL 20) £15.72, voucher number 111

21 Paid for scissors £4.92 plus VAT 86p, voucher number 112

23 Paid for sponge and car polish for van £9.30 plus VAT £1.63, voucher number 113

25 Received £14.50 from E. Bishop (use of car park), receipt number 35

27 Paid for milk £4.39, parcel post £5.42, voucher number 114

28 Paid for six desk diaries £17.94 plus VAT £3.14, voucher number 115

29 Paid for postage stamps £15.60, tea bags £3.58, voucher number 116

■ ⌄ **9** Banking – payments and receipts

In recent years, both the number of people with *bank accounts* and the services that banks offer have grown steadily. No other country in the world has a banking system as highly developed as that in the United Kingdom. It is renowned for its stability, its network of branches and the services offered.

Banks operate two main types of accounts: *deposit or savings accounts*; and *current accounts*.

Deposit accounts

Deposit means 'to put down' or 'leave', so this type of account is normally concerned with saving over a period of time. *Interest* is given on the balance held in the account. Interest is an amount paid by a bank to a customer as a reward for saving the money in the account. The rate of interest at any given time (stated as a percentage) is always displayed inside the bank. Money placed in a *deposit account* cannot be drawn on by cheque and sometimes notice may be required before money can be withdrawn.

Current accounts

These are used for regular payments into and out of a bank account. When a customer opens a *current account* the bank will issue a *cheque book* to enable the customer to make payments by cheque. The customer will also be given a *paying-in book* so that money can be paid into the account.

Practically all businesses have current accounts because of the many advantages offered with this type of account.

Advantages of a current account

- Businesses can avoid the risks involved in holding large quantities of cash on their premises.
- Payments to suppliers by cheque are more convenient and secure than cash. They also provide additional proof that payment has been made.
- Customers may wish to pay their accounts by cheque.

- Other bank services are available, such as loans or overdrafts, and advice is available on a wide range of business problems.

Bank charges

Banks give advice and offer customers many advantages and services free of charge. However, they do make charges for some of their services, and they also charge interest on any money borrowed by customers. Special arrangements can be made for customers to '*overdraw*' their current accounts. This occurs when the bank pays out more money than has been deposited in the account, and is known as a *bank overdraft*. It is used for temporary or short-term borrowing. When a bank account has been overdrawn, the abbreviation DR or O/D is printed after the balance on the bank statement.

Customers usually have to pay an *interest charge* on an overdraft. This is calculated on a daily basis on the actual amount overdrawn.

Standing orders

The *standing order* service provided by banks is a way of ensuring that specific payments are made to certain people or organisations on the date they are due. It is used by customers who want the bank to make payments for them on a regular basis. Many people use this service for paying fixed amounts that fall due on certain dates – for example, mortgage repayments or insurance premiums. The bank will ensure that the money is taken out of the customer's account and paid into the account of the person or organisation named. As standing order payments are made automatically through the banking system, this saves the customer time and expense. There is no need to remember to write cheques or pay postage costs.

Direct debits

This is another way of making regular payments out of a current account. But instead of instructing the bank to make fixed payments, the customer completes a *direct debit mandate* giving a person or an organisation permission to withdraw amounts on a regular basis.

This is a more flexible system than standing orders because the amount of the payment can easily be changed. For this reason, direct debit is particularly suitable when payments are to be made regularly but the amount may change.

Direct debit payments are set up by the business receiving the money. The company instructs *their* bank to request *your* bank to pay them by transferring the amount due from your account to their account. This can only happen if you have agreed to this method of payment in the first place.

Bank giro credit transfer

Bank giro is a system of transferring money directly from the account of one person to that of another. This system is also known as the *credit transfer service.*

The bank giro credit service provides a convenient way of receiving and paying money through the banking system. Some organisations encourage their customers to use this service by providing tear-off forms on their statements. Many people pay their telephone, gas or electricity bills by this method.

BACS

Bankers Automated Clearing Services (BACS) is a computer transfer payment system owned by the banks. This facility permits the automatic transfer of money between organisations and individuals, and is widely used for regular payments. Instead of providing the bank with individually prepared bank giro credit forms, all the details and information for the payments is supplied using magnetic media.

Cheques

To operate a current account, the bank will issue the customer with a *cheque book* and a *paying-in book*. A *cheque* is an order to the bank to pay a stated sum of money to the person named on the cheque. Each cheque is numbered with its own serial number. Most banks personalise their cheques by printing the name of the account holder, and the cheque must be signed beneath the printed name. Whether making out a cheque or accepting a cheque in payment, you should always ensure that all the necessary details are completed correctly. If they are not, the bank will refuse to accept the cheque.

There are three named participants involved when using a cheque:

- the *drawee* is the name of the bank holding the money (in this example, Westway Bank)
- the *payee* is the person to whom the cheque is made payable, who will receive the money (in this example, R. Wilding)
- the *drawer* is the account holder; this person signs the cheque (in this example, J. M. England).

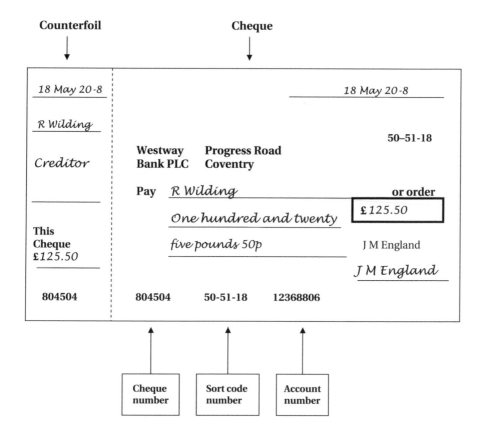

Counterfoil | Cheque

18 May 20-8

R Wilding

Creditor

This
Cheque
£125.50

804504

18 May 20-8

50–51-18

Westway   Progress Road
Bank PLC   Coventry

Pay   R Wilding   or order

One hundred and twenty   £125.50

five pounds 50p   J M England

J M England

804504   50-51-18   12368806

Cheque number

Sort code number

Account number

How to write a cheque

The drawer will normally complete four sections on a cheque:

- the date
- the payee's name
- the amount of money in words and figures
- the drawer's own signature (a specimen of which is held by the bank).

When we make out a cheque we should also copy the details on to the counterfoil, which is kept in the cheque book and used for reference purposes. By referring to the counterfoils we can quickly see how each cheque was used.

Cheque crossings

If two parallel lines are drawn down the cheque, it is a *crossed* cheque and it cannot be exchanged for cash; it *must* be paid into a bank account. Most cheques now have a general crossing printed on them as a safeguard against loss, theft and fraud.

'Refer to drawer'

In certain circumstances, the bank will refuse to *honour* (to pay) a cheque. Cheques that are not passed for payment by the drawer's bank are said to have been '*dishonoured*'. The drawer's bank will write '*Refer to drawer*' or the abbreviation *R/D* on a cheque it refuses to pay. This can be for any one of the following reasons:

- there are insufficient funds in the drawer's account
- the amount written in words does not agree with the amount in figures
- the cheque is unsigned
- the cheque has been *stopped* by the drawer (that is, the drawer has instructed the bank not to make payment)
- the cheque is *stale* (it was written more than six months before the current date)
- the cheque is *post-dated* (dated for some time in the future)
- an alteration on the cheque has not been initialled by the drawer.

Paying-in slips

Bank credit or *paying-in slips* are used to pay cash and cheques into a current account. They are completed by stating the amount to be paid in and the form it takes. Cash in notes and coins are listed collectively against the appropriate unit of currency. Cheques should be listed separately and totalled on the reverse of the paying-in slip. The total of any cheques is then written in the relevant box on the front of the slip. The paying-in slip counterfoil is completed with the same details. The completed credit slip, together with the cash/cheques, is then handed to the bank cashier. The paying-in slip counterfoil will be date-stamped by the bank cashier and returned to the customer.

Bank statements

At regular intervals, usually once a month, the bank will provide the customer with a copy of his or her account. This is known as a *statement of account* or a *bank statement*, and will give full details of all the transactions during the period, as well as details of any bank charges.

Bank statements vary in appearance, but they all have some features in common. This is a typical example:

STATEMENT

Name and address
of bank issuing the
statement

Westway Bank plc
Progress Road
Coventry
CV95 9MN

Account   J M England
Account Number   12368806
Sheet   18
Date   31 May 20-8

Date	Details	Debit	Credit	Balance
20-8				
01 May	Balance			974.86
07 May	804502	32.99		941.87
15 May	Cheque		15.00	956.87
16 May	WYHF (SO)	498.25		458.62
20 May	804503	76.50		382.12
24 May	Astor (BGC)		68.50	450.62
26 May	804504	125.50		325.12
27 May	Cheque		29.38	354.50
30 May	Tel-systems (DD)	27.50		327.00
30 May	Bank charges	1.30		325.70
		Money paid out of the bank account	Money paid into the bank account	Running balance of the bank account

As you can see from the illustration of the bank statement, money paid out of the bank appears in the debit column and money paid into the bank appears in the credit column. This is because it is seen from the bank's point of view: when there is money in the account the bank owes the money to the customer, so the customer is a creditor.

Points to remember

- A *business bank account* offers many advantages and services to a firm, and almost all businesses have a *current account*. This enables them to make *payments by cheque* and receive *payments through the banking system.*
- Most banks personalise their cheques by printing the name of the account holder; the cheque *must* be signed beneath the printed name. A *crossed cheque* cannot be cashed on demand, it must be paid into a bank account.
- Cash and cheques received by a business are paid into the bank by completing a *paying-in slip*. Details of notes and coins are listed on the front; cheques are listed on the reverse, this total is then carried forward to the front and added to the cash total. The *counterfoil* is stamped by the cashier at the bank as a proof of the deposit.

Assignments

9.1
Explain briefly the meaning of the term 'standing order'.

9.2
(a) What does the abbreviation R/D stand for?
(b) Give two reasons why a cheque may be marked R/D.

9.3
State two advantages of a current account.

9.4
What is the difference between a standing order and a direct debit?

9.5
What is a 'bank overdraft'?

9.6
Why is it necessary to complete a cheque counterfoil?

9.7
Name the three participants involved when a cheque is used.

9.8
Explain why a BACS method of payment may be chosen.

9.9
(a) Who is the drawer on a cheque?
(b) State the details that need to be completed when writing a cheque.

■ ⱱ **10** Two-column cash books

In our earlier work, the cash and bank accounts were kept in the ledger; but because of the considerable number of entries in these two accounts, they were removed from the ledger and brought together in a special book called a *cash book*.

Although the accounts for cash and bank are brought together, they still remain completely *separate* accounts, laid side by side so that both accounts are visible at the same time. For this reason it is very important to label the columns clearly and you must be careful to make entries in the correct columns. By tradition, the cash column *always* appears to the left of the bank column.

Only a responsible member of staff, usually the cashier, makes entries in the *cash book*, since these two accounts deal with money and cheques. The cash book is the book of original entry for all money received and paid out, whether in cash or by cheque.

Student cash books can be purchased from most good stationers and you will need to get one. The first single side is not used, because a cash book has the entire left-hand page for the debit side and the entire right-hand page for the credit side.

Cash column   As with our earlier cash accounts, the debit side is used to record *cash received*, and the credit side to record *cash paid out*.

Bank column   In the same way, the debit side is used to record *cheques received*, and the credit side to record *cheques paid out*.

Cash book

	Debit side					Credit side			
Date	*Particulars*	*F*	*Cash*	*Bank*	*Date*	*Particulars*	*F*	*Cash*	*Bank*

Here is an illustration showing the cash account and the bank account as they would have appeared previously, as two separate accounts.

Cash Account

20-8		£	20-8		£
1 May	Balance b/d	270	4 May	Insurance	58
7 May	E. Ashby	194	11 May	D. Riley	96
18 May	Cash sales	65	16 May	Cash purchases	160
29 May	H. Sinclair	173	27 May	Drawings	120
			31 May	Balance c/d	268
		702			702
1 Jun	Balance b/d	268			

Bank Account

20-8		£	20-8		£
1 May	Balance b/d	859	2 May	Rent	175
6 May	J. Wiseman	250	14 May	T. Norbury	487
12 May	D. Glover	393	20 May	D. King	362
24 May	B. McCann	576	31 May	Balance c/d	1,054
		2,078			2,078
1 Jun	Balance b/d	1,054			

These two accounts are now brought together, side by side, in the cash book.

Cash book

Date	Particulars	F	Cash	Bank	Date	Particulars	F	Cash	Bank
20-8					20-8				
1 May	Balances b/d		270	859	2 May	Rent			175
6 May	J. Wiseman			250	4 May	Insurance		58	
7 May	E. Ashby		194		11 May	D. Riley		96	
12 May	D. Glover			393	14 May	T. Norbury			487
18 May	Cash sales		65		16 May	Cash purchases		160	
24 May	B. McCann			576	20 May	D. King			362
29 May	H. Sinclair		173		27 May	Drawings		120	
					31 May	Balances c/d		268	1,054
			702	2,078				702	2,078
1 Jun	Balances b/d		268	1,054					

The cash and the bank accounts are totalled and balanced *separately*, in the same way that we would if they were kept apart. *Debit entries* are receipts of cash or amounts paid *into* the bank. *Credit entries* are payments by cash or amounts paid *out of* the bank.

Since it is not possible to spend more cash (notes and coins) than one actually has, the cash account will always have a debit balance. However, this is not the case with the bank account. A business may find it is short of money for a variety of reasons and the bank may be willing to make some of its money available to the business, usually in the form of an *overdraft*.

Bank overdraft

When a bank allows an overdraft it means that a customer can draw more money out of a current account than has been paid in, up to an agreed limit.

You will notice when balancing the cash book that an overdraft occurs when the total of the bank column *at the credit side* exceeds the total of the bank column *at the debit side*.

Cash sales

When a business sells goods or services for cash it will issue a receipt to the buyer. A copy of the receipt would be used to make the entry in the cash book. The description of the transaction in the cash book is '*cash sales*', as the name of the customer is not needed. The rules of double entry require the *name* of the account where the corresponding entry will be made.

Sometimes customers (debtors) pay their accounts in cash. When this happens the receipt will state the customer's name followed by (debtor). On these occasions the debtor's name must be entered in the cash book to indicate the account where the corresponding entry will be made.

Here is an illustration of a typical cash receipt for a customer:

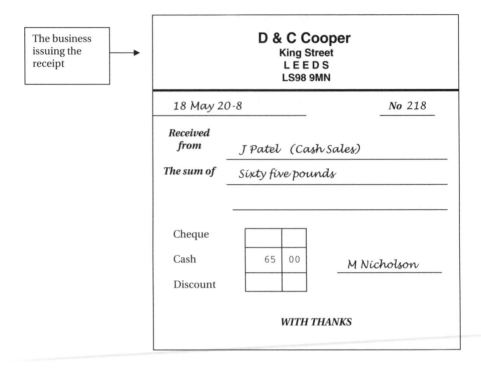

The business issuing the receipt →

D & C Cooper
King Street
L E E D S
LS98 9MN

18 May 20-8	No 218

Received from: *J Patel (Cash Sales)*

The sum of: *Sixty five pounds*

Cheque		
Cash	65	00
Discount		

M Nicholson

WITH THANKS

Cash purchases

When a business buys goods for cash they will receive a receipt from the supplier.

The receipt would be used to make the entry in the cash book. The description of the transaction in the cash book is '*cash purchases*' as the name of the supplier is not needed. The rules of double entry require the name of the account where the corresponding entry will be made.

Contra entries

Certain entries in the cash book are called *contra entries*. The word 'contra' is the Latin word for 'opposite' and indicates that the two halves of a double entry are opposite one another, one on the debit side of the cash book and the other on the credit side.

In a cash book we have two accounts placed side by side for convenience. When a contra entry occurs it will affect both the cash and bank accounts – one account receives money, the other account gives it.

Contra entries are transfers of money, they can only occur:

- *when money is taken out of the cash account and paid into the bank account* or

- *when money is taken out of the bank account and placed in the cash account*

Contra entries can sometimes cause confusion. This is because both the debit and credit entries appear in the same book.

Let us look at a typical example. On 5 June, £200 of the office cash is paid into the bank. The entries in the cash book would look like this:

Cash book

Date	Particulars	F	Cash	Bank	Date	Particulars	F	Cash	Bank
20-8					20-8				
5 Jun	Cash	C		200	5 Jun	Bank	C	200	

The credit entry shows that the cash has been reduced by £200; the cash account *gave* the money (*credit the giver*). The particulars column always shows where the corresponding entry has been made, so the word *bank* appears at the credit side.

At the debit side, the bank account is increased by £200; the bank *receives* the money (*debit the receiver*), the description *cash* explains how by naming the corresponding account involved in the transaction. Against each entry, the letter 'C' (which is short for contra) is placed in the *folio columns* to indicate that these items do not require posting as double entry has taken place in the cash book.

A contra entry can also operate the other way when money is withdrawn from the bank for business use. On 22 June, £350 is withdrawn from the bank for use in the business. The entries in the cash book would look like this:

Cash book

Date	Particulars	F	Cash	Bank	Date	Particulars	F	Cash	Bank
20-8					20-8				
22 Jun	Bank	C	350		22 Jun	Cash	C		350

The credit entry shows that the bank has been reduced by £350; the bank account *gave* the money (credit the giver). The particulars column always shows where the corresponding entry has been made, so the word *cash* appears at the credit side.

At the debit side, the cash account is increased by £350, the cash account *receives* the money (debit the receiver), the description *bank* explains how by naming the corresponding account involved in the transaction.

A letter 'C' again appears in the folio columns to indicate that double entry has taken place in the cash book.

Points to remember

- Although the cash and bank accounts have been placed side by side in the cash book, they still remain *two completely separate accounts*. It is very important to *label the columns clearly* and you must *be careful to make entries in the correct columns*. By tradition, the cash column *always* appears *to the left* of the bank column. Both the cash and bank accounts are *ledger accounts* and this new arrangement does not alter this fact and that they form an integral part of the double entry system.
- *Contra* entries are simply transfers, taking money out of one account and putting it in another.
- The *cash book* is the book of original entry for all money received and paid out, whether *in cash* or *by cheque*. The cash and bank accounts are totalled and balanced *separately*. An *overdraft* occurs when the total of the bank column *at the credit side* exceeds the total of the bank column *at the debit side*.
- When there is an *overdrawn bank balance* either at the beginning or at the end of a period, it is entered at the *credit side* of the cash book.

Assignments

Now use your cash book to work through the following assignments. Contra entries are not included in the first two assignments to enable you to gain some initial routine practice.

10.1
Robert Hurford keeps a two-column cash book. During the month of May 20-8 the following transactions took place. Enter each transaction in the cash book, balance the cash book at the end of the month, and bring down the balances.

May 1   Balances brought down from previous month: cash £262; bank £2,756
      2   Received £368 by cheque from R. Douglas
      5   Cash purchases £134
      8   Paid insurance £48 by cheque
   10   Cash sales £120
   12   Paid motor expenses £97 in cash
   19   Received £594 by cheque from S. Myers
   20   Cash sales £350
   21   Paid D. Nicholas £368 by cheque
   23   Received £469 by cheque from Bancroft Ltd
   25   Cash purchases £173

26   Paid Giles Murray £502 by cheque

28   Paid Premier Imports £436 by cheque

30   Received £375 by cheque from J. Singh

10.2

Ann Bannister keeps a two-column cash book. During the month of September 20-8 the following transactions took place. Enter each transaction in the cash book, balance the cash book at the end of the month, and bring down the balances.

Sep   1   Balances brought down from the previous month: cash £308; bank £1,062

3   Paid motor expenses £104 by cheque

4   Cash sales £158

8   Received £304 by cheque from C. M. Lupton

12   Cash drawings £170

14   Paid J. Oldridge £620 by cheque

16   Paid T. Wilson Ltd £136 by cheque

18   Received rent from sub-tenant £250 in cash

20   Received £498 by cheque from Marcus Ltd

22   Cash sales £320

24   Paid rates £290 by cheque

25   Cash purchases £84

27   Received £376 by cheque from R. Mills

28   Paid Office Supplies £52 by cheque

29   Received £94 in cash from M. Shah

30   Received £520 by cheque from Groves & Son

30   Cash purchases £168

10.3

James Chang keeps a two-column cash book. During the month of October 20-8 the following transactions took place. Enter each transaction in the cash book, balance the cash book at the end of the month, and bring down the balances.

Oct   1   Balances brought down from the previous month: cash £147; bank £850

2   Cash sales £252

3   Received £368 by cheque from F. Lewis

4   Paid rent £60 in cash

5   Banked £200 of the office cash   *(contra entry)*

8   Paid I. Robson £216 by cheque

10   Cash purchases £75

12   Cash sales £93

15   Paid Telemex £58 in cash

17   Received £498 by cheque from C. Miles

22   Withdrew £350 from the bank for business use   *(contra entry)*

25   Paid insurance £74 by cheque.

27   Cash purchases £165
28   Received £592 by cheque from M. Chinn
30   Paid Adel Plastics £408 by cheque

10.4
William Dyson keeps a two-column cash book. During the month of September 20-8 the following transactions took place. Enter each transaction in the cash book, balance the cash book at the end of the month, and bring down the balances.

Sep 1   Balances brought down from previous month: cash £248; bank £3,664
      2   Paid rates £190 by cheque
      3   Cash sales £175
      4   Received £469 by cheque from M. Roberts
      5   Banked £150 of the cash
      8   Paid motor expenses £57 by cheque
      9   Rent received from sub-tenant £250 in cash
     10   Cash purchases £96
     11   Paid Munro Ltd £395 by cheque
     12   Received £650 by cheque from B. Stevens
     14   Cash sales £293
     15   Cash drawings £300
     16   Paid D. Shaw £709 by cheque
     17   Withdrew £200 from the bank for business use
     18   Received £162 by cheque from Verity & Co
     20   Paid D. Towers £582 by cheque
     22   Cash purhases £196
     24   Received £348 by cheque from D. Chadwick
     26   Banked £250 of the cash
     28   Received £136 in cash from Botica Textiles
     30   Paid J. Kline & Co £836 by cheque

10.5
Alison D. Klerk keeps a two-column cash book. During the month of October 20-9 the following transactions took place. Enter each transaction in the cash book, balance the cash book at the end of the month, and bring down the balances.

Oct 1   Balances brought down from the previous month: cash £269; bank overdraft £3,086
      2   Paid rent by cheque £175
      3   Received £294 by cheque from J. Kendall
      4   Paid motor expenses in cash £32
      5   Paid £200 of the cash into the bank
      9   Received £68 in cash from M. Kaye
     11   Cash sales £295
     14   Paid rates £165 by cheque

17 Received £575 by cheque from L. G. Sykes
18 Paid wages in cash £180
19 Cash sales £226
20 Paid general expenses £42 by cheque
21 Received commission £267 by cheque
24 Received £142 in cash from K. Waterman
25 Paid M. Hutton £490 by cheque
26 Cash purchases £126
27 Withdrew £350 from the bank for business use
28 Paid Stylax £210 by cheque
29 Received £972 by cheque from Kurtz Enterprises

10.6
Douglas Lockwood keeps a two-column cash book. During the month of September 20-9 the following transactions took place. Enter each transaction in the cash book, balance at the end of the month, and bring down the balances.

Sep 1 Balances brought down from previous month: cash £78; bank overdraft £1,006
2 Paid rates £195 by cheque
3 Withdrew £350 from the bank for business use
4 Cash purchases £226
7 Received £492 by cheque from J. Giles & Son
8 Paid J. Carson £465 by cheque
9 Paid motor expenses £73 in cash
10 Cash sales £368
11 Paid £200 of the cash into the bank
14 Received £798 by cheque from W. Powers
15 Paid Thomas Wagner £376 by cheque
16 Drawings £350 in cash
17 Withdrew £400 from the bank for business use
18 Cash purchases £295
19 Cash sales £212
21 Received £628 by cheque from L. Spencer
24 Received £572 by cheque from T. Norbury
26 Cash sales £356
30 Received £970 by cheque from W. Freeman

■ Ⅴ ▮▮ Three-column cash books and cash discounts

Combining the cash and bank accounts together in one book has increased efficiency, but when accounts are settled the question of a *discount* may arise. In many firms payments to suppliers are timed to enable the business to receive a discount. At the same time, money will be received from customers who will have deducted discount allowed in return for prompt settlement.

The only difference between the traditional two-column cash book we looked at earlier and the *three-column cash book* is an extra column at each side. These extra columns are used to record cash discounts: the column for *discount allowed* is on the *debit side*, because a customer who is paying is allowed to take a discount. The column for *discount received* from suppliers is on the *credit side*. It is important to remember that the discount columns are *not* accounts, they are memorandum columns only, where a note is made of a cash discount as it occurs.

Cash discounts

Firms appreciate customers who pay their accounts quickly, and a *cash discount* is often offered as an incentive to encourage prompt payment. Many firms will accept a smaller amount in full settlement if payment is made within a certain period of time. The rate of cash discount, usually expressed as a percentage, and the period in which payment is to be made are quoted on the invoice. A typical example would be *'subject to 5 per cent cash discount if the account is settled within one month from date of invoice'*.

When a cash discount is offered, it is not shown as a deduction from the total value of the invoice; a customer deducts the amount of discount if payment is made within the stated time. It is still called a *cash discount* if payment is made *by cheque*. For example, A. Thompson, a customer, owes the firm £100. He pays by cheque within the stated time and the firm allows him 5 per cent cash discount (£100 less £5 = £95), so A. Thompson will pay £95 in full settlement of his account.

Discounts allowed

On the debit side of the cash book the *discount allowed* column is used to enter amounts of cash discount on the date they occur. These are *cash discounts* allowed by a firm to its customers when they pay their accounts within the time limit specified.

Look at a typical example. On 1 September, goods valued at £296 were sold on credit to Apex Casuals, subject to a 5 per cent cash discount if payment is received within one month from the date of invoice. In the sales ledger, Apex Casuals account would look like this:

Apex Casuals Account

	£	
Sep 1 Sales	296.00	

On 24 September, Apex Casuals pay their account by cheque having deducted 5 per cent cash discount. They pay £281.20 in full settlement of their account (£296 less £14.80 cash discount = £281.20). Entries in the firm's cash book would look like this:

Cash book

Date	Particulars	F	Discount allowed	Cash	Bank	Date	Particulars	F	Discount received	Cash	Bank
			£	£	£				£	£	£
24 Sep	Apex Casuals		14.80		281.20						

Details of cheque and discount are posted from the cash book to the ledger accounts. Apex Casuals account would now look like this:

Apex Casuals Account

Sep 1 Sales	296. 00	Sep 24 Bank	281.20
	‾‾‾‾‾	24 Discount allowed	14.80
	296. 00		296. 00

When discount is allowed, the customer's account *must* be reduced by the full amount of the debt being settled. Although the firm has agreed to accept less money than was originally owed in full settlement of the account, the amount of the discount allowed, in this example £14.80, must also be credited to Apex Casuals account to show that the account is fully paid. If the discount was ignored, there would be a balance on Apex Casuals account equal to the amount of discount and it would appear as though Apex Casuals still owed £14.80.

As we have seen, each time discount is allowed the customer's account must be credited with the payment *and* discount; to complete the double entry at the end of the month, the total of the discount allowed column is posted to the debit side of the discount allowed account in the nominal ledger, like this:

Discount Allowed Account

		£	
Sep 30	Cash book total	82.46	

Discounts received

In the same way as most firms encourage debtors to pay quickly by offering them cash discount, many suppliers will be trying to attract prompt payment.

On the *credit side* of the cash book the *discount received* column is used to enter amounts of cash discount on the date they occur. These are *cash discounts* received by a firm when they pay their accounts within the time limit specified. Look at a typical example. On 3 September, goods costing £250 were purchased on credit from T. G. Munro, subject to 5 per cent cash discount if payment is received within 28 days from date of invoice. In the purchase ledger, the T. G. Munro account would look like this:

T. G. Munro Account

			£
	Sep 3	Purchases	250. 00

On 28 September, the firm pays T. G. Munro's account by cheque: £250 less £12.50 cash discount = £237.50 in full settlement of his account. Entries in the firm's cash book would look like this:

Cash book

Date	Particulars	F	Discount allowed	Cash	Bank	Date	Particulars	F	Discount received	Cash	Bank
			£	£	£				£	£	£
						28 Sep	T. G. Munro		12.50		237.50

Details of cheque and discount are posted from the cash book to the ledger accounts. The T. G. Munro account would now look like this:

T. G. Munro Account

		£			£
Sep 28	Bank	237.50	Sep 3 Purchases		250. 00
28	Discount received	12.50			
		250.00			250. 00

When discount is received, a supplier's account *must* be reduced by the full amount of the debt being settled. Although T. G. Munro has agreed to accept less money than was originally owed in full settlement of the account, the amount of the discount received, in this example £12.50, must also be debited to T. G. Munro's account to show that the account is fully paid. If the discount was ignored, there would be a balance on the T. G. Munro account equal to the amount of discount and it would look as though £12.50 was still owed to T. G. Munro.

As we have seen, each time discount is received, the supplier's account must be debited with the payment and discount; at the end of the month, to complete the double entry, the total of the discount received column is posted to the credit side of the discount received account in the nominal ledger, like this:

Discount Received Account

		£
Sep 30	Cash book total	81.34

In your examinations you may be provided with documents to write up a cash book. When this happens you must ensure that you enter the correct details.

Dealing with cheques from customers

When you are writing up the cash book using cheques received from customers, you will need to record:

- the date the cheque was banked (*not* the cheque date)
- customer's business name (this is *not* always the same name as the signature on the cheque)
- amount of cheque
- amount of cash discount (this will need to be calculated).

There is an illustration of a typical example:

NB	NORTHERN BANK PLC		2 September 20-9
Banked on	Parkside Branch		
	Towers Lane LEEDS LS98 8MN		21-91-93
6 September 20-9 This was in full settlement of their account of £ 305.54	Pay *Morley Enterprises*		or order
	Two hundred and eighty six pounds 90p		£ 286.90
			CURTIS LTD
	Cheque No 793416	Branch 219193	Account No 91391291	*S Myers*

Entries in the firm's cash book would look like this:

Cash book

Date	Particulars	F	Discount allowed	Cash	Bank	Date	Particulars	F	Discount received	Cash	Bank
			£	£	£				£	£	£
6 Sep	Curtis Ltd		18.64		286.90						

Dealing with cheques issued to suppliers

When you are writing up the cash book to record details of cheques issued to suppliers and for other expenses you may be provided with cheque counterfoils. If so, you will need to record the following details:

- the date the cheque was issued
- name of the supplier (creditor)
- cash discount
- amount of cheque
- cheque number

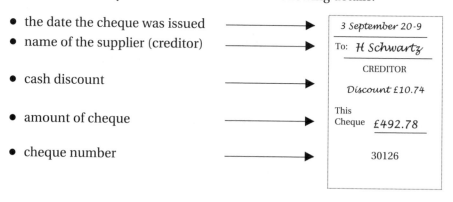

3 September 20-9

To: *H Schwartz*

CREDITOR

Discount £10.74

This Cheque *£492.78*

30126

Points to remember

- The term *cash discount* refers to the amount of the reduction given for prompt payment. It is still called cash discount if payment is made by cheque.
- To firms having sufficient funds to pay their accounts promptly cash discount offers an *additional profit*, and during the course of a year's trading could amount to a considerable sum.
- Details of cash or cheque and discount are posted from the cash book to the respective individual accounts.
- The *discount allowed* column is *at the debit side*; the *discount received* column is *at the credit side* of the cash book. At the end of the month the discount columns must be totalled but *never* balanced because they are *not* accounts.
- The discount columns are *memorandum* columns only, where a note is made of the discount as it occurs. It reminds whoever is posting entries from the cash book to remember to also post any discount to the personal accounts.
- At the end of the month, the *total discount allowed* is posted to the *debit side* of the discount allowed account; and the *total discount received* is posted to *credit side* of the discount received account to complete the double entry.
- The discount allowed account and the discount received account are in the nominal ledger, along with all other revenue and expense accounts. *Discount allowed* is an *expense* to a business, *discount received* is *additional revenue*.

Assignments

11.1

You are responsible for keeping the cash book of Morley Enterprises. On 1 September 20–9 they had opening balances of £406.72 in the cash account and £724.98 in the bank account.

You are required to:

(a) Enter the opening balances.
(b) Enter details of receipts from copies of cheques received from customers and calculate cash discounts.

NB

Banked on 6 September 20-9

This was in full settlement of their account of £305.54

NORTHERN BANK PLC
Parkside Branch
Towers Lane LEEDS LS98 8MN

2 September 20-9

21-91-93

Pay *Morley Enterprises* or order

Two hundred and eighty six pounds 90p **£ 286.90**

Cheque No	Branch	Account No
793416	219193	91391291

CURTIS LTD

S Myers

NB

Banked on 8 September 20-9

WESTWAY BANK PLC
Progress Road
COVENTRY

4 September 20-9

40-41-42

Pay *Morley Enterprises* or order

Six hundred and eighty pounds 34p **£ 680.34**

Kinsell & Co

Cheque No	Branch	Account No
321132	404142	61461760

M Dyson

NB

Banked on 18 September 20-9

This was in full settlement of their account of £604.90

NORTHERN BANK PLC
Parkside Branch
Towers Lane LEEDS LS98 8MN

10 September 20-9

21-91-93

Pay *Morley Enterprises* or order

Five hundred and seventy six pounds 28p **£ 576.28**

Cheque No	Branch	Account No
562525	219193	27432700

AZTEC SPORTSWEAR

J Patel

NB

Banked on 20 September 20-9

WESTWAY BANK PLC
Progress Road
COVENTRY

12 September 20-9

40-41-42

Pay *Morley Enterprises* or order

£ 604.32

Six hundred and four pounds 32p

De Wan Textiles

Cheque No	Branch	Account No
636129	404142	95438218

A DeWan

NORTHERN BANK PLC
Parkside Branch
Towers Lane LEEDS LS98 8MN

15 September 20-9

21-91-93

Pay   *Morley Enterprises*   or order

Two hundred and eighty one pounds 20p   £ 281.20

APEX CASUALS

Cheque No	Branch	Account No
463656	219193	42326252

E Murphy

WESTWAY BANK PLC
Progress Road
COVENTRY

20 September 20-9

40-41-42

Pay   *Morley Enterprises*   or order

Four hundred and thirty eight pounds   £ 438.76

76p   Kilroy & Ross

Cheque No	Branch	Account No
252423	404142	51541461

T McBride

(c)   Enter details of cash receipts to customers.

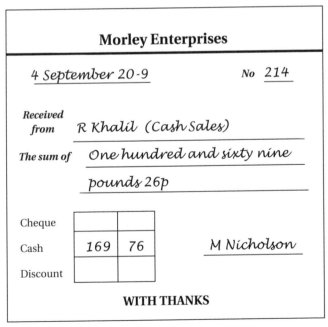

Morley Enterprises

4 September 20-9   No *214*

Received from   *R Khalil (Cash Sales)*

The sum of   *One hundred and sixty nine pounds 26p*

Cheque		
Cash	169	76
Discount		

M Nicholson

WITH THANKS

Morley Enterprises

12 September 20-9   No 215

Received
from   T Edmondson   (Debtor)

The sum of   One hundred and twenty five
pounds 82p

Cheque		
Cash	125	82
Discount		

M Nicholson

WITH THANKS

Morley Enterprises

23 September 20-9   No   216

Received
from   B Chandler   (Debtor)

The sum of   Ninety four pounds 38p

Cheque		
Cash	94	38
Discount		

M Nicholson

WITH THANKS

Morley Enterprises

27 September 20-9   No *217*

Received from   *G Howard   (Cash sales)*

The sum of   *One hundred and five*

pounds 20p

Cheque		
Cash	105	20
Discount		

M Nicholson

WITH THANKS

(d) Enter details of payments to suppliers from copies of cheque counterfoils.

3 September 20-9	
To: *H Schwartz*	
CREDITOR	
Discount £10.74	
This Cheque *£492.78*	
30126	

4 September 20-9	
To: *Contract Blinds*	
This Cheque *£295.50*	
30127	

6 September 20-9	
To: *Garside Holmes*	
CREDITOR	
Discount £19.80	
This Cheque *£508.26*	
30128	

18 September 20-9	
To: *Hudson Chase & Co*	
CREDITOR	
Discount £27.78	
This Cheque *£672.84*	
30129	

20 September 20-9	
To: *Briggs & Booth*	
CREDITOR	
Discount £10.52	
This Cheque *£315.28*	
30130	

28 September 20-9	
To: *T G Munro*	
CREDITOR	
Discount £12.50	
This Cheque *£237.50*	
30131	

(e) Enter details of cash receipts from suppliers.

S RAMSDEN	
15 September 20-9	Receipt No 105

Received with thanks from

Morley Enterprises (Cash purchases)

The sum of   Sixty pounds 76p

Cheque		
Cash	60	76
Discount		

S Ramsden

ARCHER LTD	
24 September 20-9	Receipt No 296

Received with thanks from

Morley Enterprises (Cash purchases)

The sum of   One hundred and twenty
             pounds 58p

Cheque		
Cash	120	58
Discount		

J Archer

(f) Total and balance the cash book and bring down the balances.
(g) Total the discount columns.

11.2

Andrews & Fox keep a three-column cash book. During the month of October 20–9 the following transactions took place:

Oct 1 Opening balances: £168.52 in the cash account and £998.20 in the bank account

2 Received £357.30 by cheque from S. Driver in full settlement of his account of £375.69

4 Cash purchases £102.50

6 Received £209.70 by cheque from Gladston Bros in full settlement of their account of £220.18

8 Paid motor expenses £76.32 by cheque (cheque number 34612)

10 Paid Delta Designs' account of £450.60 less 5 per cent cash discount (cheque number 34613)

12 Received £120.38 in cash from Lucus Sykes, a debtor

14 Received £592.94 by cheque from Chervilles Ltd

15 Cash sales £350.76

17 Paid Romana Products' account of £294.80 less 5 per cent cash discount (cheque number 34614)

19 Paid Sureguard Security £195.50 by cheque (cheque number 34615)

20 Received £290.80 by cheque from W. Dyson Ltd in full settlement of their account of £305.34
21 Cash purchases £176.92
23 Paid Evana Ltd account of £390.40 less 5 per cent cash discount (cheque number 34616)
24 Received £173.94 in cash from J. Hussain, a debtor
26 Received £350.28 by cheque from Cusack & Son in full settlement of their account of £367.79
27 Paid Montague Miles £250.24 by cheque (cheque number 34617)
28 Cash sales £164.86
29 Paid insurance £203.65 by cheque (cheque number 34618)
30 Received £182.42 by cheque from Adam Bates
30 Paid Star Plastics' account of £375.60 less 5 per cent cash discount (cheque number 34619)

You are required to:

(a) Enter the opening balances.
(b) Enter details of receipts and payments, including cash discounts.
(c) Total and balance the cash book and bring down the balances.
(d) Total the discount columns.

11.3

Madhur Daswani keeps a three-column cash book. During the month of May 20–9 the following transactions took place:

May 1 Opening balances: £276.52 in the cash account and £695.35 in the bank account.
3 Paid Palomo Imports' account of £304.75 by cheque (cheque number 50103)
4 Received £538.09 by cheque from Drew & Hurst in full settlement of their account of £564.99
5 Cash purchases £105.25
6 Paid R. Keaton's account of £220.00 less 2.5 per cent cash discount (cheque number 50104)
7 Received £185.72 in cash from R. Khan, a debtor
8 Paid motor expenses £69.25 by cheque (cheque number 50105)
9 Received £376.40 by cheque from Luptons Ltd in full settlement of their account of £395.20
10 Cash sales £250.98
12 Paid Douglas & Son's account of £369.80 less 5 per cent cash discount (cheque number 50106)
13 Received £480.65 by cheque from Weston Enterprises
14 Paid Ripley Signs £176.95 by cheque (cheque number 50107)
15 Cash purchases £165.39
16 Received £104.64 in cash from G. Offiah, a debtor
18 Paid Courtways' account of £296.40 less 2.5 per cent cash discount (cheque number 50108)

19 Received £198.46 by cheque from Masters Ltd in full settlement of their account of £208.38

20 Paid Murphy & Sykes £107.50 by cheque (cheque number 50109)

22 Cash sales £196.26

24 Received £204.75 by cheque from R. McQuade in full settlement of his account of £214.99

26 Paid Hyde & Son's account of £139.60 less 5 per cent cash discount (cheque number 50110)

28 Received £400.49 by cheque from Jayrose Group

You are required to:

(a) Enter the opening balances.
(b) Enter details of receipts and payments, including cash discounts.
(c) Total and balance the cash book and bring down the balances.
(d) Total the discount columns.

11.4

Harry Bairstow keeps a three-column cash book. During the month of June 20–9 the following transactions took place:

Jun 1 Opening balances: £305.96 in the cash account and there was a bank overdraft of £746.32

2 Received £370.74 by cheque from Best Textiles in full settlement of their account of £389.28

4 Paid Rodley Mills £463.95 by cheque (cheque number 46351)

6 Cash sales £175.42

7 Received £503.80 by cheque from Apex Clothes in full settlement of their account of £528.99

9 Cash purchases £105.96

12 Paid D. Crofton's account of £324.80 less 5 per cent cash discount (cheque number 46352)

13 Paid rates £195.75 by cheque (cheque number 46353)

14 Received £164.38 in cash from R. Patel, a debtor

16 Paid Vandante Ltd account of £420.40 less 2.5 per cent cash discount (cheque number 46354)

18 Received £281.69 by cheque from Shaw & Sons in full settlement of their account of £295.78

20 Cash sales £172.64

21 Paid Office Supplies £32.52 by cheque (cheque number 46355)

22 Paid J. Seymore's account of £306.20 less 5 per cent cash discount (cheque number 46356)

23 Received £294.75 by cheque from R. Lewis Ltd

23 Received £720.48 by cheque from D. Kingsley in full settlement of his account of £765.50

24 Cash purchases £158.32

26 Paid Booth and Royd £309.35 by cheque (cheque number 46357)

27 Received £95.76 in cash from B. Dixon, a debtor
28 Paid A. Thompson's account of £286.80 less 2.5 per cent cash discount (cheque number 46358)
29 Received £305.82 by cheque from T. McKenzie

You are required to:

(a) Enter the opening balances.
(b) Enter details of receipts and payments, including cash discounts.
(c) Total and balance the cash book and bring down the balances.
(d) Total the discount columns.

11.5

Wilson Singer keeps a three-column cash book. During the month of September 20–8 the following transactions took place:

Sep 1 Opening balances: £217.96 in the cash account and there was £1,095.25 in the bank account

2 Received £375.50 by cheque from Kyte Sportswear in full settlement of their account of £394.28

3 Paid motor expenses £94.72 by cheque (cheque number 20931)

6 Cash sales £169.95

8 Received £406.38 by cheque from Morton McKays

9 Paid Tartan Designs' account of £530.60 less 5 per cent cash discount (cheque number 20932)

11 Received £120.76 in cash from Buywise, a debtor

12 Paid D. Lawrence £396.98 by cheque (cheque number 20933)

14 Cash purchases £209.59

15 Received £272.76 by cheque from Kirk & Johnson in full settlement of their account of £286.40

16 Paid Pinedo Imports' account of £437.20 less 2.5 per cent cash discount (cheque number 20934)

18 Cash sales £250.75

20 Paid Realto Fabrics £394.86 by cheque (cheque number 20935)

21 Received £205.25 by cheque from Victor Shires

21 Received £320.60 by cheque from Expo Clothes in full settlement of their account of £336.63

24 Paid Hester Group's account of £650.80 less 5 per cent cash discount (cheque number 20936)

25 Received £194.38 in cash from J. Cussons, a debtor

26 Cash purchases £174.35

27 Paid Marcus King's account of £492.40 less 2.5 per cent cash discount (cheque number 20937)

28 Received £138.98 by cheque from Doyle Ltd in full settlement of their account of £145.93

29 Paid D. C. Mitchell £260.75 by cheque (cheque number 20938)

You are required to:

(a) Enter the opening balances.
(b) Enter details of receipts and payments, including cash discounts.
(c) Total and balance the cash book and bring down the balances.
(d) Total the discount columns.

11.6

Gina Howard keeps a three-column cash book. During the month of October 20–8 the following transactions took place:

Oct 1   Opening balances: £304.98 in the cash account and there was a bank overdraft of £1,012.54

      3   Paid Cable Media (Sundry expenses) £376.82 by cheque (cheque number 15292)

      4   Received £547.50 by cheque from Maximate in full settlement of their account of £574.86

      5   Cash purchases £150.95

      7   Cash sales £209.76

      9   Paid Merlins Ltd account of £320.80 less 2.5 per cent cash discount (cheque number 15293)

   12   Received £468.48 by cheque from Rogers & Shaw

   12   Received £370.04 by cheque from Bond Group in full settlement of their account of £388.54

   14   Paid Andrew Freres £216.96 by cheque (cheque number 15294)

   18   Received £192.64 in cash from J. Hakim, a debtor

   19   Paid Victoria Plastics' account of £248.40 less 5 per cent cash discount (cheque number 15295)

   20   Received £620.96 by cheque from D. Chippendale

   21   Cash purchases £109.79

   23   Paid insurance £164.50 by cheque (cheque number 15296)

   24   Received £594.36 by cheque from Douglas & Son in full settlement of their account of £624.08

   25   Cash sales £175.82

   26   Paid Woodrow Dawson's account of £130.80 less 2.5 per cent cash discount (cheque number 15297)

   27   Received £106.50 in cash from Martin Vickers, a debtor

   27   Paid D. Lorenz £250.62 by cheque (cheque number 15298)

   30   Received £872.74 by cheque from Lloyd & Young in full settlement of their account of £916.38

   30   Paid Hudson Verity's account of £308.20 less 5 per cent cash discount (cheque number 15299)

You are required to:

(a) Enter the opening balances.
(b) Enter details of receipts and payments including cash discounts.
(c) Total and balance the cash book and bring down the balances.
(d) Total the discount columns.

■ ᴍ 12 Bank reconciliation statement

If you have a current account with a bank you may receive a statement showing a balance in the bank quite different from what you expected it to be. When this happens you will need to find out why. If you keep a record of payments into your account and your spending, then explaining the difference should not be too difficult. The difference in the balances may have a clear explanation; for example, a time lapse – a cheque written yesterday would not appear on your bank statement today, because it would not have had time to pass through the bankers' clearing system. Explaining the differences between your records and those of your bank is called *reconciling* the two balances.

In a business where there have been numerous entries to record money received and paid out it may take a little longer, but the principles are the same. When we look at the closing balance in our cash book, and compare it with the balance on the bank statement on the same date we will usually find that the two balances are different. We shall need to draw up a *bank reconciliation statement* to discover the reasons for the difference in the balances. This will show if errors have been made, or there are logical reasons that will explain why this might have happened.

At any given date, there are several reasons why the bank balance in the cash book may not agree with the balance on the bank statement, and in practice the two accounts rarely show the same balance.

(a) The most common example of this surrounds the writing of cheques. We enter a cheque in the cash book on the day it is written, but our bank will learn of this only when a cheque is presented for payment. This will take a few days even if the receiver pays it into his or her bank immediately. If the receiver keeps it for a time, this increases the period our bank balance will be out of step with our cash book. Inevitable delays also occur through the bankers' clearing system, so it is very likely that there will be some cheques that have not yet been presented for payment at the firm's bank. (These are known as *unpresented cheques*.)

(b) Cheques and/or cash paid into the bank will have been entered in the firm's cash book on the date the money was banked, but this may have been late in the afternoon, and when the statement was issued the bank did not know that the money had been paid in. Such items will not yet have appeared on the bank statement.

(c)   Banks receive money on behalf of their customers. This often includes interest from investments and money received by bank giro credit transfer from customers. Money received in this way will appear on the bank statement on the date the bank receives it, but these items are not entered in the cash book until the bank statement arrives. When such items are discovered on a bank statement they should be entered at the *debit side* of the cash book.

(d)   Banks also make payments for their customers by direct debit and standing order; such items will appear on the bank statement on the date the payment is made, but these items are not entered in the cash book until the bank statement arrives. When such items are discovered on a bank statement they should be entered at the *credit side* of the cash book.

(e)   Banks make charges for some of their services. They do not send a bill but simply take money out by debiting the account with the amount of bank charges and interest on overdrafts or loans. When this happens these amounts must be entered at the *credit side* of the cash book.

(f)   Dishonoured cheques: there are several reasons why a bank may refuse to *honour* (to pay) a cheque. (See Unit 9, page 86.) Such a cheque is returned to the person who paid it in with the words *'refer to drawer'* written on it. This invites the person who paid it in to contact the person who drew the cheque and ask for an explanation. There may be a good reason, but whether there is or not, the bookkeeping entry for the dishonoured cheque is the same: *the debt must be restored.*

Let us consider a typical example. On 1 May, a debtor, Nicholas Davidson, owed the firm £250. His account would look like this:

Nicholas Davidson Account

	£	
1 May Balance b/d	250	

On 21 May we receive a cheque of £250 from Nicholas Davidson, this would be entered in the cash book at the debit side of the bank account, like this:

Cash Book

Date	Particulars	F	Discount allowed	Cash	Bank	Date	Particulars	F	Discount received	Cash	Bank
			£	£	£				£	£	£
21 May	Nicholas Davidson				250.00						

To complete double entry it is posted to the credit side of Nicholas Davidson's account, like this:

Nicholas Davidson Account

	£		£
1 May Balance b/d	250	21 May Bank	250

Nicholas Davidson's account was cleared when the cheque was received. However, a few days later, on 27 May, it was discovered that his bank would not honour (pay) the cheque. This is a *dishonoured cheque*, it would be stamped *Refer to drawer*.

Now the procedure *must be reversed*. A credit entry is made in the bank account, like this:

Cash Book

Date	Particulars	F	Discount allowed	Cash	Bank	Date	Particulars	F	Discount received	Cash	Bank
			£	£	£				£	£	£
21 May	Nicholas Davidson				250.00	27 May	Nicholas Davidson				250.00

Nicholas Davidson still owes the firm £250, so this debt must be restored to his account with a debit entry, like this:

Nicholas Davidson Account

	£		£
1 May Balance b/d	250	21 May Bank	250
27 May Bank (R/D)	250		

Bank reconciliation statement

The word *reconcile* means 'to bring together'. It often happens in business that two sets of figures should agree, but for some reason they do not. This is when we need to reconcile; that is, to make the two sets of figures agree by examining and explaining the reasons for the difference. A bank reconciliation statement, as its name suggests, is a written statement, at a particular date, that explains why there is a difference between the balance shown on the bank statement and the bank balance in the cash book. A neat copy of the bank reconciliation statement is usually placed in the cash book or filed with the bank statement for future reference.

Let us now look at a worked example. Here is a copy of our cash book (bank columns only) and of our bank statement.

Cash Book
(Bank Columns Only)

Date	Particulars	Bank	Date	Particulars	Cheque number	Bank
20–8			20–8			
1 May	Balance b/d	812.50	8 May	H. Ryder	30404	138.20
6 May	W. Bradley	196.28	18 May	A. Jackson	30405	152.64
13 May	C. Fox	324.75	20 May	E. Tyler	30406	249.50
31 May	Smithsons	162.95	31 May	Balance c/d		956.14
		1,496.48				1,496.48
1 Jun	Balance	956.14				

On 31 May 20–8 the following bank statement was received from the bank:

Bank Statement

Date	Details	Debit	Credit	Balance
20–8				
1 May	Brought forward			812.50
6 May	Cheque		196.28	1,008.78
12 May	30404	138.20		870.58
13 May	Cheque		324.75	1,195.33
15 May	Town Estates (DD)	120.50		1,074.83
26 May	30406	249.50		825.33
27 May	Jordans (BGC)		593.94	1,419.27
30 May	Bank charges	10.35		1,408.92

1 To illustrate the best procedure, we must first compare each item in the cash book with the bank statement. It is useful to tick each entry in the cash book that is also on the bank statement and each entry on the statement that is also in the cash book, like this:

Cash Book
(Bank Columns Only)

Date	Particulars	Bank	Date	Particulars	Cheque number	Bank
20–8			20–8			
1 May	Balance b/d	✓ 812.50	8 May	H. Ryder	30404	✓ 138.20
6 May	W. Bradley	✓ 196.28	18 May	A. Jackson	30405	152.64
13 May	C. Fox	✓ 324.75	20 May	E. Tyler	30406	✓ 249.50
31 May	Smithsons	162.95	31 May	Balance c/d		956.14
		1,496.48				1,496.48
1 Jun	Balance	956.14				

Bank Statement

Date	Details	Debit	Credit	Balance
20–8				
1 May	Brought forward			✓ 812.50
6 May	Cheque		✓ 196.28	1,008.78
12 May	30404	✓ 138.20		870.58
13 May	Cheque		✓ 324.75	1,195.33
15 May	Town Estates (DD)	120.50		1,074.83
26 May	30406	✓ 249.50		825.33
27 May	Jordans (BGC)		593.94	1,419.27
30 May	Bank charges	10.35		1,408.92

It is the unticked entries that will help to explain why the balances are different. Unticked items on the bank statement normally represent money *received* or *payments* made by the bank. These items have not yet been entered in the cash book.

There are three unticked items on the statement. The first is on 15 May, Town Estates (direct debit). This is a regular payment for rent and will need to be entered at the credit side of the cash book.

The second unticked item is on 27 May, from Jordans, a customer, who has paid his account by instructing his bank to pay directly through the banking system instead of sending a cheque. This money has been received into our bank account but we had not been informed. This amount will need to be entered on the debit side of the cash book.

The third unticked item is on 30 May, for bank charges, this means the bank has made a charge for its services. This amount has been taken out of our account but we had not been notified of the bank's actions. This will need to be entered on the credit side of the cash book.

2 The next step is to bring the cash book up to date by entering these three items in the cash book and recalculating the balance, like this:

Cash Book
(Bank Columns Only)

Date	Particulars		Bank	Date	Particulars	Cheque Number		Bank
20–8				20–8				
1 May	Balance b/d	✓	812.50	8 May	H. Ryder	30404	✓	138.20
6 May	W. Bradley	✓	196.28	18 May	A. Jackson	30405		152.64
13 May	C. Fox	✓	324.75	20 May	E. Tyler	30406	✓	249.50
31 May	Smithsons		162.95	31 May	Balance c/d			956.14
			1,496.48					1,496.48
31 May	Balance b/d		956.14	31 May	Town Estates (DD)			120.50
31 May	Jordans (BGC)		593.94	31 May	Bank charges			10.35
				31 May	Balance c/d			1,419.23
			1,550.08					1,550.08
1 Jun	Balance b/d		1,419.23					

There are two items entered in the cash book that are not on the bank statement. First, the unticked item on the credit side on 18 May represents a cheque sent to A. Jackson that has not yet been presented to the bank for payment. This item is an *unpresented cheque* that will be adjusted on the bank reconciliation statement. Unpresented cheques are added back to the cash book balance, since the bank thinks we still have this money.

The second unticked item on the debit side of the cash book represents a cheque received from Smithsons that was paid into the bank on 31 May, the last day of the month. Clearly, the bank has not yet increased the account with the value of this cheque because it has not yet appeared on the bank statement. This item is known as a *bank lodgement* also called *bank deposits* (money paid into the bank) and must be explained on the bank reconciliation statement.

3 The final step is to draw up a brief statement to reconcile the differences that remain, like this:

- Enter correct date of the reconciliation statement.
- Enter the balance at bank as per the cash book.
- Enter details of unpresented cheques.
- Enter subtotal.
- Enter details of bank deposits.
- Calculate balance as per bank statement.

Bank reconciliation statement as at 31 May 20–8

	£
Balance as per cash book	1,419.23
Add: Unpresented cheque (30405)	152.64
	1,571.87
Less: Bank deposit not yet entered	
on bank statement	162.95
Balance as per bank statement	1,408.92

Frequently, more than one cheque is paid into the bank using a single paying-in slip; details of each cheque are entered on the reverse. It is the total of the cheques on the paying-in slip that appears on the bank statement. For example: if cheques of £300 and £250 were paid into the bank on the same day, they would be shown on the bank statement as £550.

Bank overdrafts

Take care if there is a bank overdraft; that is, a credit balance in the cash book (a debit balance on the bank statement). When a bank account is overdrawn any amounts drawn out of the bank will cause the overdraft to *increase*, while amounts paid in will cause the overdraft to *decrease* and the adjustments needed to reconcile will be the reverse.

When a bank account is overdrawn the abbreviation DR or O/D is usually placed after the balance on the bank statement.

Points to remember

- When comparing the cash book with the bank statement you must realise that in the cash book all *receipts* are shown as *debit entries* and all *payments* as *credit entries*; on a bank statement the entries are shown *exactly the reverse way around*. This is because the bank statement is kept from the bank's point of view.
- Always compare the cash book with the bank statement and tick each item that appears on both. It is only the remaining *unticked items* that will require attention.
- Unticked items on the bank statement will usually need to be entered in the cash book.
- Unticked items at the debit side of the cash book will usually be money paid into the bank that has not yet been entered on the bank statement (*bank deposits*).
- Unticked items at the credit side of the cash book will usually be cheques drawn but not yet presented for payment (*unpresented cheques*).
- A *bank reconciliation statement* is a brief report drawn up to explain any differences that remain. Its purpose is to prove that while there might be a difference between the balance in the cash book and the balance shown on the bank statement, there are usually logical reasons why this might have happened.
- When more than one cheque is paid into the bank using a single paying-in slip details of each cheque are entered on the reverse. It is the *total of the cheques* on the paying-in slip that appears on the bank statement.

Assignments

Now complete the following assignments.

12.1

Morley Enterprises cash book for the month of September 20–9 is shown below:

Cash Book
(Bank Columns Only)

Date	Particulars	Bank	Date	Particulars	Cheque Number	Bank
20–9			20–9			
1 Sep	Balance b/d	724.98	3 Sep	H. Schwartz	30126	492.78
6 Sep	Curtis Ltd	286.90	4 Sep	Contract Blinds	30127	295.50
8 Sep	Kinsell & Co.	680.34	6 Sep	Garside Holmes	30128	508.26
18 Sep	Aztec Sportswear	576.28	18 Sep	Hudson Chase & Co	30129	672.84
20 Sep	De Wan Textiles	604.32	20 Sep	Briggs & Booth	30130	315.28
24 Sep	Apex Casuals	281.20	28 Sep	T. G. Munro	30131	237.50
30 Sep	Kilroy & Ross	438.76	30 Sep	Balance c/d		1,070.62
		3,592.78				3,592.78
30 Sep	Balance b/d	1,070.62				

On 30 September Morley Enterprises received the following bank statement.

Bank Statement

Date	Details	Debit	Credit	Balance
20–9				
1 Sep	Brought forward			724.98
6 Sep	30126	492.78		232.20
6 Sep	Cheque		286.90	519.10
7 Sep	30127	295.50		223.60
8 Sep	Cheque		680.34	903.94
15 Sep	L. D. Council (DD)	137.20		766.74
18 Sep	Cheque		576.28	1,343.02
20 Sep	T. Kay Group (SO)	104.94		1,238.08
20 Sep	Cheque		604.32	1,842.40
23 Sep	30129	672.84		1,169.56
24 Sep	Cheque		281.20	1,450.76
27 Sep	30130	315.28		1,135.48
28 Sep	Roberts Ltd (BGC)		497.76	1,633.24
30 Sep	Bank charges	13.04		1,620.20

You are required to:

(a) Reconcile the cash book with the bank statement.
(b) Make the entries necessary to update the cash book on 30 September 20–9.
(c) Total and balance the bank columns of the cash book and calculate the revised bank balance.
(d) Prepare a bank reconciliation statement dated 30 September 20–9.
(e) Starting with the balance as per the cash book, list any unpresented cheques and subtotal the reconciliation statement.
(f) Enter details of bank deposits not yet entered on the bank statement.
(g) Calculate the balance as per bank statement.

12.2

Andrews & Fox cash book for the month of October 20–9 is shown below:

Cash Book
(Bank Columns Only)

Date	Particulars	Bank	Date	Particulars	Cheque Number	Bank
20–9			20–9			
1 Oct	Balance b/d	998.20	8 Oct	Motor expenses	34612	76.32
2 Oct	S. Driver	357.30	10 Oct	Delta Designs	34613	428.07
6 Oct	Gladston Bros	209.70	17 Oct	Romana Products	34614	280.06
14 Oct	Chervilles Ltd	592.94	19 Oct	Sureguard Security	34615	195.50
20 Oct	W. Dyson Ltd	290.80	23 Oct	Evana Ltd	34616	370.88
26 Oct	Cusack & Son	350.28	27 Oct	Montague Miles	34617	250.24
30 Oct	Adam Bates	182.42	29 Oct	Insurance	34618	203.65
			30 Oct	Star Plastics	34619	356.82
			31 Oct	Balance c/d		820.10
		2,981.64				2,981.64
31 Oct	Balance b/d	820.10				

On 31 October, Andrews & Fox received the following bank statement:

Bank Statement

Date	Details	Debit	Credit	Balance
20–9				
1 Oct	Brought forward			998.20
2 Oct	Cheque		357.30	1,355.50
4 Oct	Medleys (DD)	114.50		1,241.00
6 Oct	Cheque		209.70	1,450.70
14 Oct	34613	428.07		1,022.63
14 Oct	Cheque		592.94	1,615.57
16 Oct	34612	76.32		1,539.25
20 Oct	Cheque		290.80	1,830.05
26 Oct	34616	370.88		1,459.17
26 Oct	Cheque		350.28	1,809.45
27 Oct	34615	195.50		1,613.95
28 Oct	Catlow Ltd (BCG)		607.25	2,221.20
30 Oct	YDC (SO)	213.76		2,007.44
30 Oct	34617	250.24		1,757.20
30 Oct	Bank charges	10.50		1,746.70

You are required to:

(a) Reconcile the cash book with the bank statement.
(b) Make the entries necessary to update the cash book on 31 October 20–9.
(c) Total and balance the bank columns of the cash book and calculate the revised bank balance.
(d) Prepare a bank reconciliation statement dated 31 October 20–9.
(e) Starting with the balance as per the cash book, list any unpresented cheques and subtotal the reconciliation statement.
(f) Enter details of bank deposits not yet entered on the bank statement.
(g) Calculate the balance as per the bank statement.

12.3

Madhur Daswani's cash book for the month of May 20–9 is shown below:

Cash Book
(Bank Columns Only)

Date	Particulars	Bank	Date	Particulars	Cheque Number	Bank
20–9			20–9			
1 May	Balance b/d	695.35	3 May	Palomo Imports	50103	304.75
4 May	Drew & Hurst	538.09	6 May	R. Keaton	50104	214.50
9 May	Luptons Ltd	376.40	8 May	Motor expenses	50105	69.25
13 May	Weston Enterprises	480.65	12 May	Douglas & Son	50106	351.31
19 May	Masters Ltd	198.46	14 May	Ripley Signs	50107	176.95
24 May	R. McQuade	204.75	18 May	Courtways	50108	288.99
28 May	Jayrose Group	400.49	20 May	Murphy & Sykes	50109	107.50
			26 May	Hyde & Son	50110	132.62
			31 May	Balance c/d		1,248.32
		2,894.19				2,894.19
31 May	Balance b/d	1,248.32				

On 31 May, Madhur Daswani received the following bank statement:

Bank Statement

Date	Details	Debit	Credit	Balance
20–9				
1 May	Brought forward			695.35
4 May	Cheque		538.09	1,233.44
8 May	50103	304.75		928.69
9 May	Cheque		376.40	1,305.09
12 May	50105	69.25		1,235.84
13 May	Cheque		480.65	1,716.49
19 May	50107	176.95		1,539.54
19 May	Cheque		198.46	1,738.00
20 May	50104	214.50		1,523.50
21 May	AOW Group (SO)	136.72		1,386.78
22 May	Cheque		204.75	1,591.53
26 May	50109	107.50		1,484.03
28 May	Lock Ltd (BGC)		592.58	2,076.61
30 May	Bank charges	12.65		2,063.96
30 May	Smythe Group (BACS)		436.94	2,500.90

You are required to:

(a) Reconcile the cash book with the bank statement.
(b) Make the entries necessary to update the cash book on 31 May 20–9.
(c) Total and balance the bank columns of the cash book and calculate the revised bank balance.

(d) Prepare a bank reconciliation statement dated 31 May 20–9.
(e) Starting with the balance as per the cash book, list any unpresented cheques and subtotal the reconciliation statement.
(f) Enter details of bank deposits not yet entered on the bank statement.
(g) Calculate the balance as per the bank statement.

12.4

Harry Bairstow's cash book for the month of June 20–9 is shown below:

Cash Book
(Bank Columns Only)

Date	Particulars	Bank	Date	Particulars	Cheque Number	Bank
20–9			20–9			
2 Jun	Best Textiles	370.74	1 Jun	Balance b/d		746.32
7 Jun	Apex Clothes	503.80	4 Jun	Rodley Mills	46351	463.95
18 Jun	Shaw & Sons	281.69	12 Jun	D. Crofton	46352	308.56
23 Jun	R. Lewis Ltd	294.75	13 Jun	Rates	46353	195.75
23 Jun	D. Kingsley	720.48	16 Jun	Vandante Ltd	46354	409.89
29 Jun	T. McKenzie	305.82	21 Jun	Office Supplies	46355	32.52
30 Jun	Balance c/d	559.58	22 Jun	J. Seymore	46356	290.89
			26 Jun	Booth & Royd	46357	309.35
			28 Jun	A. Thompson	46358	279.63
		3,036.86				3,036.86
			30 Jun	Balance b/d		559.58

On 30 June, Harry Bairstow received the following bank statement.

Bank Statement

Date	Details	Debit	Credit	Balance
20–9				
1 Jun	Brought forward			746.32 **O/D**
2 Jun	Cheque		370.74	375.58 **O/D**
7 Jun	46351	463.95		839.53 **O/D**
7 Jun	Cheque		503.80	335.73 **O/D**
10 Jun	Lex Group (BACS)		752.76	417.03
17 Jun	46353	195.75		221.28
18 Jun	Cheque		281.69	502.97
20 Jun	46352	308.56		194.41
23 Jun	Cheques		1,015.23	1,209.64
24 Jun	Interpak (DD)	29.50		1,180.14
25 Jun	46355	32.52		1,147.62
26 Jun	Conrad Ltd (BGC)		496.48	1,644.10
28 Jun	46356	290.89		1,353.21
30 Jun	46357	309.35		1,043.86
30 Jun	Bank charges	34.26		1,009.60

You are required to:

(a) Reconcile the cash book with the bank statement.
(b) Make the entries necessary to update the cash book on 30 June 20–9.
(c) Total and balance the bank columns of the cash book and calculate the revised bank balance.
(d) Prepare a bank reconciliation statement dated 30 June 20–9.
(e) Starting with the balance as per the cash book, list any unpresented cheques and subtotal the reconciliation statement.
(f) Enter details of bank deposits not yet entered on the bank statement.
(g) Calculate the balance as per the bank statement.

12.5

Wilson Singer's cash book for the month of September 20–8 is shown below:

Cash Book
(Bank Columns Only)

Date	Particulars	Bank	Date	Particulars	Cheque Number	Bank
20–8			20–8			
1 Sep	Balance b/d	1,095.25	3 Sep	Motor expenses	20931	94.72
2 Sep	Kyte Sportswear	375.50	9 Sep	Tartan Designs	20932	504.07
8 Sep	Morton McKays	406.38	12 Sep	D. Lawrence	20933	396.98
15 Sep	Kirk & Johnson	272.76	16 Sep	Pinedo Imports	20934	426.27
21 Sep	Victor Shires	205.25	20 Sep	Realto Fabrics	20935	394.86
21 Sep	Expo Clothes	320.60	24 Sep	Hester Group	20936	618.26
28 Sep	Doyle Ltd	138.98	27 Sep	Marcus King	20937	480.09
30 Sep	Balance c/d	361.28	29 Sep	D. C. Mitchell	20938	260.75
		3,176.00				3,176.00
			30 Sep	Balance b/d		361.28

On 30 September, Wilson Singer received the following bank statement:

Bank Statement

Date	Details	Debit	Credit	Balance
20–8				
1 Sep	Brought forward			1,095.25
2 Sep	Cheque		375.50	1,470.75
7 Sep	20931	94.72		1,376.03
8 Sep	Cheque		406.38	1,782.41
15 Sep	20933	396.98		1,385.43
15 Sep	Cheque		272.76	1,658.19
18 Sep	20932	504.07		1,154.12
20 Sep	Keys Estates (SO)	250.50		903.62
21 Sep	Cheques		525.85	1,429.47
26 Sep	20935	394.86		1,034.61
27 Sep	Frazers (BACS)		825.95	1,860.56
30 Sep	20937	480.09		1,380.47
30 Sep	Bank charges	12.50		1,367.97
30 Sep	Y. D. Council (DD)	101.24		1,266.73
30 Sep	20934	426.27		840.46

You are required to:

(a) Reconcile the cash book with the bank statement.
(b) Make the entries necessary to update the cash book on 30 September 20–8.
(c) Total and balance the bank columns of the cash book and calculate the revised bank balance.
(d) Prepare a bank reconciliation statement dated 30 September 20–8.
(e) Starting with the balance as per the cash book, list any unpresented cheques and subtotal the reconciliation statement.
(f) Enter details of bank deposits not yet entered on the bank statement.
(g) Calculate the balance as per the bank statement.

12.6

Gina Howard's cash book for the month of October 20–8 is shown below:

Cash Book
(Bank Columns Only)

Date	Particulars	Bank	Date	Particulars	Cheque Number	Bank
20–8			20–8			
4 Oct	Maximate	547.50	1 Oct	Balance b/d		1,012.54
12 Oct	Rogers & Shaw	468.48	3 Oct	Sundry expenses	15292	376.82
12 Oct	Bond Group	370.04	9 Oct	Merlins Ltd	15293	312.78
20 Oct	D. Chippendale	620.96	14 Oct	Andrew Freres	15294	216.96
24 Oct	Douglas & Son	594.36	19 Oct	Victoria Plastics	15295	235.98
30 Oct	Lloyd & Young	872.74	23 Oct	Insurance	15296	164.50
			26 Oct	Woodrow Dawson	15297	127.53
			27 Oct	D. Lorenz	15298	250.62
			30 Oct	Hudson Verity	15299	292.79
			31 Oct	Balance c/d		483.56
		3,474.08				3,474.08
31 Oct	Balance b/d	483.56				

On 31 October, Gina Howard received the following bank statement.

Bank Statement

Date	Details	Debit	Credit	Balance
20–8				
1 Oct	Brought forward			1,012.54 O/D
4 Oct	Cheque		547.50	465.04 O/D
6 Oct	Karline (DD)	138.90		603.94 O/D
12 Oct	Cheques		838.52	234.58
14 Oct	15293	312.78		78.20 O/D
16 Oct	Salmon Group (BGC)		690.96	612.76
18 Oct	15292	376.82		235.94
20 Oct	Cheque		620.96	856.90
23 Oct	15295	235.98		620.92
24 Oct	Cheque		594.36	1,215.28
26 Oct	15294	216.96		998.32
28 Oct	Briggs Ltd (BACS)		407.80	1,406.12
29 Oct	15296	164.50		1,241.62
30 Oct	Bank charges	25.84		1,215.78
30 Oct	15298	250.62		965.16

You are required to:

(a) Reconcile the cash book with the bank statement.
(b) Make the entries necessary to update the cash book on 31 October 20–8.
(c) Total and balance the bank columns of the cash book and calculate the revised bank balance.
(d) Prepare a bank reconciliation statement dated 31 October 20–8.
(e) Starting with the balance as per the cash book, list any unpresented cheques and subtotal the reconciliation statement.
(f) Enter details of bank deposits not yet entered on the bank statement.
(g) Calculate the balance as per the bank statement.

12.7
Simms Enterprises keeps a three-column cash book. During the month of May 20–8 the following transactions took place:

May 1	Opening balances: £280.78 in the cash account and £762.30 in the bank account
2	Received £375.50 by cheque from T. Lonsdale in full settlement of his account of £394.28
3	Paid Digitel £176.92 by cheque (cheque number 20514)
5	Cash purchases £105.30
8	Received £247.95 by cheque from A. Brown & Sons
10	Paid Riley & Clark's account of £420.60 less 5 per cent cash discount (cheque number 20515)
12	Received £104.38 in cash from S. Groves, a debtor
14	Paid Chapela Ltd £294.06 by cheque (cheque number 20516)
16	Paid L. Wiseman's account of £176.80 less 2.5 per cent cash discount (cheque number 20517)
18	Received £490.62 by cheque from Aspinall Ltd in full settlement of their account of £515.15
18	Received £209.88 by cheque from E. Foxhill
20	Cash purchases £165.92
21	Paid Mollitex £350.46 by cheque (cheque number 20518)
23	Received £126.24 in cash from H. Khan, a debtor
24	Paid Sharp Electronics' account of £430.80 less 2.5 per cent cash discount (cheque number 20519)
25	Paid motor expenses £94.24 by cheque (cheque number 20520)
25	Received £308.36 from Moss Linton in full settlement of their account of £323.78
26	Cash sales £190.56
28	Paid Dean & Gill's account of £250.40 less 5 per cent cash discount (cheque number 20521)
30	Received £82.36 in cash from C. Botica, a debtor
30	Received £585.25 by cheque from King Bros in full settlement of their account of £614.52

You are required to:

(a) Enter the opening balances.
(b) Enter details of receipts and payments including cash discounts.
(c) Total and balance the cash book and bring down the balances.
(d) Total the discount columns.

On 31 May, Simms Enterprises received the following bank statement:

Bank Statement

Date	Details	Debit	Credit	Balance
20–8				
1 May	Brought forward			762.30
2 May	Cheque		375.50	1,137.80
5 May	Parkway (DD)	176.94		960.86
8 May	Cheque		247.95	1,208.81
9 May	20514	176.92		1,031.89
12 May	Benson Group (BGC)		420.36	1,452.25
15 May	20515	399.57		1,052.68
18 May	Cheques		700.50	1,753.18
20 May	W. Y. Council (SO)	69.25		1,683.93
21 May	20517	172.38		1,511.55
25 May	Cheque		308.36	1,819.91
28 May	20519	420.03		1,399.88
28 May	20516	294.06		1,105.82
29 May	Qualpak (BACS)		750.50	1,856.32
30 May	20520	94.24		1,762.08

You are required to:

(a) Reconcile the cash book with the bank statement.
(b) Make the entries necessary to update the cash book on 31 May 20–8.
(c) Total and balance the bank columns of the cash book and calculate the revised bank balance.
(d) Prepare a bank reconciliation statement dated 31 May 20–8.
(e) Starting with the balance as per the cash book, list any unpresented cheques and subtotal the reconciliation statement.
(f) Enter details of bank deposits not yet entered on the bank statement.
(g) Calculate the balance as per the bank statement.

■ ∨ **13** Analysed purchases and purchase returns day books

In business, there are many transactions of a similar nature. For example, there are usually numerous purchases on credit. The purpose of *day books* is to group together all like transactions and so reduce the number of entries that need to be made in the ledger.

Because all business activities really start with a document, day books are also known as *'books of original entry'*.

Purchase invoices

In many businesses, most of the purchases will be made on a credit basis (to be paid for at a future date) rather than paid for immediately with cash.

When a business buys goods on credit an invoice is made out by the supplier showing full details of the goods, prices and any trade discount. This is known as a *purchase invoice*. It is the original document that provides the financial information that will subsequently be recorded in the ledger. In practice you will find that invoices will differ in appearance, each business having its own individual design.

When invoices are received from suppliers they should always be checked to ensure that they are genuine and accurate. These procedures should be carried out:

- Check that the goods were ordered. (Invoices are sometimes received for goods that have not been ordered.)
- Check all goods have been received in good condition and details correspond with the order. (It may be that only part of the order has been received.)
- Check prices charged on the invoice are correct.
- Check that all calculations are accurate.

Analysed purchases day book

Only when the checking procedures have been carried out should the purchase invoices be entered in the *purchases day book*. This book contains details of all credit purchases of goods for resale. When a purchase invoice is received this document is the original accounting record of the transaction. Day books are also known as *journals* (the word 'journal' is the French word for *day book*). Cash purchases are *never* entered in the purchases day book. When goods are bought and payment is made immediately in cash, the original entry is made in the *cash book* (*credit cash account* and *debit purchases account*).

A modern purchases day book is simply a list, in date order, of all purchases on credit, showing:

- date
- name of supplier
- amount of goods analysed into relevant columns
- amount of VAT
- total amount of invoice.

We can look at a typical example. Kaymar Cards analyses its purchase invoices into two departments, Greetings cards and Gift wrap. This invoice has been received from a supplier:

Van Leer Varley
Lockwood Lane
WAKEFIELD
WK7 8NP

VAT Registration No 719 3578 29   Telephone 01924 5532

INVOICE

Kaymar Cards
Manor Road
COVENTRY
CV96 1MN

Date 2 November 20-4

Invoice No 2097

Qty	Description	Unit price £	£	£
144	Embossed birthday cards	0.72 each	103.68	
144	Musical Christmas cards	1.05 each	151.20	
250 boxes	Assorted Christmas cards	1.59 a box	397.50	
			652.38	
	Less trade discount 15%		97.86	
			554.52	
	VAT at 17.5%		97.04	
				651.56

Trade discount is simply a way of calculating prices. You do not need to worry about trade discount, it is *never* entered in day books or in any account. When writing up the day books you will record the figure after any trade discount has been deducted. The entries in the analysed day book for this invoice would look like this:

Purchases Day Book

Date 20–4	Details	Greetings cards	Gift wrap	VAT	Invoice total
2 Nov	Van Leer Varley	554.52		97.04	651.56

Now look at another invoice received from a supplier:

Delta designs
Lockwood Trading Estate
SHEFFIELD
S50 6AM

VAT Registration No 719 3578 29   Telephone 0114 70926

INVOICE

Kaymar Cards
Manor Road
COVENTRY
CV96 1MN

Date 6 November 20-4

Invoice No 7895

Qty	Description	Unit Price £	£	£
450 rolls	Gold foil gift wrap 5m	1.29 a roll	580.50	
400 rolls	Silver foil gift wrap 5m	1.29 a roll	516.00	
			1,096.50	
	Less trade discount 10%		109.65	
				986.85
250 boxes	Deluxe Christmas cards	2.89 a box	722.50	
	Less trade discount 15%		108.38	614.12
				1,600.97
	VAT at 17.5%			280.17
				1,881.14

The entries in the purchases day book for this invoice would look like this:

Purchases Day Book

Date 20–4	Details	Greetings cards	Gift wrap	VAT	Invoice total
2 Nov	Van Leer Varley	554.52		97.04	651.56
6 Nov	Delta Designs	614.12	986.85	280.17	1,881.14

This invoice is received from Henry Carters:

Henry Carters
Queen Street
Morley
LS78 8ER

VAT Registration No 308 9674 50   Telephone 0113 25716

Invoice

Kaymar Cards
Manor Road
Coventry
CV96 1MN

Invoice No 8492

Date 10 November 20-4

Quantity	Description	£	£	£
144 rolls	Disney gift wrap 5m	1.39 a roll	200.16	
144 rolls	Celebration gift wrap 5m	1.29 a roll	185.76	
			385.92	
	Less trade discount 10%		38.59	
				347.33
	VAT at 17.5%			60.78
				408.11

The entries in the purchases day book for this invoice would look like this:

Purchases Day Book

Date 20–4	Details	Greetings cards	Gift wrap	VAT	Invoice total
2 Nov	Van Leer Varley	554.52		97.04	651.56
6 Nov	Delta Designs	614.12	986.85	280.17	1,881.14
10 Nov	Henry Carters		347.33	60.78	408.11

Another invoice is received from Van Leer Varley:

Van Leer Varley
Lockwood Lane
WAKEFIELD
WK7 8NP

VAT Registration No 719 3578 29   Telephone 01924 5532

INVOICE

Kaymar Cards
Manor Road
COVENTRY
CV96 1MN

Date 16 November 20–4

Invoice No 2104

Qty	Description	Unit Price £	£	£
500 rolls	Christmas gift wrap 10m	0.99 a roll	495.00	
500 rolls	Christmas gift wrap 5m	0.65 a roll	325.00	
			820.00	
	Less trade discount 10%		82.00	
				738.00
100	Embossed birthday cards	0.72 each	72.00	
	Less trade discount 15%		10.80	61.20
				799.20
	VAT at 17.5%			139.86
				939.06

The entries in the analysed day book for this invoice would look like this:

Purchases Day Book

Date 20–4	Details	Greetings cards	Gift wrap	VAT	Invoice total
2 Nov	Van Leer Varley	554.52		97.04	651.56
6 Nov	Delta Designs	614.12	986.85	280.17	1,881.14
10 Nov	Henry Carters		347.33	60.78	408.11
16 Nov	Van Leer Varley	61.20	738.00	139.86	939.06

Another invoice is received from Henry Carters:

Henry Carters
Queen Street
Morley
LS78 8ER

VAT Registration No 308 9674 50   Telephone 0113 25716

Invoice

Kaymar Cards
Manor Road
Coventry
CV96 1MN

Invoice No 8510

Date 20 November 20-4

Quantity	Description	£	£	£
144 rolls	Celebration gift wrap 5m	1.29 a roll	185.76	
144 rolls	Christmas gift wrap 10m	0.95 a roll	136.80	
			322.56	
	Less trade discount 10%		32.26	
				290.30
144	Cute birthday cards	0.62 each	89.28	
250 boxes	Christmas card specials	1.59 a box	397.50	
			486.78	
	Less trade discount 15%		73.02	
				413.76
				704.06
	VAT at 17.5%			123.21
				827.27

The entries in the purchases day book for this invoice would look like this:

Purchases Day Book

Date 20–4	Details	Greetings cards	Gift wrap	VAT	Invoice total
2 Nov	Van Leer Varley	554.52		97.04	651.56
6 Nov	Delta Designs	614.12	986.85	280.17	1,881.14
10 Nov	Henry Carters		347.33	60.78	408.11
16 Nov	Van Leer Varley	61.20	738.00	139.86	939.06
20 Nov	Henry Carters	413.76	290.30	123.21	827.27

Entries are made for a certain period, usually a month. At the end of the month all the columns are totalled. This is an illustration of the completed purchases day book for the month of November 20–4.

Purchases Day Book

Date 20–4	Details	Greetings cards	Gift wrap	VAT	Invoice total
2 Nov	Van Leer Varley	554.52		97.04	651.56
6 Nov	Delta Designs	614.12	986.85	280.17	1,881.14
10 Nov	Henry Carters		347.33	60.78	408.11
16 Nov	Van Leer Varley	61.20	738.00	139.86	939.06
20 Nov	Henry Carters	413.76	290.30	123.21	827.27
30 Nov		1,643.60	2,362.48	701.06	4,707.14

The total of all the analysis columns should always equal the addition of the *Invoice total column*. This method of checking is known as *cross casting* and will usually reveal any mistakes, either in the addition of the columns or if an incorrect amount has been entered in the analysis columns.

The important rule of the purchases day book is that each supplier's account is credited, and the purchases and VAT accounts are debited from this original source.

Personal accounts are not affected by the analysis. At the end of the period each supplier's account in the purchase ledger is credited with the total amount of each invoice, *including VAT*, like this:

Purchase Ledger

Van Leer Varley Account

	2 Nov	Purchases	651.56
	16 Nov	Purchases	939.06

Delta Designs Account

	6 Nov	Purchases	1,881.14

Henry Carters Account

	10 Nov	Purchases	408.11
	20 Nov	Purchases	827.27

All the personal accounts have been credited with the total value of each invoice *including VAT* because this is the amount the firm will have to pay its suppliers. We can now see how the information given in the analysis columns provides the figures that are posted to the nominal ledger. This is achieved by having separate purchases accounts for each department. One entry is made to correspond with the total *purchases value* for each department, like this:

Nominal Ledger

Purchases Account – Greetings Cards

30 Nov Total PDB	1,643.60	

Purchases Account – Gift Wrap

30 Nov Total PDB	2,362.48	

Value Added Tax Account

30 Nov Total PDB	701.06	

It is immediately evident that this procedure is more efficient and considerably reduces the number of entries in the purchases and VAT accounts. If you check the totals you will find out that the debit entries exactly equal the credit entries, so our double entry is correct. To save space, only a few examples have been given, but the real value is seen when the number of entries is very large. Only five invoices are shown in the illustration, but for some firms, during a period of a month this could easily be 500.

In practice you may find a variety of methods in use for dealing with numerous credit purchase transactions, but all will eventually result in the same ledger entries.

Credit notes

In any business where goods are bought it is likely that some will need to be returned. Goods are returned for many reasons: it may be that the goods supplied were the wrong size or colour, they may be faulty, or they may have been damaged in transit. Whatever the reason, when goods are returned the necessary entries must be made in the accounts. When goods are returned a *credit note* is issued. A credit note is a type of refund document reducing the amount owed by the buyer. A credit note is made out by the seller showing full details of the goods returned, prices and any trade discount. The top copy is sent to the customer and the seller keeps copies of all credit notes for his own records. It is the original document that provides the financial information that will subsequently be recorded in the ledger accounts.

When credit notes are received from suppliers they should always be checked to ensure that they are accurate. When the checking procedures have been carried out the credit notes should be entered in the purchase returns day book. This book contains details of all credit notes received from suppliers. When a credit note is received this document is the original accounting record of the transaction.

Purchase returns day book

A modern purchase returns day book is simply a list, in date order, of all credit notes, showing:

- date
- name of supplier
- amount of goods analysed into relevant columns
- amount of VAT
- total amount of credit note.

We can look at a typical example. This credit note has been received from a supplier:

Van Leer Varley
Lockwood Lane
WAKEFIELD
WK7 8NP

VAT Registration No 719 3578 29

Telephone 01924 5532

CREDIT NOTE

Kaymar Cards
Manor Road
COVENTRY
CV96 1MN

Date 12 November 20-4

Credit Note No 125

Quantity	Description	Unit price £	£	£
20	Musical Christmas cards	1.05 each	21.00	
25 boxes	Assorted Christmas cards	1.59 a box	39.75	
			60.75	
	Less trade discount 15%		9.11	
			51.64	
	VAT at 17.5%		9.04	
				60.68

The entries in the analysed purchase returns day book for this credit note would look like this:

Purchases Returns Day Book

Date 20–4	Details	Greetings cards	Gift wrap	VAT	Total
12 Nov	Van Leer Varley	51.64		9.04	60.68

Another credit note is received from Delta Designs:

Delta designs
Lockwood Trading Estate
SHEFFIELD
S50 6AM

VAT Registration No 719 3578 29   Telephone 0114 70926

Credit Note

Kaymar Cards
Manor Road
COVENTRY
CV96 1MN

Date 17 November 20-4

Credit Note No 019

Qty	Description	Unit Price £	£	£
50 rolls	Gold foil gift wrap 5m Less trade discount 10%	1.29 a roll	64.50 6.45	
				58.05
25 boxes	Deluxe Christmas cards Less trade discount 15%	2.89 a box	72.25 10.84	
				61.41
				119.46
	VAT at 17.5%			20.90
				140.36

The entries in the analysed purchase returns day book for this credit note would look like this:

Purchases Returns Day Book

Date 20–4	Details	Greetings cards	Gift wrap	VAT	Total
12 Nov	Van Leer Varley	51.64		9.04	60.68
17 Nov	Delta Designs	61.41	58.05	20.90	140.36

Another credit note is received from Henry Carters:

Henry Carters
Queen Street
Morley
LS78 8ER

VAT Registration No 308 9674 50

Telephone 0113 25716

Credit Note

Kaymar Cards
Manor Road
Coventry
CV96 1MN

Credit Note No 148

Date 29 November 20-4

Quantity	Description	£	£	£
44 rolls	Celebration gift wrap 5m Less trade discount 10%	1.29 a roll	56.76 5.68	
				51.08
20 boxes	Christmas card specials Less trade discount 15%	1.59 a box	31.80 4.77	
				27.03
				78.11
	VAT at 17.5%			13.67
				91.78

Now the entries in the purchase returns day book for this credit note would look like this:

Purchases Returns Day Book

Date 20–4	Details	Greetings cards	Gift wrap	VAT	Total
12 Nov	Van Leer Varley	51.64		9.04	60.68
17 Nov	Delta Designs	61.41	58.05	20.90	140.36
29 Nov	Henry Carters	27.03	51.08	13.67	91.78

Entries are made for a certain period, usually a month. At the end of the month all the columns are totalled. This is an illustration of the completed purchase returns day book for the month of November 20–4.

Purchases Returns Day Book

Date 20–4	Details	Greetings cards	Gift wrap	VAT	Total
12 Nov	Van Leer Varley	51.64		9.04	60.68
17 Nov	Delta Designs	61.41	58.05	20.90	140.36
29 Nov	Henry Carters	27.03	51.08	13.67	91.78
30 Nov		140.08	109.13	43.61	292.82

The total of all the analysis columns should always equal the addition of the *Total* column. This method of checking is known as *cross casting* and will usually reveal any mistakes, either in the addition of the columns or if an incorrect amount has been entered in the analysis columns.

The important rule of the purchase returns day book is that each supplier's account is debited and the purchase returns and VAT accounts are credited from this original source. Personal accounts are not affected by the analysis. The original purchases have been inserted so that the entries you need to consider are meaningful; it would be unrealistic to show returns if we had not purchased goods in the first place.

At the end of the period each supplier's account in the purchase ledger is debited with the total amount of each credit note, *including VAT*, like this:

Purchase Ledger

Van Leer Varley Account

12 Nov Purchase returns	60.68	2 Nov Purchases	651.56
		16 Nov Purchases	939.06

Delta Designs Account

17 Nov Purchase returns	140.36	6 Nov Purchases	1,881.14

Henry Carters Account

29 Nov Purchase returns	91.78	10 Nov Purchases	408.11
		20 Nov Purchases	827.27

All the personal accounts have been debited with the total value of each credit note *including VAT*.

We can now see how the information given in the analysis columns provides the figures that are posted to the nominal ledger. This is achieved by having separate purchase returns accounts for each department. One entry is made to correspond with the total *purchase returns value* for each department, like this:

Nominal Ledger

Purchase Returns Account – Greetings Cards

		30 Nov Total PRDB	140.08

Purchase Returns Account – Gift Wrap

		30 Nov Total PRDB	109.13

Value Added Tax Account

30 Nov Total PDB	701.06	30 Nov Total PRDB	43.61

Points to remember

- *Analysed day books* provide firms with *useful information* regarding which products sell best, or which department is most profitable.
- All *personal accounts of suppliers* are posted with the total value *including VAT*. To complete the double entry the goods value only for each product or department is entered in the purchases and purchase returns accounts. All VAT is collected together in the VAT account.
- *Trade discount* is simply a way of calculating prices and *no entry for trade discount should be made in the day books* or in any ledger account.
- *Cash purchases* are *never* entered in the purchases day book. The book of original entry for all cash purchases is the *cash book*.

Assignments

13.1

You are responsible for compiling, in date order, the analysed purchases and purchase returns day books for West Park Centre. The firm analyses its invoices and credit notes into two departments, Camping and Gardening. At the end of the month you are required to post the analysed day books to the purchase and nominal ledgers and balance all purchase ledger accounts.

During the month of February 20–5 the following invoices and credit notes were received:

Dalesman Products
Moorfield Lane
SKIPTON
SK9 8ER

VAT Registration No 392 4864 52   Telephone 01756 2984

Invoice

West Park Centre   Invoice No 256
Ring Road
LEEDS   Date 2 February 20-5
LS78 1MN

Quantity	Description	Unit price £	£	£
10	Explorer rucksacks	29.95	299.50	
10	Camping stoves	24.50	245.00	
			544.50	
	Less trade discount 20%		108.90	
				435.60
	VAT at 17.5%			76.23
				511.83

Stanley Engineering
Brook Lane
LEEDS
LS74 8ER

VAT Registration No 839 3576 78

Telephone 0113 26214

INVOICE

West Park Centre
Ring Road
LEEDS
LS78 1MN

Date 7 February 20-5

Invoice No SE 2872

Quantity	Description	Unit Price £	£	£
10	Hover garden lawn mowers	35.95	359.50	
6	Electric garden lawn mowers	29.50	177.00	
				536.50
10	Camping stoves	19.99	199.90	
20	Camping lamps	10.50	210.00	
				409.90
				946.40
	VAT at 17.5%			165.62
				1,112.02

Dalesman Products
Moorfield Lane
SKIPTON
SK9 8ER

VAT Registration No 392 4864 52

Telephone 01756 2984

Credit Note

West Park Centre
Ring Road
LEEDS
LS78 1MN

Credit Note No 74

Date 14 February 20-5

Quantity	Description	Unit price £	£	£
1	Explorer rucksack	29.95	29.95	
2	Camping stoves	24.50	49.00	
			78.95	
	Less trade discount 20%		15.79	
				63.16
	VAT at 17.5%			11.05
				74.21

Earltex Supplies
Tunstall Road
YORK
YO62 5JO

VAT Registration No 294 3852 15

Telephone 01904 5824

Invoice

West Park Centre
Ring Road
LEEDS
LS78 1MN

Date 15 February 20-5

Invoice No 6347

Quantity	Description	Unit Price £	£	£
10	Garden forks	12.95	129.50	
10	Garden spades	14.50	145.00	
			274.50	
	Less trade discount 10%		27.45	
				247.05
12	Camping cook kits	15.95	191.40	
12	Camping tables	14.99	179.88	
12	Camping lanterns	5.50	66.00	
			437.28	
	Less trade discount 20%		87.46	
				349.82
				596.87
	VAT at 17.5%			104.45
				701.32

Stanley Engineering
Brook Lane
LEEDS
LS74 8ER

VAT Registration No 839 3576 78

Telephone 0113 26214

CREDIT NOTE

West Park Centre
Ring Road
LEEDS
LS78 1MN

Date 17 February 20-5

Credit Note No 315

Quantity	Description	Unit Price £	£	£
1	Electric garden lawn mower	29.50	29.50	
4	Camping stoves	19.99	79.96	
				109.46
	VAT at 17.5%			19.16
				128.62

Dalesman Products
Moorfield Lane
SKIPTON
SK9 8ER

VAT Registration No 392 4864 52   Telephone 01756 2984

Invoice

West Park Centre   Invoice No 262
Ring Road
LEEDS   Date 20 February 20-5
LS78 1MN

Quantity	Description	Unit price £	£	£
20	Explorer rucksacks	29.95	599.00	
20	Trail blazer rucksacks	24.75	495.00	
			1,094.00	
	Less trade discount 20%		218.80	
				875.20
	VAT at 17.5%			153.16
				1,028.36

Earltex Supplies
Tunstall Road
YORK
YO62 5JO

VAT Registration No 294 3852 15   Telephone 01904 5824

Invoice

West Park Centre
Ring Road
LEEDS
LS78 1MN

Date 24 February 20-5

Invoice No 6362

Quantity	Description	Unit Price £	£	£
10	Camping tables	14.99	149.90	
20	Camping lanterns	5.50	110.00	
			259.90	
	Less trade discount 20%		51.98	
				207.92
20	Garden spades	14.50	290.00	
20	Garden forks	12.95	259.00	
			549.00	
	Less trade discount 10%		54.90	
				494.10
				702.02
	VAT at 17.5%			122.85
				824.87

13.2

You are responsible for compiling, in date order, the analysed purchases and purchase returns day books for Pick-up Parts. The firm analyses its invoices and credit notes into two departments, Tyres and Exhausts. At the end of the month you are required to post the analysed day books to the purchase and nominal ledgers and balance all purchase ledger accounts.

During the month of May 20–5 the following invoices and credit notes were received:

May 2   Auto Factors: invoice number 3762
         Tyres £309.86, Exhausts £274.90 plus VAT £102.33,
         invoice total £687.09
      7   Mitchells Ltd: invoice number M2815
         Tyres £672.50 plus VAT £117.69, invoice total £790.19
     14   Auto Factors: credit note number CN510
         Exhausts £47.28, Tyres £59.65 plus VAT £18.71,
         credit note total £125.64
     16   Euro Universal: invoice number 386
         Tyres £407.60, Exhausts £318.58 plus VAT £127.08,
         invoice total £853.26
     18   Mitchells Ltd: credit note number 159
         Tyres £94.50 plus VAT £16.54, credit note total £111.04
     20   Auto Factors: invoice number 3785
         Exhausts £205.76, Tyres £494.80 plus VAT £122.60,
         invoice total £823.16
     24   Mitchells Ltd: invoice number M2828
         Tyres £392.75 plus VAT £68.73, invoice total £461.48
     28   Euro Universal: credit note number 105
         Exhausts £79.50, Tyres £62.49 plus VAT £24.85,
         credit note total £166.84

13.3

You are responsible for compiling, in date order, the analysed purchases and purchase returns day books for Europas Fashions. The firm analyses its invoices and credit notes into two departments, Jackets and Jeans. At the end of the month you are required to post the analysed day books to the purchase and nominal ledgers and balance all purchase ledger accounts.

During the month of November 20–5 the following invoices and credit notes were received:

Nov 2   Hongtai Imports: invoice number H3015
         Jeans £460.58, Jackets £374.90, plus VAT £146.21,
         invoice total £981.69
      5   James Wyatt Ltd: invoice number 1874
         Jackets £502.76, Jeans £296.38, plus VAT £139.85,
         invoice total £938.99
     10   Hongtai Imports: credit note number 380
         Jeans £48.50, Jackets £39.45, plus VAT £15.39,
         credit note total £103.34
     14   Focus Marketing: invoice number 2059
         Jeans £407.32, plus VAT £71.28, invoice total £478.60
     17   James Wyatt Ltd: invoice number 1882
         Jackets £364.20, Jeans £590.75, plus VAT £167.12,
         invoice total £1,122.07
     23   Focus Marketing: credit note number 34
         Jeans £39.95 plus VAT £6.99, credit note total £46.94

25 Hongtai Imports: invoice number H3026
Jeans £205.20, Jackets £278.50, plus VAT £84.65,
invoice total £568.35
27 James Wyatt Ltd: credit note number 272
Jackets £49.92, Jeans £38.78, plus VAT £15.52,
credit note total £104.22

13.4

You are responsible for compiling, in date order, the analysed purchases
and purchase returns day books for Marcus Cavendish. The firm analyses
its invoices and credit notes into two departments, China and Cutlery. At
the end of the month you are required to post the analysed day books to the
purchase and nominal ledgers and balance all purchase ledger accounts.

During the month of February 20–6 the following invoices and credit
notes were received:

Feb 2 Ainsley Sykes: invoice number 1574
Cutlery £519.50, China £208.76, plus VAT £127.45,
invoice total £855.71
4 Ultimate Designs: invoice number 860
China £326.48, Cutlery £290.20, plus VAT £107.92,
invoice total £724.60
6 Kilncroft Ltd: invoice number 10368
China £450.42 plus VAT £78.82, invoice total £529.24
15 Ultimate Designs: credit note number 156
Cutlery £40.38, China £73.56, plus VAT £19.94,
credit note total £133.88
18 Ainsley Sykes: invoice number 1586
Cutlery £462.90, China £375.56, plus VAT £146.73,
invoice total £985.19
20 Kilncroft Ltd: credit note number 38
China £32.78 plus VAT £5.74, credit note total £38.52
24 Ultimate Designs: invoice number 876
Cutlery £509.74, China £128.90, plus VAT £111.76,
invoice total £750.40
26 Ainsley Sykes: credit note number 207
China £39.20, Cutlery £84.36, plus VAT £21.62,
credit note total £145.18

13.5

You are responsible for compiling, in date order, the analysed purchases
and purchase returns day books for Kerterama Ltd. The firm analyses its
invoices and credit notes into two departments, Curtains and Cushions. At
the end of the month you are required to post the analysed day books to the
purchase and nominal ledgers and balance all purchase ledger accounts.

During the month of May 20–6 the following invoices and credit notes
were received:

May 3   Yorkshire Fabrics: invoice number 3015
             Cushions £89.50, Curtains £420.76, plus VAT £89.30,
             invoice total £599.56

      7   Kirk Mills Ltd: invoice number 1076
             Curtains £704.20 plus VAT £123.24, invoice total £827.44

    12   Yorkshire Fabrics: credit note number 139
             Cushions £20.50, Curtains £58.26, plus VAT £13.78,
             credit note total £92.54

    15   Venture Textiles: invoice number 3078
             Cushions £186.30, Curtains £498.62, plus VAT £119.86,
             invoice total £804.78

    18   Kirk Mills Ltd: credit note number KM47
             Curtains £92.70 plus VAT £16.22, credit note total £108.92

    20   Yorkshire Fabrics: invoice number 3025
             Cushions £138.26, Curtains £394.78, plus VAT £93.28,
             invoice total £626.32

    25   Venture Textiles: credit note number C480
             Curtains £69.30, Cushions £28.52, plus VAT £17.12,
             credit note total £114.94

    28   Kirk Mills Ltd: invoice number 1084
             Cushions £115.78, Curtains £409.50, plus VAT £91.92,
             invoice total £617.20

■ ⊻ 14 Analysed sales and sales returns day books

In business there are many transactions of a similar nature: for example, there are usually numerous sales on credit. The purpose of *day books* is to group together all like transactions and so reduce the number of entries that need to be made in the ledger.

Because all business activities really start with a document, day books are also known as '*books of original entry*'.

Sales invoices

In many businesses, most of the sales will be made on a credit basis (to be paid for at a future date) rather than for immediate cash. When goods are sold on credit, an invoice is made out by the seller showing full details of the goods, prices and any trade discount. This is known as a *sales invoice*. This is the original document that provides the financial information that will be recorded subsequently in the ledger. In practice, you will find that invoices will differ in appearance, with each business having its own individual design.

For convenience, invoices are frequently prepared in sets, with each copy being used for a specific purpose. This enables a firm to properly organise the sending of the goods, and ensures that they can confirm the goods have been received safely. The exact number of copies will vary from one firm to another, but the seller will keep at least one copy of each sales invoice for his/her own records. Extra copies may be used as:

Advice notes

These are sent to the customer *before* the goods are despatched. Their purpose is to notify the customer that the goods are on the way, stating the method of transport and when the goods are expected to arrive. If the goods do not arrive within a reasonable time, the customer will notify the seller, so that enquiries can be made to establish what has happened to the goods.

Delivery notes

These are sent *with the goods*, so the customer can check immediately that all the items listed have been received.

Analysed sales day book

When the sales invoices have been made out, the top copy is sent to the customer, and copy invoices are entered in the *sales day book*. This book contains details of all credit sales. Day books are also known as *journals* (the word journal is simply the French word for 'day book').

Cash sales are *never* entered in the sales day book. When goods are sold and payment is received immediately in cash, the original entry is in the *cash book* (*debit cash account* and *credit sales account*).

A modern sales day book is simply a list, in date order, of all sales on credit, showing:

- date
- name of customer
- amount of goods analysed into relevant columns
- amount of VAT
- total amount of invoice.

We can now look at a typical example. Activity Zone analyses its sales invoices into two departments: Tents and Sleeping bags. This invoice has been sent to a customer:

```
                        Activity Zone
                     78 Commercial Road
                        TADCASTER
                          TA59 8TP

VAT Registration No 624 8512 68                    Telephone 01937 6882

                            INVOICE

  Camping & Leisure Centre                 Date 3 February 20-6
  Ring Road
  LEEDS                                    Invoice No 2842
  LS97 8DN
```

Quantity	Description	Unit price £	£	£
6	2-person Dome tents	25.99	155.94	
6	3-person Dome tents	35.95	215.70	
				371.64
10	Resteasy sleeping bags	16.99	169.90	
20	Sonata sleeping bags	18.50	370.00	
				539.90
				911.54
	VAT at 17.5%			159.52
				1,071.06

The entries in the analysed sales day book for this invoice would look like this:

Sales day book

Date 20–6	Details	Tents	Sleeping bags	VAT	Invoice total
3 Feb	Camping & Leisure Centre	371.64	539.90	159.52	1,071.06

This invoice was sent to another customer:

Activity Zone
78 Commercial Road
TADCASTER
TA59 8TP

VAT Registration No 624 8512 68   Telephone 01937 6882

INVOICE

D E Cooper Ltd
174 High Street
HALIFAX
HA56 8MD

Date 5 February 20-6

Invoice No 2843

Quantity	Description	Unit price £	£	£
25	Sonata sleeping bags	18.50	462.50	
20	Everwarm sleeping bags	17.95	359.00	
10	Explorer sleeping bags	19.75	197.50	
			1,019.00	
	VAT at 17.5%		178.32	
				1,197.32

Now the entries in the sales day book would look like this:

Sales day book

Date 20–6	Details	Tents	Sleeping bags	VAT	Invoice total
3 Feb	Camping & Leisure Centre	371.64	539.90	159.52	1,071.06
5 Feb	D. E. Cooper Ltd		1,019.00	178.32	1,197.32

This invoice has been sent to Hills and Fells:

Activity Zone
78 Commercial Road
TADCASTER
TA59 8TP

VAT Registration No 624 8512 68   Telephone 01937 6882

INVOICE

Hills and Fells
Plaza Centre
BARWICK IN ELMET
LS92 9TZ

Date 9 February 20-6

Invoice No 2844

Quantity	Description	Unit price £	£	£
2	4-person Oregon trail tents	159.99	319.98	
2	6-person Oregon trail tents	195.95	391.90	
				711.88
6	Explorer sleeping bags	19.75	118.50	
6	Sonata sleeping bags	18.50	111.00	
				229.50
				941.38
	VAT at 17.5%			164.74
				1,106.12

Now the entries in the sales day book would look like this:

Sales day book

Date 20–6	Details	Tents	Sleeping bags	VAT	Invoice total
3 Feb	Camping & Leisure Centre	371.64	539.90	159.52	1,071.06
5 Feb	D. E. Cooper Ltd		1,019.00	178.32	1,197.32
9 Feb	Hills and Fells	711.88	229.50	164.74	1,106.12

Another invoice is sent to Camping & Leisure Centre:

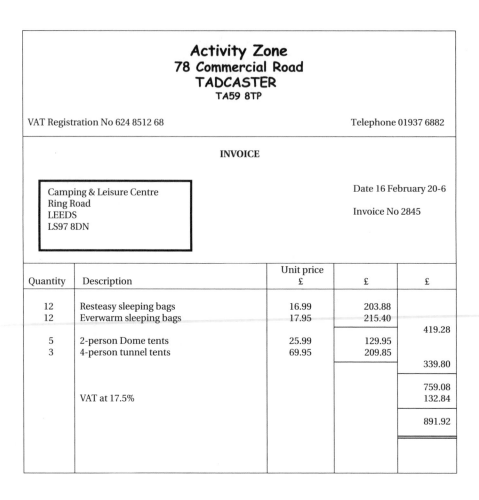

Now the entries in the sales day book would look like this:

Sales day book

Date 20–6	Details	Tents	Sleeping bags	VAT	Invoice total
3 Feb	Camping & Leisure Centre	371.64	539.90	159.52	1,071.06
5 Feb	D. E. Cooper Ltd		1,019.00	178.32	1,197.32
9 Feb	Hills and Fells	711.88	229.50	164.74	1,106.12
16 Feb	Camping & Leisure Centre	339.80	419.28	132.84	891.92

Another invoice is sent to D. E. Cooper Ltd:

Activity Zone
78 Commercial Road
TADCASTER
TA59 8TP

VAT Registration No 624 8512 68   Telephone 01937 6882

INVOICE

D E Cooper Ltd
174 High Street
HALIFAX
HA56 8MD

Date 20 February 20-6

Invoice No 2846

Quantity	Description	Unit price £	£	£
10	Seville sleeping bags	19.50	195.00	
10	Explorer sleeping bags	19.75	197.50	
10	Everwarm sleeping bags	17.95	179.50	
			572.00	
	VAT at 17.5%		100.10	
				672.10

The entries in the sales day book for this invoice would look like this:

Sales day book

Date 20–6	Details	Tents	Sleeping bags	VAT	Invoice total
3 Feb	Camping & Leisure Centre	371.64	539.90	159.52	1,071.06
5 Feb	D. E. Cooper Ltd		1,019.00	178.32	1,197.32
9 Feb	Hills and Fells	711.88	229.50	164.74	1,106.12
16 Feb	Camping & Leisure Centre	339.80	419.28	132.84	891.92
20 Feb	D. E. Cooper Ltd		572.00	100.10	672.10

Entries are made for a certain period, usually a month. At the end of the month all the columns are totalled. Here is an illustration of the completed sales day book for the month of February 20–6:

Sales day book

Date 20–6	Details	Tents	Sleeping bags	VAT	Invoice total
3 Feb	Camping & Leisure Centre	371.64	539.90	159.52	1,071.06
5 Feb	D. E. Cooper Ltd		1,019.00	178.32	1,197.32
9 Feb	Hills and Fells	711.88	229.50	164.74	1,106.12
16 Feb	Camping & Leisure Centre	339.80	419.28	132.84	891.92
20 Feb	D. E. Cooper Ltd		572.00	100.10	672.10
28 Feb		1,423.32	2,779.68	735.52	4,938.52

The total of all the analysis columns should always equal the total of the *Invoice total* column. This method of checking is known as *cross casting* and will usually reveal any mistakes, either in the addition of the columns or if an incorrect amount has been entered in any of the analysis columns.

The important rule of the sales day book is that each customer's account is debited and the sales and VAT accounts are credited from this original source. Personal accounts are not affected by the analysis.

At the end of the period, each customer's account in the sales ledger is debited with the total amount of each invoice, *including VAT*, like this:

Sales ledger

Camping & Leisure Centre Account

3 Feb	Sales	1,071.06
16 Feb	Sales	891.92

D. E. Cooper Ltd Account

5 Feb	Sales	1,197.32
20 Feb	Sales	672.10

Hills and Fells Account

9 Feb	Sales	1,106.12

All the personal accounts have been debited with the total value of each invoice *including VAT*, because this is the amount the customers will have to pay.

We can now see how the information given in the analysis columns provides the figures that are posted to the nominal ledger. This is achieved by having separate sales accounts for each department. One entry is made to correspond with the total *sales value* for each department, like this:

Nominal ledger

Sales Account – Tents

	28 Feb Total SDB	1,423.32

Sales Account – Sleeping Bags

	28 Feb Total SDB	2,779.68

Value Added Tax Account

	28 Feb Total SDB	735.52

It is immediately evident that this procedure is more efficient and considerably reduces the number of entries in the sales and VAT accounts. If you check the totals you will find that the debit entries exactly equal the credit entries, so our double entry is correct. To save space, only a few examples have been used, but the real benefit is seen when the number of entries is very large. Only five invoices are shown in the illustration, but for some firms, during a month this could easily be 500.

In practice, you may find a variety of methods in use for dealing with numerous credit sales transactions, but all will result eventually in the same ledger entries.

Credit notes

In any business where goods are sold it is likely that some will need to be returned. Goods are returned for many reasons: it may be that the goods supplied were the wrong size or colour, they may be faulty, or they may have been damaged in transit. Whatever the reason, when goods are returned the necessary entries must be made in the accounts. When goods are returned a *credit note* is issued. This is a type of refund document, which reduces the amount owed by the buyer. A credit note is made out by the seller showing full details of the goods returned, prices and any trade discount. The top copy is sent to the customer and the seller keeps copies of all credit notes for his/her own records. This is the original document that provides the financial information that will subsequently be recorded in the ledger accounts.

Entries are made in the *sales returns day book* from the copies of the credit notes.

Sales returns day book

A modern sales returns day book is simply a list, in date order, of all credit notes, showing:

- date
- name of customer
- amount of goods analysed into relevant columns
- amount of VAT
- total amount of credit note.

We can look at a typical example here. This credit note has been sent to Hills and Fells:

Activity Zone
78 Commercial Road
TADCASTER
TA59 8TP

VAT Registration No 624 8512 68

Telephone 01937 6882

CREDIT NOTE

Hills and Fells
Plaza Centre
BARWICK IN ELMET
LS92 9TZ

Date 22 February 20-6

Credit Note No C159

Quantity	Description	Unit price £	£	£
1	4-person Oregon trail tent	159.99	159.99	
	VAT at 17.5%		28.00	
				187.99

The entries in the analysed sales returns day book for this credit note would look like this:

Sales returns day book

Date 20–6	Details	Tents	Sleeping bags	VAT	Total
22 Feb	Hills and Fells	159.99		28.00	187.99

Another credit note is sent to Camping & Leisure Centre:

Activity Zone
78 Commercial Road
TADCASTER
TA59 8TP

VAT Registration No 624 8512 68

Telephone 01937 6882

CREDIT NOTE

Camping & Leisure Centre
Ring Road
LEEDS
LS97 8DN

Date 25 February 20-6

Credit Note No C160

Quantity	Description	Unit price £	£	£
1	2-person Dome tent	25.99	25.99	
1	3-person Dome tent	35.95	35.95	
				61.94
2	Sonata sleeping bags	18.50		37.00
				98.94
	VAT at 17.5%			17.31
				116.25

The entries in the analysed sales returns day book for this credit note would look like this:

Sales returns day book

Date 20–6	Details	Tents	Sleeping bags	VAT	Total
22 Feb	Hills and Fells	159.99		28.00	187.99
25 Feb	Camping & Leisure Centre	61.94	37.00	17.31	116.25

Entries are made for a certain period, usually a month. At the end of the month all the columns are totalled. This is an illustration of the completed sales returns day book for the month of February 20–6:

Sales returns day book

Date 20–6	Details	Tents	Sleeping bags	VAT	Total
22 Feb	Hills and Fells	159.99		28.00	187.99
25 Feb	Camping & Leisure Centre	61.94	37.00	17.31	116.25
28 Feb		221.93	37.00	45.31	304.24

The total of all the analysis columns should always equal the addition of the *Total* column. This method of checking is known as *cross casting* and will usually reveal any mistakes, either in the addition of the columns or if an incorrect amount has been entered in any of the analysis columns.

The important rule of the sales returns day book is that each *customer's account* is *credited* and the *sales returns and VAT accounts* are *debited* from this original source. Personal accounts are not affected by the analysis. The original sales have been inserted so that the entries you need to consider are meaningful: it would be unrealistic to show returns if the company had not sold goods in the first place.

At the end of the period, the customer's account in the sales ledger is credited with the total amount of each credit note, *including VAT*, like this:

Sales ledger

Camping & Leisure Centre Account

3 Feb	Sales	1,071.06	25 Feb	Sales returns	116.25
16 Feb	Sales	891.92			

Hills and Fells Account

9 Feb	Sales	1,106.12	22 Feb	Sales returns	187.99

The customers' accounts have been credited with the total value of each credit note *including VAT*.

We can now see how the information given in the analysis columns provides the figures that are posted to the nominal ledger. This is achieved by having separate sales returns accounts for each department. One entry is made to correspond with the total *sales returns value* for each department, like this:

Nominal ledger

Sales Returns Account – Tents

28 Feb	Total SRDB	221.93				

Sales Returns Account – Sleeping Bags

28 Feb	Total SRDB	37.00				

Value Added Tax Account

28 Feb	Total SRDB	45.31	28 Feb	Total SDB	735.52

Points to remember

- Analysed *day books* provide firms with useful information regarding which products sell best or which department is most profitable.
- All personal accounts of customers are posted with the total value *including VAT*. To complete the double entry the goods value only for each product or department is entered in the sales and sales returns accounts. All VAT is collected together in the VAT account.
- Cash sales are *never* entered in the sales day book; the book of original entry for all cash sales is the *cash book*.

Assignments

14.1

You are responsible for compiling, in date order, the analysed sales and sales returns day books for Otterman Supplies. The firm analyses its invoices and credit notes into two departments, Quilts and Pillows. At the end of the month you are required to post the analysed day books to the sales and nominal ledgers and balance all sales ledger accounts.

During the month of May 20–6 the following invoices and credit notes were sent to customers:

Otterman Supplies
Greenside Trading Estate
HARROGATE
HA72 9PM

VAT Registration No 276 6203 78

Telephone 01423 6104

Invoice

Homecraft Ltd
34 Market Street
WAKEFIELD
WA62 5MT

Invoice No 1352

Date 2 May 20-6

Quantity	Description	Unit price £	£	£
10	Single feather quilts	19.50	195.00	
10	Double hollow fibre quilts	18.95	189.50	
				384.50
10	Feather pillows	5.50	55.00	
20	Polyester pillows	3.75	75.00	
				130.00
				514.50
	VAT at 17.5%			90.04
				604.54

Otterman Supplies
Greenside Trading Estate
HARROGATE
HA72 9PM

VAT Registration No 276 6203 78

Telephone 01423 6104

Invoice

Tradeways
Headingley Road
LEEDS
LS78 6DR

Invoice No 1353

Date 4 May 20-6

Quantity	Description	Unit price £	£	£
50	Travel pillows	4.99	249.50	
50	Anti-allergy pillows	7.50	375.00	
50	Polyester pillows	3.75	187.50	
				812.00
	VAT at 17.5%			142.10
				954.10

Otterman Supplies
Greenside Trading Estate
HARROGATE
HA72 9PM

VAT Registration No 276 6203 78

Telephone 01423 6104

Invoice

Windsor Stores
Bridge Street
BIRMINGHAM
B92 8TL

Invoice No 1354

Date 7 May 20-6

Quantity	Description	Unit price £	£	£
50	Support pillows	10.50	525.00	
50	Polyester pillows	3.75	187.50	
				712.50
10	Single fibre fill quilts	7.50	75.00	
10	Double fibre fill quilts	9.75	97.50	
				172.50
				885.00
	VAT at 17.5%			154.88
				1,039.88

Otterman Supplies
Greenside Trading Estate
HARROGATE
HA72 9PM

VAT Registration No 276 6203 78   Telephone 01423 6104

Credit Note

Homecraft Ltd   Credit Note No 136
34 Market Street
WAKEFIELD   Date 12 May 20-6
WA62 5MT

Quantity	Description	Unit price £	£	£
1	Single feather quilt	19.50	19.50	
2	Double hollow fibre quilts	18.95	37.90	
				57.40
4	Polyester pillows	3.75		15.00
				72.40
	VAT at 17.5%			12.67
				85.07

Otterman Supplies
Greenside Trading Estate
HARROGATE
HA72 9PM

VAT Registration No 276 6203 78

Telephone 01423 6104

Invoice

Tradeways
Headingley Road
LEEDS
LS78 6DR

Invoice No 1355

Date 14 May 20-6

Quantity	Description	Unit price £	£	£
20	Anti-allergy pillows	7.50	150.00	
20	Feather pillows	5.50	110.00	
				260.00
20	Single hollow fibre quilts	15.95	319.00	
20	Double hollow fibre quilts	18.95	379.00	
				698.00
				958.00
	VAT at 17.5%			167.65
				1,125.65

Otterman Supplies
Greenside Trading Estate
HARROGATE
HA72 9PM

VAT Registration No 276 6203 78

Telephone 01423 6104

Credit Note

Windsor Stores
Bridge Street
BIRMINGHAM
B92 8TL

Credit Note No 137

Date 18 May 20-6

Quantity	Description	Unit price £	£	£
5	Support pillows	10.50	52.50	
2	Polyester pillows	3.75	7.50	
				60.00
1	Double fibre fill quilt	9.75		9.75
				69.75
	VAT at 17.5%			12.21
				81.96

Otterman Supplies
Greenside Trading Estate
HARROGATE
HA72 9PM

VAT Registration No 276 6203 78

Telephone 01423 6104

Invoice

Windsor Stores
Bridge Street
BIRMINGHAM
B92 8TL

Invoice No 1356

Date 21 May 20-6

Quantity	Description	Unit price £	£	£
10	Single feather quilts	19.50	195.00	
10	Double feather quilts	27.99	279.90	
10	Double all seasons quilts	24.95	249.50	
				724.40
	VAT at 17.5%			126.77
				851.17

Otterman Supplies
Greenside Trading Estate
HARROGATE
HA72 9PM

VAT Registration No 276 6203 78

Telephone 01423 6104

Credit Note

Tradeways
Headingley Road
LEEDS
LS78 6DR

Credit Note No 138

Date 26 May 20-6

Quantity	Description	Unit price £	£	£
5	Travel pillows	4.99	24.95	
3	Anti-allergy pillows	7.50	22.50	
				47.45
	VAT at 17.5%			8.30
				55.75

14.2

You are responsible for compiling, in date order, the analysed sales and sales returns day books for Shandley Group. The firm analyses its invoices and credit notes into two departments, Paint and Wallpaper. At the end of the month you are required to post the analysed day books to the sales and nominal ledgers and balance all sales ledger accounts.

During the month of November 20–6 the following invoices and credit notes were sent to customers:

Nov 2 Nulooks Stores: Invoice number 2021
Wallpaper £396.50, Paint £274.82 plus VAT £117.48,
invoice total £788.80

3 Foyle & Barker: Invoice number 2022
Paint £590.76 plus VAT £103.38, invoice total £694.14

8 Creative Designs: Invoice number 2023
Wallpaper £407.20, Paint £350.96 plus VAT £132.68,
invoice total £890.84

12 Foyle & Barker: Credit note number 319
Paint £46.74 plus VAT £8.18, credit note total £54.92

14 Nulooks Stores: Invoice number 2024
Wallpaper £524.62, Paint £207.38 plus VAT £128.10,
invoice total £860.10

18 Creative Designs: Credit note number 320
Paint £38.54, Wallpaper £56.30, plus VAT £16.60,
credit note total £111.44

26 Foyle & Barker: Invoice number 2025
Wallpaper £319.78, plus VAT £55.96, invoice total £375.74

28 Nulooks Stores: Credit note number 321
Wallpaper £29.50, Paint £37.84 plus VAT £11.78,
credit note total £79.12

14.3

You are responsible for compiling, in date order, the analysed sales and sales returns day books for Speedy Supplies. The firm analyses its invoices and credit notes into two departments, Handles and Hinges. At the end of the month you are required to post the analysed day books to the sales and nominal ledgers and balance all sales ledger accounts.

During the month of February 20–7 the following invoices and credit notes were sent to customers:

Feb 2 Keywise Centre: Invoice number 4036
Handles £270.58, Hinges £42.50, plus VAT £54.79,
invoice total £367.87

5 Sureguard Solutions: Invoice number 4037
Hinges £56.20, Handles £304.50, plus VAT £63.12,
invoice total £423.82

9 James Moss Ltd: Invoice number 4038
Handles £398.76, plus VAT £69.78, invoice total £468.54

14 Keywise Centre: Credit note number CN56
Hinges £9.50, Handles £24.58, plus VAT £5.96,
credit note total £40.04

18 James Moss Ltd: Invoice number 4039
Handles £507.20, Hinges £90.24, plus VAT £104.55,
invoice total £701.99

20 Sureguard Solutions: Credit note number CN57
Hinges £16.36, Handles £45.92, plus VAT £10.90,
credit note total £73.18

24 Keywise Centre: Invoice number 4040
Hinges £80.70, plus VAT £14.12, invoice total £94.82

26 James Moss Ltd: Credit note number CN58
Handles £52.48, plus VAT £9.18, credit note total £61.66

14.4

You are responsible for compiling, in date order, the analysed sales and sales returns day books for Colorcraft Ltd. The firm analyses its invoices and credit notes into two departments, Blinds and Curtains. At the end of the month you are required to post the analysed day books to the sales and nominal ledgers and balance all sales ledger accounts.

During the month of May 20–7 the following invoices and credit notes were sent to customers:

May 1 Abbeygales Ltd: Invoice number 4716
Curtains £490.58, Blinds £217.64, plus VAT £123.94,
invoice total £832.16

3 Thomas Fannelli: Invoice number 4717
Curtains £576.92, plus VAT £100.96, invoice total £677.88

6 Style Interiors: Invoice number 4718
Blinds £409.60, Curtains £286.42, plus VAT £121.80,
invoice total £817.82

10 Abbeygales Ltd: Credit note number 94
Curtains £52.50, Blinds £27.98, plus VAT £14.08,
credit note total £94.56

14 Thomas Fannelli: Invoice number 4719
Blinds £305.20, Curtains £418.76, plus VAT £126.69,
invoice total £850.65

18 Style Interiors: Credit note number 95
Blinds £72.80 plus VAT £12.74, credit note total £85.54

22 Abbeygales Ltd: Invoice number 4720
Curtains £294.30, Blinds £148.50, plus VAT £77.49,
invoice total £520.29

27 Thomas Fannelli: Credit note number 96
Blinds £36.24, Curtains £40.62, plus VAT £13.45,
credit note total £90.31

14.5

You are responsible for compiling, in date order, the analysed sales and sales returns day books for Avenger Sportswear. The firm analyses its invoices and credit notes into two departments, Shirts and Shorts. At the end of the month you are required to post the analysed day books to the sales and nominal ledgers and balance all sales ledger accounts.

During the month of November 20–7 the following invoices and credit notes were sent to customers:

Nov 2   Sport & Leisure Ltd: Invoice number 1069
      Shorts £120.68, Shirts £295.90, plus VAT £72.90,
      invoice total £489.48

    4   K. Pointers: Invoice number 1070
      Shirts £307.50, Shorts £91.39, plus VAT £69.81,
      invoice total £468.70

  10   Sport & Leisure Ltd: Credit note number 72
      Shorts £26.50, Shirts £38.92, plus VAT £11.45,
      credit note total £76.87

  12   D. McKenzie Ltd: Invoice number 1071
      Shorts £309.26, Shirts £362.28, plus VAT £117.52,
      invoice total £789.06

  15   K. Pointers: Credit note number 73
      Shirts £47.36 plus VAT £8.29, credit note total £55.65

  18   Sport & Leisure Ltd: Invoice number 1072
      Shorts £162.75, Shirts £394.72, plus VAT £97.56,
      invoice total £655.03

  20   D. McKenzie Ltd: Credit note number 74
      Shorts £50.28, Shirts £25.70, plus VAT £13.30,
      credit note total £89.28

  24   D. McKenzie Ltd: Invoice number 1073
      Shirts £405.36, Shorts £113.52, plus VAT £90.80,
      invoice total £609.68

15 Trading, profit and loss accounts and balance sheets

What is the purpose of trading and profit and loss accounts?

People set up in business to try and make a profit, but if the business is not successful they may lose money. To calculate how much profit or loss has been made, a *trading and profit and loss account* is prepared. Businesses usually prepare trading and profit and loss accounts once a year, although they could be prepared for six months or any other time period required. Their main purpose is to see how profitably the business is being run, and to enable the owners to compare the results achieved with those of previous years. They are often referred to as the *final accounts* of a business.

To enable two types of profit to be calculated, a trading and profit and loss account is divided into two sections: the *trading account* (top section) is where the *gross profit* is calculated; the *profit and loss account* (lower section) is where the *net profit* is calculated.

Trading account

This is the first of the two *final accounts* normally made out once a year to discover the gross profit of a business.

Gross profit is what the business has gained from the trading activity of buying and selling, it is the difference between *sales* and the *cost of goods sold*. The best explanation of gross profit is:

sales *less* cost of goods sold = gross profit

The trading account, like every other account, must follow the rules of double entry. The trading account cannot be debited unless some other account is credited; and the trading account cannot be credited unless another account is debited.

To illustrate this, we shall gradually build up a trading account observing the rules of double entry. To do this we shall need the information in the ledger account balances. In business, all the sales during the year are collected together in the sales account, and the last entry would look like this:

Sales Account

		20-8		£
		31 Dec	Balance b/d	24,000

At the end of the accounting period the sales account is closed (leaving it ready to start a new financial year) and the total sales figure is transferred to the trading account by making a debit entry in the sales account, like this:

Sales Account

20-8		£	20-8		£
31 Dec	Transfer to trading A/c	24,000	31 Dec	Balance b/d	24,000

The corresponding credit entry will be in the trading account, like this:

Trading Account for the year ended 31 December 20-8

		£
	Sales	24,000

All the purchases during the year are collected together in the purchases account. The last entry would look like this:

Purchases Account

20-8		£	
31 Dec	Balance b/d	15,250	

At the end of the accounting period the account is closed (leaving it ready to start a new financial year) and the total purchases figure is transferred to the trading account by making a credit entry in the purchases account, like this:

Purchases Account

20-8		£	20-8		£
31 Dec	Balance b/d	15,250	31 Dec	Transfer to trading A/c	15,250

The corresponding debit entry will be in the trading account, like this:

Trading Account for the year ended 31 December 20-8

	£		£
Purchases	15,250	Sales	24,000

We have not yet arrived at the *cost of goods sold*. This is because in real life it would be almost impossible to have sold everything that had been purchased during the year; there would still be some stock remaining at the end of the year. Therefore the value of the unsold stock must be deducted from the purchases to arrive at the *cost of goods sold* figure. To find the value of the unsold goods, a *stocktaking* is carried out at the end of the financial year. Stocktaking means counting every item in stock and then finding its value. Accountants follow certain rules to value stock, and in normal circumstances it is valued at cost – that is, the price paid for it. The value of the unsold goods is called the *closing stock* and is deducted from the purchases in the trading account, like this:

Trading Account for the year ended 31 December 20-8

	£		£
Purchases	15,250	Sales	24,000
Less closing stock	2,000		
Cost of goods sold	13,250		

We are now ready to calculate the gross profit; that is, sales £24,000 *less* cost of goods sold £13,250, making a gross profit of £10,750. The trading account is then completed like this:

Trading Account for the year ended 31 December 20-8

	£		£
Purchases	15,250	Sales	24,000
Less closing stock	2,000		
Cost of goods sold	13,250		
Gross profit c/d	10,750		
	24,000		24,000
		Gross profit b/d	10,750

At this point a stock account is opened and the value of the unsold goods is placed at the debit side, like this:

Stock Account

20-8		£	
31 Dec	Balance b/d	2,000	

The debit balance remains on the stock account until the end of the next trading period. Clearly, the closing stock at the end of this trading period will become the opening stock for the next trading period.

Profit and loss account

Gross profit shows what the business has gained from the buying and selling activity. However, in carrying out this activity many expenses are incurred, such as wages, rent, rates, insurance, telephone, electricity and so on. The profit when all expenses have been taken into consideration is the *net profit*. A good explanation of net profit is:

gross profit less expenses = net profit

As the main source of income comes from trading (buying and selling), the profit and loss account begins with the balance of gross profit from the trading account, like this:

Profit and Loss Account for the year ended 31 December 20-8

Expenses		£
	Gross profit b/d	10,750

Like every other account, the profit and loss account must follow the rules of double entry. In every transfer to the profit and loss account we shall be doing the same sort of closing entry as we did in the trading account, to transfer the balances on the accounts we use.

To illustrate this, we shall gradually build up a profit and loss account observing the rules of double entry. To do this we shall need the information in the ledger account balances. In business, all expenses incurred during the year are recorded in separate accounts. Using a typical wages account as an example, the last entry would look like this:

Wages Account

20-8		£	
31 Dec	Balance b/d	3,200	

At the end of the accounting period this account is closed (leaving it ready to start a new financial year) and the total wages figure is transferred to the profit and loss account by making a credit entry in the wages account, like this:

Wages Account

20-8		£	20-8		£
31 Dec	Balance b/d	3,200	31 Dec	Profit and loss	3,200

The corresponding debit entry will be in the profit and loss account, like this:

Profit and Loss Account for the year ended 31 December 20-8

Expenses	£		£
Wages	3,200	Gross profit b/d	10,750

In the same way, all the remaining expense accounts are closed, leaving them ready to start a new financial year. Each balance is transferred to the profit and loss account by making a credit entry in each expense account, like this:

Rent Account

20-8		£	20-8		£
31 Dec	Balance b/d	850	31 Dec	Profit and loss	850

Telephone Account

20-8		£	20-8		£
31 Dec	Balance b/d	500	31 Dec	Profit and loss	500

Motor Expenses Account

20-8		£	20-8		£
31 Dec	Balance b/d	300	31 Dec	Profit and loss	300

Electricity Account

20-8		£	20-8		£
31 Dec	Balance b/d	650	31 Dec	Profit and loss	650

The corresponding debit entry for each expense account will appear in the profit and loss account, like this:

Profit and Loss Account for the year ended 31 December 20-8

Expenses	£		£
Wages	3,200	Gross profit b/d	10,750
Rent	850		
Telephone	500		
Motor expenses	300		
Electricity	650		

We are now ready to discover the net profit. To calculate the amount of net profit we need to deduct the *total expenses* from the *gross profit*; that is, gross profit £10,750 less total expenses £5,500 making a *net profit* of £5,250. The profit and loss account is then completed like this:

Profit and Loss Account for the year ended 31 December 19-8

Expenses	£		£
Wages	3,200	Gross profit b/d	10,750
Rent	850		
Telephone	500		
Motor expenses	300		
Electricity	650		
Net profit	5,250		
	10,750		10,750

The expenses incurred in running a business are often referred to as the *overheads*. As we have seen, the surplus when the overhead expenses are deducted is called *net profit*. 'Net' means *clear*, and is the true profit after *all* expenses have been met. If the expenses are greater than the gross profit a *net loss* will occur.

Final accounts are always dated for the particular period of time for which profit is being calculated. Normally this is one year, as shown in the examples, but there is nothing to prevent profit being calculated for six months or for any other time period. Because a trading account is always followed immediately by a profit and loss account they are usually shown under a combined heading, like this:

Trading and Profit and Loss Account for the year ended 31 December 20-8

	£		£
Purchases	15,250	Sales	24,000
Less closing stock	2,000		
Cost of goods sold	13,250		
Gross profit c/d	10,750		
	24,000		24,000
Wages	3,200	Gross profit b/d	10,750
Rent	850		
Telephone	500		
Motor expenses	300		
Electricity	650		
Net profit	5,250		
	10,750		10,750

When we have discovered the net profit of the business (shown as a debit entry in the profit and loss account) the profit belongs to the owner so a corresponding entry must be made in the owner's capital account. As we saw in Chapter 2, the first entry in the capital account is made when the owner introduces capital into the business. On 1 January the capital account would look like this:

Capital Account

		20-8		£
		1 Jan	Bank	5,000

At the end of the accounting period the net profit is transferred by making a credit entry in the capital account, like this:

Capital Account

		20-8		£
		1 Jan	Bank	5,000
		31 Dec	Net profit	5,250

Net profit increases capital, but if a loss had been made a *debit entry* would be needed in the capital account to reduce it. We are now ready to complete the account. To do this we must transfer any drawings to the capital account. Sometimes the owner of a business will take money or goods out of the business for his/her private use. Whether taken as money or goods, these withdrawals are known in bookkeeping as *drawings* withdrawals of capital. During the year, a record is kept in the drawings account of all money or goods taken by the owner for personal use. At the end of the financial year the drawings account is totalled and transferred to the capital account. The drawings account would show all the separate amounts drawn by the owner, week by week, during the year, but the last entry would look like this:

Drawings Account

20-8		£			
31 Dec	Balance b/d	800			

At the end of the year the drawings account is closed (leaving it ready for the following year's entries). The total drawings are transferred to the capital account by making a credit entry in the drawings account, like this:

Drawings Account

20-8		£	20-8		£
31 Dec	Balance b/d	800	31 Dec	Capital account	800

The corresponding debit entry is in the capital account, like this:

Capital Account

20-8		£	20-8		£
31 Dec	Drawings	800	1 Jan	Bank	5,000
			31 Dec	Net profit	5,250

The capital account can now be completed and balanced ready to start a new year, like this:

Capital Account

20-8		£	20-8		£
31 Dec	Drawings	800	1 Jan	Bank	5,000
31 Dec	Balance c/d	9,450	31 Dec	Net profit	5,250
		10,250			10,250
			20-9		
			1 Jan	Balance b/d	9,450

Balance sheets

After the trading and profit and loss account has been prepared, some accounts will still remain. These accounts cannot be closed because they must be carried forward into the next trading period. All balances remaining will be assets, capital or liabilities. All other balances should have been closed off when the trading and profit and loss account was completed. It is the balances which remain that are used to prepare a balance sheet. This is usually done on the last day of the trading period to show the financial position at that moment in time.

Balance sheets are *not* part of the double entry system. It is useful to remember that if you see the word '*account*' you will know that it is part of the double entry system and will involve debit and credit entries. If the word '*account*' is not used the entry is *not* part of the double entry system. For example:

Trial balance – this is a list of balances to check if the records are correct.
Balance sheet – this is a list of balances arranged according to whether they are assets, capital or liabilities.

The most common accounting method used for small businesses is the *traditional style balance sheet* arranged in *order of permanence*. Generally, before starting to prepare the final accounts, the balances on the accounts are shown in a trial balance. We can now look at William Dyson's trial balance drawn up after his first year of trading. This is used in the examples shown in this chapter.

Each balance listed in the trial balance is used only once. To illustrate this important rule, the balances already used to prepare the trading and profit and loss account have been ticked.

Trial balance as at 31 December 20-8

		DR	CR
		£	£
✓	Sales		24,000
✓	Purchases	15,250	
✓	Wages	3,200	
✓	Rent	850	
✓	Telephone	500	
✓	Motor expenses	300	
✓	Electricity	650	
	Fixtures and fittings	550	
	Office equipment	1,200	
	Motor vehicle	5,000	
	Debtors	1,050	
	Creditors		850
	Bank	425	
	Cash	75	
	Capital		5,000
	Drawings	800	
		29,850	29,850

We can now prepare a balance sheet using the balances that remain and the closing stock. The value the of closing stock is *never* included in a trial balance, because the actual amount is not known until after the close of business at the end of the financial year, when the stock of unsold goods must be counted and valued. The closing stock of a business is available to sell in the following year, so we must include this figure as an asset on the balance sheet.

Balance sheet as at 31 December 20-8

	£	£		£	£
Fixed assets			Capital at start	5,000	
Fixtures & fittings	550		*Add* net profit	5,250	
Office equipment	1,200			10,250	
Motor vehicle	5,000	6,750	*Less* drawings	800	9,450
Current assets			*Current liabilities*		
Closing Stock	2,000		Creditors		850
Debtors	1,050				
Bank	425				
Cash	75	3,550			
		10,300			10,300

It is a rule of accounting that balance sheets should be arranged in such a way that anyone reading them can immediately appreciate the important features of a business. For this reason, a balance sheet shows items grouped together under various headings. Assets are divided into two sections: *fixed assets* and *current assets*.

Fixed assets

These assets are for continuing use in a business and will be retained over a long period of time. Examples are land, premises, buildings, plant and machinery, fixtures and fittings, furniture, office equipment and motor vehicles. On a balance sheet, fixed assets are listed *in order of permanence*, with the longest-lasting placed first. Motor vehicles are placed last because they are usually kept for only a few years. The general rule for a fixed asset is that it would be kept for *more than one year*.

Current assets

Current assets consist of cash and items that the firm intends to turn into cash within a short period of time, including bank balances. The general rule for a current asset is that it will be kept for *less than one year*. Examples are stock (closing stock at the end of the trading period because it has been bought for resale), debtors (customers who are due to pay their accounts in the near future), cash at bank and cash in hand. On a balance sheet these are listed in order of permanence for realisation into cash. Stock is listed first because it is considered to be the most difficult to convert into cash. Debtors are next, as they have promised to pay within one month; money in the bank can easily be obtained by drawing it out; and cash in hand is already in cash form.

Liabilities

Liabilities are debts owed by a business that must be paid sooner or later. Just as the assets are arranged into two groups, it is useful to show the liabilities under three separate headings.

Capital

This is the owner's original investment in the business. To show how the capital was calculated, full details of the *capital account* are displayed on the balance sheet, beginning with the capital at the start of a trading period, adding the net profit and deducting the drawings. This enables anyone looking at the balance sheet to see the profits earned in that trading period.

Long-term liabilities

These are usually *formal loans* that may be repayable over many years. Good examples are loans from a bank, building society, private investor or a finance company. A legal contract is made with the owner of the business, stating the amount of the loan, the terms of repayment and the period of time for repayment (number of years). Loans represent amounts of money that do not have to be repaid in the near future. The general rule is that they are payable more than twelve months after the balance sheet date.

Current liabilities

These are debts that will need to be paid in the near future. *Creditors* are a good example, as they are due to be paid within one month. Another example would be a *bank overdraft*, as these are only intended to be a short-term facility. Overdrafts are a way of helping a firm to overcome a temporary shortage of cash.

Points to remember

- *Trading* and *profit and loss accounts* are prepared to discover the profit or loss of a business during a trading period. As with every other account, they follow the rules of double entry.
- *Headings are essential* and must state clearly the period of time concerned, usually 'for the year ending . . .'.
- *Stocks* can sometimes present a problem. *Closing stock* at the end of one trading period will clearly be the *opening stock* for the next trading period. When opening stock appears in a trial balance it must be included in the calculation of the *cost of goods sold*. Look at it like this: what the previous year hands over is the stock which starts the new year, then more stock is bought (purchases). At the end of the year a stocktaking is carried out to find the value of the closing stock. A trading account that included both stock figures would look like this:

	£
Opening stock	2,500
Add purchases	18,500
	21,000
Less closing stock	1,750
= Cost of goods sold	19,250

- *Opening stock* will be listed in a trial balance and dated for the first day of the new trading period; *closing stock* is always given as additional information and *never* included in a trial balance.

Continued

- The surplus when all expenses are deducted from the *gross profit* is called *net profit*; this means clear profit.
- A *net loss* will occur when the total expenses are greater than the gross profit.
- A *balance sheet* is *not* an account. It is a financial statement that lists a firm's assets, capital and liabilities at a given moment in time, usually the end of its trading year. It is prepared after the trading and profit and loss account has been completed, using the balances that remain and the closing stock.
- On a balance sheet, a *bank overdraft* would be listed under *current liabilities* because money is owing to the bank. A balance sheet has five main sections; items in each group are listed, then totalled.

There are still many things to learn about final accounts, but we must first practise using our present knowledge by preparing a number of final accounts.

Assignments

15.1

From the following trial balance of Sandra Ramsden, who has been trading for one year, you are required to draw up a trading and profit and loss account and balance sheet for the year ended 31 December 20-6.

Trial balance as at 31 December 20-6

	DR £	CR £
Sales		20,662
Purchases	15,269	
Rent	650	
Insurance	155	
Motor expenses	545	
Wages	2,568	
Equipment	2,850	
Motor vehicle	1,100	
Debtors	2,350	
Creditors		1,682
Cash at Bank	1,864	
Cash in hand	68	
Drawings	925	
Capital at 1 January 20-6		6,000
	28,344	28,344

Closing stock at 31 December 20-6 was £2,868

15.2

The following trial balance was taken from the books of Michael Seymour after one year's trading. You are required to prepare a trading and profit and loss account and balance sheet for the year ending 31 December 20-7.

Trial balance as at 31 December 20-7

	DR £	CR £
Purchases	14,650	
Sales		18,874
Rates	720	
General expenses	490	
Wages and salaries	3,105	
Motor expenses	382	
Insurance	220	
Premises	7,700	
Fixtures & fittings	1,750	
Motor vehicle	3,900	
Debtors	2,865	
Creditors		1,926
Cash at bank	1,646	
Cash in hand	122	
Drawings	1,250	
Capital at 1 January 20-7		18,000
	38,800	38,800

Stock at 31 December 20-7 was £3,235

15.3

From the following trial balance of Pauline Ellis you are required to prepare a trading and profit and loss account for the year ended 31 May 20-7 and a balance sheet as at that date.

Trial balance as at 31 May 20-7

	DR £	CR £
Capital on 1 June 20-6		20,508
Purchases	23,308	
Sales		27,974
Debtors	3,670	
Creditors		2,018
Stock at 1 June 20-6	2,342	
Rent	760	
Lighting & heating expenses	520	
Salaries and wages	2,950	
Fixtures and fittings	2,500	
Cash at bank	4,438	
Cash in hand	170	
Insurance	280	
Motor vehicles	6,750	
Motor expenses	612	
Drawings	2,200	
	50,500	50,500

Stock at 31 May 20-7 was £5,995

15.4

From the following trial balance of Frederick Allen, you are required to draw up a trading and profit and loss account for the year ending 31 October 20-7 and a balance sheet as at that date.

Trial balance as at 31 October 20-7

	DR	CR
	£	£
Sales		35,650
Purchases	28,452	
Stock at 1 November 20-6	5,425	
Premises	15,000	
Fixtures and fittings	5,600	
Motor vehicles	8,800	
Loan – T. Wiseman		6,000
Debtors	4,926	
Creditors		4,124
Rates	970	
Electricity	644	
General expenses	933	
Salaries and wages	3,850	
Insurance	617	
Drawings	2,450	
Bank overdraft		2,326
Cash in hand	338	
Motor expenses	795	
Capital on 1 November 20-6		30,700
	78,800	78,800

Stock at 31 October 20-7 was £4,965

15.5

On 31 March 20-8 the following trial balance was taken from the books of James Conway:

Trial balance as at 31 March 20-8

	DR £	CR £
Capital on 1 April 20-7		38,200
Cash at bank	13,326	
Cash in hand	234	
Debtors	15,808	
Creditors		13,864
Stock at 1 April 20-7	16,940	
Motor van	7,000	
Sales		45,736
Purchases	28,435	
Telephone	672	
Insurance	593	
Premises	12,000	
Rates	764	
Loan – J. Graham		5,000
General expenses	316	
Wages	4,800	
Motor expenses	412	
Drawings	1,500	
	102,800	102,800

Stock at 31 March 20-8 was £15,420

You are required to prepare a trading and profit and loss account for the year ended 31 March 20-8 and a balance sheet as at that date.

15.6

David Nicholson is the owner of a textile business. He has completed his trading and profit and loss account for the year ended 31 December 20-2. The following balances remain in his ledger:

	£
Net profit	18,500
Capital at 1 January 20-2	25,750
Drawings	5,000
Debtors	3,475
Creditors	1,025
Motor vehicles	16,500
Office equipment	5,650
Furniture and fittings	3,800
Bank	5,380
Cash	520
Stock at 31 December 20-2	4,950

You are required to:

(a) Prepare a balance sheet as at 31 December 20-2 clearly showing all the items under the appropriate headings.
(b) David Nicholson had taken drawings in four equal instalments, by cheque, at the end of each quarter.

You are required to write up the drawings account and the capital account, including all relevant dates and transfers, and balance the accounts for the year ended 31 December 20-2.

15.7

Anne Parfitt owns a retail carpet business. After her trading and profit and loss account for the year ended 31 May 20-5 was completed, the following balances remain in her ledger:

	£
Net profit	29,720
Premises	48,000
Motor vehicles	12,750
Equipment	7,500
Debtors	4,318
Creditors	3,804
Cash	572
Loan – Northern Bank	5,000
Capital at 1 June 20-4	45,250
Drawings	7,000
Bank overdraft	1,726
Stock at 31 May 20-5	5,360

You are required to:

(a)   Prepare a balance sheet as at 31 May 20-5 clearly showing all the items under the appropriate headings.
(b)   Anne Parfitt had taken drawings in four equal instalments, by cheque, at the end of each quarter.

   You are required to: write up the drawings account and the capital account, including all relevant dates and transfers, and balance the accounts for the year ended 31 May 20-5.

■ M̌ **16** Further trading and profit and loss accounts

In any business where goods are bought and sold it is likely that some will need to be returned. Sometimes goods will be returned to suppliers (*purchase returns*) and sometimes goods will be returned to the firm by its customers (*sales returns*). In our first look at the trading account in Chapter 15 returns were not included. This was quite deliberate, to ensure that our first set of final accounts would be straightforward. So that the entries you need to consider are meaningful, we have assumed that William Dyson has continued his business for another year. In Chapter 15 we prepared Dyson's final accounts after his first year of trading. He started without any stock, so there was closing stock only. For his second year of trading, to 31 December 20-9, both opening and closing stock figures will be used in the calculations. As you will see, last year's closing stock now becomes the opening stock and is included in Dyson's trial balance.

William Dyson
Trial balance as at 31 December 20-9

	DR £	CR £
Sales		36,000
Purchases	21,500	
Sales returns	650	
Purchase returns		980
Stock at 1 January 20-9	2,000	
Carriage inwards	320	
Carriage outwards	760	
Discount received		250
Discount allowed	240	
Wages	5,450	
Rent	900	
Telephone	680	
Motor expenses	490	
Electricity	750	
Fixtures and fittings	2,500	
Office equipment	1,350	
Motor vehicle	7,000	
Debtors	3,480	
Creditors		1,602
Bank overdraft		518
Loan from City Bank		2,000
Cash	230	
Capital at 1 January 20-9		9,450
Drawings	2,500	
	50,800	50,800

On 31 December 20-9 closing stock was valued at £3,240.

Remember this important rule: *each balance listed in a trial balance is used once only*. To illustrate this process, look back to the trial balance and tick each item when it is used to prepare the trading and profit and loss account for the second year of trading, to 31 December 20-9.

Sales returns

One of the most vital figures in any business is the *net sales*, often referred to as the *turnover*. The word 'net' means 'clear' and indicates that any returns have been deducted from the sales figure to obtain the correct turnover.

Good style presentation of final accounts is essential so that important figures can be seen instantly. To do this, the value of any sales returns (goods that have been returned by customers) are deducted from the sales, in the trading account, like this:

Trading and Profit and Loss Account for the year ended 31 December 20-9

			£
	Sales		36,000
	Less sales returns		650
			35,350

Purchase returns

We must now find the accurate purchases figure by deducting the value of any purchase returns (goods which have been returned to suppliers) from our purchases, in the trading account, like this:

Trading and Profit and Loss Account for the year ended 31 December 20-9

	£		£
Opening stock	2,000	Sales	36,000
Add purchases	21,500	*Less* sales returns	650
	23,500		35,350
Less purchase returns	980		
	22,520		

Carriage inwards

When goods are bought, the cost of transport may be included in the purchase price, or there may be an additional charge. When an extra charge is made for delivery, it increases the cost of the goods being purchased. Although most of the business expenses are included in the profit and loss account, *carriage inwards* is dealt with in the trading account. This is because it is a direct expense incurred in bringing goods into the firm and consequently increases the cost of the purchases.

Whenever carriage inwards is charged on goods purchased, a separate record is kept of these costs in the *carriage inwards account*. Because these additional costs have increased the price of the goods purchased, carriage inwards is added in the trading account, like this:

Trading and Profit and Loss Account for the year ended 31 December 20-9

	£		£
Opening stock	2,000	Sales	36,000
Add purchases	21,500	*Less* sales returns	650
	23,500		35,350
Less purchase returns	980		
	22,520		
Add carriage inwards	320		
	22,840		
Less closing stock	3,240		
Cost of goods sold	19,600		
Gross profit c/d	15,750		
	35,350		35,350
		Gross profit b/d	15,750

Carriage outwards

Carriage outwards are the costs incurred in transporting goods sold to customers. A separate record is kept in the *carriage outwards account* of these expenses. Because these costs are directly related to selling they are *always* entered with the other expenses in the profit and loss account.

Discount allowed

Discount allowed to customers for prompt payment means a firm has agreed to accept less money than was originally owed. This is another expense, and a record is kept of these expenses in the *discount allowed account*. Because these costs are directly related to selling they are *always* entered with the other expenses in the profit and loss account.

Discount received

Discount received from suppliers makes more profit. It is added to the gross profit in the profit and loss account along with any other items of income such as rent received and commission received.

All incomes received are positioned immediately below the gross profit.

We are now ready to discover the *net profit*. As you will see, discount received has been added to the gross profit, then we deduct the total of all expenses to find the amount of net profit. The calculation is: £16,000 less total expenses of £9,270 = a net profit of £6,730.

The profit and loss account is then completed like this:

Trading and Profit and Loss Account for the year ended 31 December 20-9

	£		£
Opening stock	2,000	Sales	36,000
Add purchases	21,500	*Less* sales returns	650
	23,500		35,350
Less purchase returns	980		
	22,520		
Add carriage inwards	320		
	22,840		
Less closing stock	3,240		
Cost of goods sold	19,600		
Gross profit c/d	15,750		
	35,350		35,350
Carriage outwards	760	Gross profit b/d	15,750
Discount allowed	240	Discount received	250
Wages	5,450		
Rent	900		
Telephone	680		
Motor expenses	490		
Electricity	750		
Net profit	6,730		
	16,000		16,000

The expenses incurred in running a business are often referred to as the *overheads*. As we have seen, the surplus when the overhead expenses are deducted is called *net profit*. This is the true profit after all expenses have been met. A *net loss* will occur if the expenses are greater than the income received.

Final accounts are always dated for the particular period of time for which profit is being calculated. This is normally one year, but there is nothing to prevent profit being calculated for six months or any other time period.

If you have clearly marked each item on the trial balance when it was used to prepare the trading and profit and loss account, you will see that all the remaining balances are assets, capital or liabilities. We can now prepare a balance sheet using these balances and the closing stock.

William Dyson
Balance sheet as at 31 December 20-9

	£	£		£	£
Fixed assets			**Capital** at 1 Jan 20-9	9,450	
Fixtures & fittings	2,500		*Add* net profit	6,730	
Office equipment	1,350			16,180	
Motor vehicle	7,000	10,850	*Less* drawings	2,500	13,680
			Long-term liabilities		
			Loan from City Bank		2,000
Current assets			**Current liabilities**		
Closing stock	3,240		Creditors	1,602	
Debtors	3,480		Bank overdraft	518	2,120
Cash	230	6,950			
		17,800			17,800

You may need to look back to Chapter 15 to see what happens to the accounts that appear in the trading and profit and loss account. At the end of the financial year all balances on the accounts that are needed to calculate profit are transferred to the trading and profit and loss account. This process of closing accounts (leaving them ready to start a new year) and transferring the balances always follows the rules of double entry.

Other trading account expenses

As we have seen, the cost of carriage inwards is an additional expense that increases the cost of the goods purchased. Similarly, any costs incurred in bringing goods into a saleable condition may be charged to the trading account. Such costs may include heating, labour or wages costs.

Normally, all expenses (except carriage inwards) will appear in the profit and loss section. However, in examination questions you may be required to add part of the cost of any expense to the trading section. This is a typical example:

> *One quarter of the wages costs are to be charged to the trading account and three-quarters to the profit and loss account.*

To do this, you will need to divide the wages figure by four, to obtain one quarter. This amount should then be *added* in the trading account, after deducting the closing stock. The remaining three-quarters should be listed with all other expenses in the profit and loss section. A specific instruction will be given in the question if any expense item is to be included in the trading account.

Final accounts in the services sector

So far we have looked at the final accounts for people who are traders, buying and selling goods. However, many firms do not deal in goods but instead provide services – such as accountants, doctors, solicitors, hairdressers, insurance brokers, business consultants.

When final accounts are prepared for people who provide services there will not be a trading account, because goods are not bought and sold. Instead a profit and loss account and a balance sheet will be drawn up.

Points to remember

- *Carriage inwards* and *carriage outwards* often cause confusion and are frequently included in examination questions. They are both *expenses* and will appear as *debit balances* in their ledger accounts and a trial balance.
- *Carriage inwards* is the expense of paying for transport when goods are purchased and it *increases the cost of goods*. Although most expenses are included in the profit and loss account, carriage inwards is *always* added to the net purchases in the trading account.
- *Carriage outwards* are the costs involved in transporting goods sold to customers, they are always entered with the other expenses in the profit and loss account.
- *Discounts received* from suppliers are shown as income in the profit and loss account along with any other income, such as rent received and commission received. Such incomes *increase profit* and are positioned immediately below the gross profit.
- *Discounts allowed* to customers for prompt payment are entered with the other *expenses* in the profit and loss account.
- *Net profit* is the true profit after all expenses have been met. A *net loss* will occur if the expenses are greater than the income received.
- Many firms do not deal in goods, but instead supply *services*, such as accountants or business consultants. When final accounts are prepared for people who provide services there will not be a trading account, because goods are not bought and sold. Instead a profit and loss account and a balance sheet will be drawn up.

Assignments

16.1

Ann Bannister extracted the following trial balance from her books on 31 December 20-7:

Trial balance as at 31 December 20-7

	DR £	CR £
Capital on 1 January 20-7		30,200
Debtors and creditors	14,950	10,735
Sales returns	562	
Purchase returns		415
Bank	4,620	
Cash	513	
Stock at 1 January 20-7	21,190	
Rent	1,855	
Wages and salaries	9,890	
Carriage outwards	251	
Insurance	365	
Carriage inwards	204	
Sales		98,650
Purchases	76,990	
Motor vehicle	5,500	
Motor expenses	932	
Furniture and fittings	4,420	
Drawings	2,330	
Loan – D. Conway		5,000
General expenses	428	
	145,000	145,000

Stock at 31 December 20-7 was £22,560

You are required to prepare a trading and profit and loss account and balance sheet for the year ended 31 December 20-7.

16.2

David Allen is the owner of an electrical business. On 30 September 20-7 the following trial balance was taken from his books:

Trial balance as at 30 September 20-7

	DR £	CR £
Sales		69,480
Purchases	45,612	
Stock at 1 October 20-6	9,842	
Salaries and wages	7,838	
Insurance	556	
Sales and purchase returns	872	684
Rent and rates	740	
Carriage inwards	485	
Carriage outwards	414	
Motor expenses	526	
Discount received		452
Discount allowed	322	
Motor vehicles	7,500	
Fixtures and fittings	2,900	
Drawings	2,500	
Debtors	10,765	
Creditors		8,984
Bank	5,628	
Capital on 1 October 20-6		16,900
	96,500	96,500

Stock at 30 September 20-7 was £8,975

You are required to prepare a trading and profit and loss account for the year ended 30 September 20-7 together with a balance sheet as at that date.

16.3

John Roberts is a retail trader. On 30 April 20-5 the following trial balance was taken from his books.

Trial balance as at 30 April 20-5

	DR £	CR £
Capital on 1 May 20-4		24,640
Furniture and equipment	9,400	
Postage and stationery	1,680	
Sales returns	1,320	
Rates	760	
Insurance	450	
Wages and salaries	7,480	
Purchases and sales	27,510	46,800
Drawings	5,000	
Creditors		2,580
Carriage inwards	270	
Cash	180	
Bank overdraft		3,480
Sundry expenses	430	
Stock at 1 May 20-4	6,560	
Loan from City Bank		3,000
Freehold premises	16,500	
Debtors	2,960	
	80,500	80,500

Stock at 30 April 20-5 was valued at £6,740

You are required to prepare a trading and profit and loss account for the year ended 30 April 20-5 together with a balance sheet as at that date.

16.4

On 31 December 20-6 the following trial balance was taken from the books of James Giles:

Trial balance as at 31 December 20-6

	DR £	CR £
Capital on 1 January 20-6		25,090
Equipment	6,000	
Furniture and fittings	3,700	
Sales		36,000
Purchases	27,500	
Drawings	4,800	
Carriage outwards	490	
Sundry expenses	322	
Cash	170	
Bank	3,792	
Purchase returns		1,250
Carriage inwards	430	
Wages	5,880	
Printing and stationery	390	
Debtors and creditors	9,700	5,980
Rent	550	
Insurance	226	
Commissions received		480
Stock at 1 January 20-6	4,850	
	68,800	68,800

Stock on 31 December 20-6 was valued at £6,500

You are required to prepare a trading and profit and loss account for the year ended 31 December 20-6 and a balance sheet as at that date.

16.5

Nicholas Davidson owns a small business. On 30 September 20-7 the following trial balance was taken from his books:

Trial balance as at 30 September 20-7

	DR £	CR £
Salaries	8,250	
Rent and rates	1,500	
Cash	120	
Bank overdraft		2,890
Debtors and creditors	8,810	5,650
Sales returns	580	
Sundry expenses	256	
Stock at 1 October 20-6	5,995	
Carriage outwards	397	
Discounts received		842
Motor vehicles	9,400	
Insurance	564	
Telephone	290	
Purchases and sales	28,640	38,800
Capital on 1 October 20-6		25,218
Vehicle expenses	768	
Fixtures and fittings	8,500	
Drawings	4,330	
Loan from City Bank		5,000
	78,400	78,400

Stock at 30 September 20-7 was £6,870

You are required to prepare a trading and profit and loss account for the year ended 30 September 20-7 and a balance sheet as at that date.

16.6

Brian Stone, a sole trader, extracted the following trial balance from his books at the close of business on 31 October 20-7:

Trial balance as at 31 October 20-7

	DR £	CR £
Freehold land and buildings	25,000	
Motor van	3,500	
Purchases and sales	62,880	84,600
Bank	2,990	
Cash	520	
Stock at 1 November 20-6	4,740	
Debtors and creditors	7,500	4,950
Carriage inwards	675	
Carriage outwards	890	
Motor expenses	465	
Rates	750	
Sundry expenses	390	
Sales and purchase returns	820	982
Drawings	3,500	
Stationery and printing	376	
Discounts allowed	246	
Discounts received		378
Wages and salaries	9,058	
Capital at 1 November 20-6		33,390
	124,300	124,300

Stock at 31 October 20-7 was valued at £7,650.

You are required to prepare a trading and profit and loss account for the year ended 31 October 20-7, and a balance sheet as at that date.

■ ☑ **17** Calculating depreciation for fixed assets

What is depreciation?

Everyone knows how quickly motor vehicles decrease in value. This loss in value is known as *depreciation.*

Fixed assets are those held for long-term use in a business, but that does not mean they are kept for ever. Some fixed assets, such as buildings, may have very long lives, while others such as motor vehicles are regularly replaced.

Most fixed assets will decrease in value over their useful lifetime. Depreciation is the name given to this loss in value.

Causes of depreciation

Physical deterioration   Caused by wear and tear in normal use.
Obsolescence   Caused by the asset becoming obsolete or out of date because of new technology or improved methods.
Inadequacy   Caused by growth or changes in the size of a business that makes the asset incapable of achieving increased productivity.

Balance sheet value of fixed assets

Some fixed assets, such as machinery, equipment and motor vehicles, are in constant use over a period of time and consequently their value will decrease. The balance sheet of a business summarises its financial position and must show assets at their actual value. In order to determine the correct value of a fixed asset any reduction in value should be taken into consideration, otherwise the balance sheet would not show the true financial position.

For example, a new motor van bought this year may cost £14,000. By next year it will be worth less, probably around £12,000, and in five years' time it will be worth a fraction of its original cost. The motor van cannot be kept on the books valued at £14,000 down the years. Every year it is depreciated by a fair amount depending on an estimate of its fall in value.

Depreciation can be defined as part of the cost of a fixed asset which is *used up* during its period of use. By calculating and deducting an estimated amount for depreciation each year, a business can effectively spread the cost of a fixed asset over its expected useful life.

Depreciation is an expense of production and is charged to the profit and loss account in the same way as such items as wages, rent, insurance and so on. Calculating depreciation involves three important factors:

(i)   cost of the asset
(ii)   anticipated life
(iii)   disposal value

The cost of the asset is the price paid at the time it is purchased. The anticipated life is an estimate of the number of years it will be kept by the business. The disposal value is an estimate of its value at the end of its useful life to the business. *Disposal value* is also known as *residual value*. This forecast of its useful life is usually based on a firm's previous experience of similar types of fixed assets.

Methods of calculating depreciation

There are several ways of calculating depreciation and the method chosen will normally depend on the type of fixed asset. The two main methods are the *straight line method* and the *reducing balance method*.

Straight line method

With this method, the cost of the fixed asset, less any estimated disposal value, is divided equally by the number of years' of use:

$$\text{Amount of annual depreciation} = \frac{\text{original cost} - \text{disposal value}}{\text{number of years' use}}$$

Suppose a motor vehicle cost £15,000; it is anticipated that it will be kept for three years; and at the end of that time it will have an estimated disposal value of £6,000.

This would be expressed as: Cost £15,000 less £6,000 (disposal value) = £9,000 divided by 3 = £3,000. This is the depreciation charge for each of the three years. Expressed as a fraction:

$$\text{Annual depreciation} = \frac{£15,000 - £6,000}{3} = £3,000$$

The calculations would be like this:

	£
Cost	15,000
First year depreciation	3,000
	12,000
Second year depreciation	3,000
	9,000
Third year depreciation	3,000
Disposal value	6,000

With this method, the depreciation charge is the same each year. It is also known as the *equal instalment method* because it results in the same amount of depreciation being charged each year.

Reducing balance method

With this method, a fixed percentage rate for depreciation is deducted from the cost in the first year. In the second and later years the same percentage is taken, but of the reduced balance (cost less depreciation already charged). This method is also known as the *diminishing balance method*.

Suppose a machine is bought costing £10,000 and depreciation is to be charged at 20 per cent per annum, the calculations for the first three years would be:

	£
Cost	10,000
First year: depreciation (20% of £10,000)	2,000
	8,000
Second year: depreciation (20% of £8,000)	1,600
	6,400
Third year: depreciation (20% of £6,400)	1,280
	5,120

Using this method, much larger amounts are charged in the early years of the asset's life, and much smaller amounts during the later years. This is often considered to be an advantage, because a business enjoys greater efficiency from an asset in its early years. Repair and maintenance costs are greater in the later years, and these higher costs are then offset by a lower depreciation charge.

It is important to realise that depreciation has nothing to do with putting aside money to replace an asset, it is merely a way of spreading the cost over a period of time.

Depreciation charge for part of a year

Until now we have been concerned only with calculations of depreciation on fixed assets that have been in a business for a complete financial year.

In practice, assets may be bought or sold at any time during the year. When an asset is purchased or sold during a business's financial year, we must consider how much depreciation is to be charged for the year in which it is purchased or sold. The normal procedure is to provide for a full year's depreciation in the year of purchase, and make no charge for depreciation in the year of sale.

In examinations, you should read the question carefully because you may be expected to calculate the depreciation charge for part of a year. For example, either of the following may happen:

(a) no depreciation is charged during year of purchase or sale; or
(b) depreciation is to be calculated according to number of months the asset is owned by business.

This is a typical question:

A business that prepares its accounts annually to 31 December purchased a new motor van on 1 July 20-4 costing £15,000.

It is anticipated that the van will be kept for four years and depreciation is to be calculated at 40 per cent using the reducing balance method. In the first year, depreciation is to be calculated according to the number of months it is owned.

You are required to show the calculations for depreciation for each year, from the year of purchase to the year ending 31 December 20-7.

Solution: The motor van was purchased on 1 July 20-4. The charge for depreciation for the year ending 31 December 20-4 should be for six months (number of months of ownership). This is calculated as follows: 40 per cent of £15,000 = £6,000; divided by 12 = £500 per month. This figure is then multiplied by six (the number of months the van has been owned); 6 × £500 = £3,000, which is the depreciation charge for the first year 20-4.

		£
Cost		15,000
20-4	depreciation (40% for six months)	3,000
		12,000
20-5	depreciation (40% of £12,000)	4,800
		7,200
20-6	depreciation (40% of £7,200)	2,880
		4,320
20-7	depreciation (40% of £4,320)	1,728
		2,592

Points to remember

- *Depreciation* means a *reduction in value*, caused usually by normal wear and tear. The purpose of depreciation is to *spread the cost* of the asset over its expected useful life. By calculating an amount for depreciation each year these losses are spread over the lifetime of the asset. It is also important to recognise that *assets must be correctly valued on a balance sheet*; if we do otherwise the balance sheet will not give a true and fair view of the assets. On a balance sheet the assets are shown at cost less amounts of depreciation charged to date.
- The *straight line method* of depreciation reduces the original cost of the asset by the same amount each year. This is expressed as the original cost, less any disposal value, divided by the number of years of use.
- The *reducing balance method* is calculated by a fixed percentage rate each year. This percentage rate is deducted from the cost in the first year. In the second and later years the same percentage is taken *of the reduced balance* (cost less depreciation already charged). This method is also known as the *diminishing balance method*.
  This method gives a higher depreciation charge in the early years of the asset's life, and less in the later years. This is sometimes an advantage, as the cost of repairs often increases towards the end of its expected working life.

Assignments

All calculations to the nearest pound.

17.1
A packing machine was purchased for £20,000. The business plans to use it for five years, and it is estimated that at the end of that time it will have a disposal value of £5,000. Depreciation is to be calculated by the straight line method.

You are required to calculate the amount of depreciation for each of the five years.

17.2
John Preston purchased a delivery van on 1 January 20-7 costing £8,000. He anticipated he would keep it for three years, and it would then be sold for an estimated figure of £2,744. He decided to calculate depreciation at the rate of 30 per cent per annum, using the reducing balance method.

You are required to calculate the depreciation charges for each of the three years.

17.3

Michael Johnson purchased a new fork-lift machine costing £10,500. He expects to keep it for four years and at the end of that time its residual value is estimated to be £2,520.

You are required to show your calculations for depreciation for each of the four years using:

(a) the straight line method; and
(b) the reducing balance method at a rate of 30 per cent.

17.4

Ross Brothers purchased a new machine in July 20-7 costing £3,000. It is estimated it will have a useful life of five years, and a disposal value at the end of this time of £712. Accounts are prepared to 31 December each year and a full year's depreciation is provided in the year of purchase.

You are required to show your calculations for depreciation for each of the five years using:

(a) the straight line method; and
(b) the reducing balance method at a rate of 25 per cent.

17.5

D. Armstrong's accounts are prepared to 31 December each year. He provides depreciation for his motor vehicles at a rate of 20 per cent per annum using the diminishing balance method.

On 1 January 20-5, Armstrong bought a motor van costing £6,500. On 1 April 20-6 Armstrong purchased a further delivery van costing £7,500. In the year of purchase depreciation is to be calculated according to the number of months owned.

You are required to show your calculations for depreciation, for each vehicle, for the years to 31 December 20-7.

17.6

K. Gillow prepares his accounts annually to 30 June. He depreciates all his machinery at a rate of 30 per cent per annum on the reducing balance method. Details of the machines and the dates of purchase are as follows:

	£
Machine type 'M' purchased on 1 August 20-5 cost	3,000
Machine type 'D' purchased on 1 January 20-6 cost	4,000
Machine type 'W' purchased on 1 June 20-6 cost	5,000
Machine type 'B' purchased on 1 March 20-7 cost	6,000

In the year of purchase, depreciation is to be calculated according to the number of months owned.

You are required to show your calculations of depreciation, for each machine, for each year, from the year of purchase to the year ending 30 June 20-8.

■ ☑ **18** Double entry system for depreciation

The accounting records are exactly the same for both the straight-line method and the reducing balance method of calculating depreciation. It is the *amounts* that vary according to the method chosen.

It was illustrated in the previous chapter that as an asset decreases in value we reduce its book valuation to correspond with our estimate of its loss in value. Assets must be shown on a balance sheet at a true and fair value, and the loss suffered must be charged against the profits. The depreciation charged each year is an *expense* and is set against the profits earned by the business at the end of the financial year. There are two methods of recording depreciation in the double entry accounts.

Method 1 Direct depreciation

With this method, the depreciation is shown in the fixed asset account reducing its value each year, and in a depreciation expense account.

This is a typical example: on 1 January 20-6 a firm bought a new motor van costing £16,000, paying by cheque. The motor van is to be depreciated at a rate of 25 per cent per annum using the reducing balance method. The double entry accounts for the year ending 31 December 20-6 would appear like this, as a credit entry in the Motor van account:

Motor Van Account

20-6		£	20-6		£
1 Jan	Bank	16,000.00	31 Dec	Depreciation	4,000.00
			31 Dec	Balance c/d	12,000.00
		16,000.00			16,000.00
20-7					
1 Jan	Balance b/d	12,000.00			

A corresponding debit entry in the depreciation account, like this:

Depreciation Account

20-6		£		
31 Dec	Motor van	4,000.00		

Because depreciation is an *expense* it will need to be charged to the profit and loss account. At the end of the accounting period the depreciation account is closed (leaving it ready to start a new financial year) and the amount of depreciation is transferred to the profit and loss account by making a credit entry, like this:

Depreciation Account

20-6		£	20-6		£
31 Dec	Motor van	4,000.00	31 Dec	Profit & loss	4,000.00

A corresponding debit entry will appear in the profit and loss account, like this:

Profit and Loss Account for the Year Ended 31 December 20–6

	£	
Depreciation – motor van	4,000.00	

On the balance sheet, the fixed asset is shown at its original cost, less the depreciation charge, like this:

Balance sheet as at 31 December 20-6

		£	
Fixed assets			
Motor van	16,000		
Less			
depreciation	4,000	12,000.00	

In subsequent years the value of the asset continues to decrease in the ledger account and appears on the balance sheet at the *reduced* figure.

Using the same example, the entries you need to consider are now completed in the ledger accounts for the first three years:

Motor Van Account

20-6		£	20-6		£
1 Jan	Bank	16,000.00	31 Dec	Depreciation	4,000.00
			31 Dec	Balance c/d	12,000.00
		16,000.00			16,000.00
20-7			20-7		
1 Jan	Balance b/d	12,000.00	31 Dec	Depreciation	3,000.00
			31 Dec	Balance c/d	9,000.00
		12,000.00			12,000.00
20-8			20-8		
1 Jan	Balance b/d	9,000.00	31 Dec	Depreciation	2,250.00
			31 Dec	Balance c/d	6,750.00
		9,000.00			9,000.00
20-9					
1 Jan	Balance b/d	6,750.00			

Depreciation Account

20-6		£	20-6		£
31 Dec	Motor van	4,000.00	31 Dec	Profit & loss	4,000.00
20-7			20-7		
31 Dec	Motor van	3,000.00	31 Dec	Profit & loss	3,000.00
20-8			20-8		
31 Dec	Motor van	2,250.00	31 Dec	Profit & loss	2,250.00

The entries in the profit and loss accounts for the three years would look like this:

Profit and Loss Account for the Year Ended 31 December 20-6

	£	
Depreciation – motor van	4,000.00	

Profit and Loss Account for the Year Ended 31 December 20-7

	£	
Depreciation – motor van	3,000.00	

Profit and Loss Account for the Year Ended 31 December 20-8

	£
Depreciation – motor van	2,250.00

It is important to remember that, with this method, the motor van is shown at its original cost on the balance sheet *in the first year only*, and in later years at its *reduced* value, as shown in the ledger account, like this:

Balance sheet as at 31 December 20-6

		£
Fixed assets		
Motor van	16,000	
Less		
depreciation	4,000	12,000.00

Balance sheet as at 31 December 20-7

		£
Fixed assets		
Motor van	12,000	
Less		
depreciation	3,000	9,000.00

Balance sheet as at 31 December 20-8

		£
Fixed assets		
Motor van	9,000	
Less		
depreciation	2,250	6,750.00

Method 2 Providing for depreciation (modern method)

With this method, the asset account remains at its original cost and no entries for depreciation are made in the asset account. Instead, the amount of depreciation is accumulated in a separate *provision for depreciation account*. As each annual charge is credited to the provision for depreciation account, the balance on that account increases to equal the accumulated depreciation that is shown on the balance sheet each year.

This method has been used for many years by most limited companies, because company balance sheets show fixed assets at cost less total depreciation to date. The double entry is:

Debit the profit and loss account.
Credit the provision for depreciation account.

Using the same example as before, below is an illustration showing the double entry accounts using the now-preferred modern method.

On 1 January 20-6 a firm bought a new motor van costing £16,000. It is to be depreciated at a rate of 25 per cent per annum using the reducing balance method. The double entry accounts for the years ending 31 December 20-6, 20-7 and 20-8 would appear like this:

Motor Van Account

20-6		£	
1 Jan	Bank	16,000.00	

Provision for Depreciation Account – Motor Van

20-6		£	20-6		£
31 Dec	Balance c/d	4,000.00	31 Dec	Profit & loss	4,000.00
20-7			20-7		
31 Dec	Balance c/d	7,000.00	1 Jan	Balance b/d	4,000.00
			31 Dec	Profit & loss	3,000.00
		7,000.00			7,000.00
20-8			20-8		
31 Dec	Balance c/d	9,250.00	1 Jan	Balance b/d	7,000.00
			31 Dec	Profit & loss	2,250.00
		9,250.00			9,250.00
20-9			20-9		
			1 Jan	Balance b/d	9,250.00

Entries in the relevant profit and loss accounts for the three years would look like this:

Profit and Loss Account for the Year Ended 31 December 20-6

	£	
Depreciation (motor van)	4,000.00	

Profit and Loss Account for the Year Ended 31 December 20-7

	£	
Depreciation (motor van)	3,000.00	

Profit and Loss Account for the Year Ended 31 December 20-8

	£	
Depreciation (motor van)	2,250.00	

It is important to remember that, with this method, the motor van is shown on the balance sheet each year *at its original cost, less depreciation to date*, like this:

Balance sheet as at 31 December 20-6

		£	
Fixed assets			
Motor van	16,000		
Less depreciation	4,000	12,000.00	

Balance sheet as at 31 December 20-7

		£	
Fixed assets			
Motor van	16,000		
Less depreciation to date	7,000	9,000.00	

Balance sheet as at 31 December 20-8

		£	
Fixed assets			
Motor van	16,000		
Less depreciation to date	9,250	6,750.00	

A balance sheet should always represent a true and fair view; with this method, the fixed asset is shown at its realistic value. This value is called its *net book value*. It is usual to keep a separate provision account for each type of fixed asset.

One aspect of this method of accounting for depreciation that often causes problems to students is the name *provision for depreciation account*. It gives an impression that money has been set aside that can be used to purchase a replacement for the fixed asset when its working life is over. This is a mistaken impression. The provision for depreciation account is simply an account in which the amount of depreciation written off an asset is accumulated each year. The actual value of the asset at any given time is found by deducting the depreciation to date from the original cost.

Disposal of fixed assets

When a fixed asset is sold it is unlikely that it will realise a figure exactly equal to its value in the accounts. The annual charge made for depreciation is an *estimate* of its fall in value during each year's use by a business. Only when a fixed asset is scrapped or sold will the true accuracy of the estimates be determined.

If an asset is sold for *more than* its net book value we say there is *a profit on disposal*. Similarly, an asset may be sold for *less than* its net book value, in which case we say there is *a loss on disposal*. In fact, a profit on disposal is not a true profit; it simply means that the amount of depreciation to be written off has been overestimated. A loss on disposal simply means that the amount of depreciation to be written off has been underestimated.

Look at this example: on 1 February 20-9, the motor van was sold for £7,000. The net book value of the motor van is £6,750, so this would result in a profit on the sale of £250. On the sale of the motor van, the following entries are needed:

(i) Open a motor van disposals account, make a debit entry with the original cost price of the asset, namely £16,000:

Disposal Account – Motor Van

20-9		£		
1 Feb	Motor van	16,000.00		

The corresponding credit entry is in the original motor van account, opened when the vehicle was purchased.

Motor Van Account

20-6		£	20-9		£
1 Jan	Bank	16,000.00	1 Feb	Disposal account	16,000.00

(ii) Next, a debit entry in the provision for depreciation account to transfer the accumulated depreciation to the disposal account.

Provision for Depreciation Account – Motor Van

20-9		£	20-9		£
1 Feb	Disposal account	9,250.00	1 Jan	Balance b/d	9,250.00

The corresponding credit entry is in the disposal account:

Disposal Account – Motor Van

20-9		£	20-9		£
1 Feb	Motor van	16,000.00	1 Feb	Provision for depreciation	9,250.00

(iii) Next, a debit entry in the bank account for the amount received from the sale of the vehicle:

Cash book – (Bank Column)

20-9		£		
1 Feb	Motor van	7,000.00		

The corresponding credit entry for the remittance is in the disposal account:

Disposal Account – Motor Van

20-9		£	20-9		£
1 Feb	Motor van	16,000.00	1 Feb	Provision for depreciation	9,250.00
			1 Feb	Bank	7,000.00

When a fixed asset is over-depreciated and sold for *more than* the estimated disposal value, this profit will be transferred at the end of the financial year to the profit and loss account.

Now we can look at the completed entries, showing the transfer at the end of the financial year.

(iv) A debit entry in the disposal account, like this:

Disposal Account – Motor Van

20-9		£	20-9		£
1 Feb	Motor van	16,000.00	1 Feb	Provision for depreciation	9,250.00
31 Dec	Profit on sale	250.00	1 Feb	Bank	7,000.00
		16,250.00			16,250.00

The corresponding credit entry will appear in the profit and loss account, like this:

Profit and Loss Account for the Year Ended 31 December 20-9

	£
Profit on sale of van	250.00

Now we can look at an example of a fixed asset that is under-depreciated and sold for *less than* the estimated disposal value. Using the same example as above, if instead of being sold at £7,000 (a profit on sale), the motor van was sold for £6,000, this would result in a loss on the sale of £750. Now look at the accounting entries. There is a credit entry in the disposal account, like this:

Disposal Account – Motor Van

20-9		£	20-9		£
1 Feb	Motor van	16,000.00	1 Feb	Provision for depreciation	9,250.00
			1 Feb	Bank	6,000.00
			31 Dec	Profit and loss	750.00
		16,000.00			16,000.00

And a corresponding debit entry in the profit and loss account, like this:

Profit and Loss Account for the year ended 31 December 20-9

	£	
Loss on sale of van	750.00	

A disposal account is a *collecting together account* that brings together all the information relevant to the disposal of a fixed asset.

Points to remember

- The two main ways of calculating depreciation are the *straight-line method* and the *reducing balance method*. Whichever method is used, or requested in examinations, the double entry records are the same; it is the *amounts* which vary according to the method used.
- Depreciation is an *expense* and is charged to the *profit and loss account*. The *cost of fixed assets* is debited to the relevant *ledger accounts*. The *annual depreciation* is credited either to the same account, or as is now more likely, to a separate *provision for depreciation account*. It is usual to keep a *separate provision account* for each fixed asset.
- As each annual charge is credited to the provision account, the balance on that account *increases* to equal the accumulated depreciation. On each year's balance sheet, the fixed asset is shown at the cost price, less the accumulated depreciation to date.
  When a fixed asset is *sold*, both its cost and its accumulated depreciation are removed from their respective ledger accounts and transferred into a *fixed asset disposals account*.

Assignments

18.1
Graham Dyson purchased machinery for £3,000 in April 20-4. It is expected to have an effective working life of five years and its estimated disposal value at the end of this period is £712.

You are required to show the machinery and the provision for depreciation accounts for the five years. Depreciation is to be calculated at a rate of 25 per cent per annum on the reducing balance method. Accounts are prepared annually to 31 December and a full year's depreciation is provided in the year of purchase.

18.2
David Allen purchased a vehicle costing £23,000 on 1 January 20-3. Its useful life is anticipated to be five years. At the end of this time it is

estimated to be worth £3,000. A provision for depreciation is to be established and depreciation charges calculated on the fixed instalment method. Accounts are prepared to 31 December each year.

You are required to:

(a) Prepare the vehicle account and the provision for depreciation account for the five years to 31 December 20-7.
(b) Show the balance sheet entry at the end of each year.

18.3

Brian Tate purchased machinery costing £25,000 in March 20-5. It is the firm's policy to depreciate machinery by direct depreciation on the machinery account, using the reducing balance method at a rate of 20 per cent per annum. A full year's depreciation is charged in the year of purchase and the financial year ends on 30 September.

You are required to:

(a) Show the entries for three years, 20-5, 20-6 and 20-7, on the machinery account and the depreciation account.
(b) Show the entries for three years, 20-5, 20-6 and 20-7, in the profit and loss account and the balance sheet.

18.4

James Clayton purchased a motor van on 1 June 20-5 costing £10,800, paying by cheque. It was estimated he would keep it for three years, providing depreciation at a rate of 33.3 per cent per annum by the reducing balance method. On 1 June 20-8 the van was sold for £3,000 cash. Final accounts are prepared to 31 May each year.

You are required to write up for the years 20-5, 20-6, 20-7, 20-8 and 20-9:

(a) (i)   motor van account
    (ii) provision for depreciation account
    (iii) disposal account
(b) show the relevant extract entries in the profit and loss accounts
(c) show the relevant extract entries of the balance sheets.

18.5

William Evans is a sole trader, and his financial year ends on 31 December each year. On 4 January 20-5 he purchased machinery costing £15,500, paying by cheque. Evans plans to use the machinery for four years and estimates that at the end of that time its residual value will be £3,000.

A provision for depreciation was established and depreciation was calculated on the straight line method. On 3 January 20-9 the machinery was sold for £3,250.

You are required to draw up for the years 20-5, 20-6, 20-7, 20-8 and 20-9:

(a) machinery account
(b) provision for depreciation account
(c) disposal account

(d) the relevant extracts for each year in the profit and loss account and the balance sheet.

18.6
(i) What is meant by depreciation, and why is it important for a business to provide for depreciation?
(ii) A. Swain is a haulage contractor. On 1 January 20-6 he purchased three tipper lorries for £4,800 each. Mr Swain estimated that his lorries would have an effective working life of five years with a disposal value of £300 each. The straight line method of depreciation is to be used. The financial year ends on 31 December. One of the lorries kept breaking down and was sold on 1 January 20-8 for £2,500.

You are required to show the relevant entries for the years 20-6, 20-7 and 20-8 in the following ledger accounts:

(a) Lorries
(b) Lorries disposal
(c) Provision for depreciation on lorries

18.7
The financial year end of Hodgson (Builders Merchants) Ltd is 31 December. The company's policy is to depreciate its motor vans at 20 per cent per annum, using the straight line method, and to calculate a full year's depreciation on the assets in existence at the end of the financial year, regardless of when they were purchased or sold. The company's vans were purchased and sold as follows:

			£
1 January 19-9	Purchased	AB 101 T	2,500
1 July 20-0	Purchased	CD 202 V	3,000
31 March 20-1	Purchased	EF 303 W	2,000
31 March 20-1	Sold	AB 101 T	1,000
1 April 20-2	Purchased	GH 404 X	3,500
31 August 20-2	Sold	CD 202 V	2,000

You are required to draw up for the years 19-9, 20-0, 20-1 and 20-2:

(a) (i) Motor van account
    (ii) Provision for depreciation of motor vans account
    (iii) Disposal of motor vans account
(b) Extracts of the profit and loss accounts
(c) Extracts of the balance sheets.

■ ☑ 19 Bad debts and provision for bad and doubtful debts

In business, most transactions are carried out on a credit basis. This means that the goods or services are received immediately but payment is made at a later date. Credit is not usually given to customers until references from other suppliers have been obtained regarding the customers' ability to pay their debts promptly.

Bad debts

A *debtor* is a person who owes a firm money. A debtor who cannot or will not pay his/her debts is known as a *bad debtor* and the amount owing is referred to as a *bad debt*. Once it is discovered that a debt is never going to be collected, the account can no longer be regarded as an asset to the business.

Usually many attempts will have been made in an effort to recover the outstanding amount. However, regardless of the circumstances, if a debtor cannot pay what is owed it is a business loss, and must be treated in the same way as other losses and expenses. There are three possibilities:

(a) a debt may be entirely bad;
(b) a debt may be partially bad (some part payment is received); or
(c) a debt written off may eventually be recovered.

A debt that is entirely bad

Consider a typical example. Edward Hemingway is a debtor for the sum of £95. On 8 July 20-7 he is declared bankrupt and we are informed the amount owing will not be paid. It is decided to write off the amount owing as a bad debt. At the beginning of July, Edward Hemingway's account in the sales ledger would look like this:

Edward Hemingway Account

20-7		£	
1 Jul	Balance b/d	95.00	

To write off this debt, two entries are required. A debit entry in a bad debts account, like this:

Bad Debts Account

20-7		£		
8 Jul	Edward Hemingway	95.00		

And then a corresponding credit entry to close Edward Hemingway's account, like this:

Edward Hemingway Account

20-7		£	20-7		£
1 Jul	Balance b/d	95.00	8 Jul	Bad debts account	95.00

Note that the debtor's account would be ruled off and clearly marked in red pen *BAD DEBTOR*, to prevent any further credit being made available.

A bad debts account is a *collecting together* account that brings together all bad debts incurred during a financial year. Only at the end of the financial year is the bad debts account totalled and the balance transferred to the profit and loss account.

At the end of the accounting period the bad debts account is closed (leaving it ready to start a new financial year) and the balance is transferred to the profit and loss account by making a credit entry, like this:

Bad Debts Account

20-7		£	20-7		£
8 Jul	Edward Hemingway	95.00	31 Dec	Profit & loss	95.00

A corresponding debit entry will appear in the profit and loss account, like this:

Profit and Loss Account for the year ended 31 December 20-7

Expenses	£	
Bad debts	95.00	

A debt that is partially bad

Occasionally, a debtor comes to an arrangement to repay only part of the debt. This type of voluntary agreement to settle a debt by paying only a portion of the amount owed is called a 'composition with the creditors'. Sometimes a debtor may go into voluntary liquidation or be declared bankrupt and his/her assets sold for the benefit of the creditors. In these circumstances, the money received would be debited in the bank or cash account, and the unpaid portion would be written off to the bad debts account.

Here is a typical example of a debt that is partially bad. Brian Forbes, who owes the firm £268, has been declared bankrupt. On 20 August 20-7 a cheque for 50 pence in the pound is received in full settlement of the debt. At the beginning of August, Brian Forbes' account in the sales ledger would look like this:

Brian Forbes Account

20-7		£			
1 Aug	Balance b/d	268.00			

On 20 August a cheque for £134 is received. This would need a debit entry in the bank account, like this:

Bank Account

20-7		£		
20 Aug	Brian Forbes	134.00		

The credit entry would be in Brian Forbes account, like this:

Brian Forbes Account

20-7		£	20-7		£
1 Aug	Balance b/d	268.00	20 Aug	Bank	134.00

Only the balance remaining on Brian Forbes' account of £134 is to be written off as a bad debt. A debit entry is made in the bad debts account, like this:

Bad Debts Account

20-7		£		
20 Aug	Brian Forbes	134.00		

A corresponding credit entry to close Brian Forbes' account, like this:

Brian Forbes Account

20-7		£	20-7		£
1 Aug	Balance b/d	268.00	20 Aug	Bank	134.00
			20 Aug	Bad debts	134.00
		268.00			268.00

Bad debts recovered

When a debtor's account has been closed it is eventually removed from the ledger and stored in a file of *dead* accounts. Because of the bankruptcy laws and the limitations imposed on bankrupts, some debtors do their best to repay their debts. Sometimes bad debts are recovered, often many years later. When this happens it is a pleasant surprise and an unexpected profit of the business.

This is a typical example of a bad debt recovered. Suppose we receive a cheque for £187 from A. Slowman, with a letter saying that he is now in a position to repay his debt. Because A. Slowman's account was written off several years ago it no longer exists in the ledger. In this situation, a debit entry would be made in the bank account for the money received, like this:

Bank Account

20-9		£		
8 Mar	A. Slowman	187.00		

A corresponding credit entry is made in the bad debts account where it will offset any bad debts that occur during the current financial year:

Bad Debts Account

			20-9		£
			8 Mar	Bank (A. Slowman)	187.00

Note that no entries are made in the debtor's *dead* account.

Provision for bad and doubtful debts

Even when bad debtors have been removed, the accounts do not represent a *true and fair view* of the debtors. Accountants know from experience that there will always be some debtors who will be unable to pay their debts. On a balance sheet, the figure for total debtors appears as an asset, therefore this figure should be as accurate as possible.

Practically every business suffers from bad debts, but a good business will know from experience approximately what percentage of debts will eventually prove to be bad debts. With this in mind, most firms set aside a certain sum of money to guard against the likelihood of future bad debts. A *provision* is the name given to the sum of money set aside. This is usually quoted as a percentage of the debtors' total. Here is a typical example. On 31 December 20-6 the debtors' total amounted to £15,000. It is estimated that 4 per cent of debts (that is, £600) would eventually prove to be bad debts, and it is decided to make a provision for these out of the profits for the year. The ledger entries needed to start a provision for bad debts are, first, a debit entry in the profit and loss account, like this:

Profit and Loss Account for the year ended 31 December 20-6

Expenses	£	
Provision for bad debts	600.00	

Then a corresponding credit entry in a provision for bad debts account, like this:

Provision for Bad Debts Account

	20-6		£
	31 Dec	Profit and loss	600.00

The provision for bad debts account is totalled and balanced at the end of each financial year. Any adjustment to the provision – increase or decrease – is then made on this account.

On the balance sheet, in order to show a true and fair view of debtors, the amount of the provision for bad debts is deducted from the total debtors, like this:

Balance sheet as at 31 December 20-6 (extract)

		£	
Current assets			
Debtors	15,000		
Less provision			
for bad debts	600	14,400	

Increasing the provision

The provision for bad debts is usually reviewed each year, and any change since the previous year is then adjusted. Using the same firm as an example, suppose that at the end of the following year – 31 December 20-7 – the bad debts provision needed to be increased, because the provision is to be kept at 4 per cent, but debtors had risen to £18,000. A provision of £600 had been brought forward from the previous year, but now a total provision of £720 (that is, 4 per cent of £18,000) is required, an increase of £120. To make this adjustment, the provision for bad debts account is credited with the *extra* £120, like this:

Provision for Bad Debts Account

20-6		£	20-6		£
31 Dec	Balance c/d	600.00	31 Dec	Profit and loss	600.00
			20-7		
			1 Jan	Balance b/d	600.00
			31 Dec	Profit and loss	120.00

A corresponding debit entry is made in the profit and loss account, like this:

Profit and Loss Account for the year ended 31 December 20-7

Expenses	£	
Provision for bad debts	120.00	

The balance sheet now shows debtors at a more realistic value, with the amount of the provision for bad debts deducted from the debtors' total, like this:

Balance sheet as at 31 December 20-7 (extract)

		£	
Current assets			
Debtors	18,000		
Less provision			
for bad debts	720	17,280	

Decreasing the provision

When the provision is reviewed at the end of the following year it is very likely that it will need to be adjusted. Using the same firm as an example, suppose that at the end of the following year – 31 December 20-8 – the bad debts provision needed to be reduced. This is because the provision is to be kept at 4 per cent, but debtors had fallen to £16,000. A provision of £720 had been brought forward from the previous year, but now a total provision of £640 (that is, 4 per cent of £16,000) is required – a reduction of £80. To make this adjustment, a *debit* entry is made in the provision for bad debts account of £80 to *reduce* it, like this:

Provision for Bad Debts Account

20-6		£	20-6		£
31 Dec	Balance c/d	600.00	31 Dec	Profit and loss	600.00
20-7			20-7		
31 Dec	Balance c/d	720.00	1 Jan	Balance b/d	600.00
			31 Dec	Profit and loss	120.00
		720.00			720.00
20-8			20-8		
31 Dec	Profit and loss	80.00	1 Jan	Balance b/d	720.00

And a corresponding credit entry is made in the profit and loss account, like this:

Profit and Loss Account for the year ended 31 December 20-8

Expenses	£		£
		Reduction in provision	80.00

On the balance sheet, the amount of the revised provision is deducted from the total debtors, like this:

Balance sheet as at 31 December 20-8 (extract)

		£	
Current assets			
Debtors	16,000		
Less provision			
for bad debts	640	15,360	

Look carefully at the illustration below showing all the entries in the provision for bad debts account for the three years 20-6, 20-7 and 20-8:

Provision for Bad Debts Account

20-6		£	20-6		£
31 Dec	Balance c/d	600.00	31 Dec	Profit and loss	600.00
20-7			20-7		
31 Dec	Balance c/d	720.00	1 Jan	Balance b/d	600.00
			31 Dec	Profit and loss	120.00
		720.00			720.00
20-8			20-8		
31 Dec	Profit and loss	80.00	1 Jan	Balance b/d	720.00
31 Dec	Balance c/d	640.00			
		720.00			720.00
			20-9		
			1 Jan	Balance b/d	640.00

Points to remember

- A debtor who cannot pay his debts is known as a *bad debtor*, and the amount owing is referred to as a *bad debt*.
- When a bad debt occurs, the bad debts account is debited with the relevant amount, and the debtor's account is credited with the same amount. A *bad debts account* is a *collecting together account* that brings together all bad debts incurred during a financial year. Only at the end of the financial year is the bad debts account totalled and the balance transferred to the profit and loss account.
- Many firms make a *provision* for debts that might eventually prove to be bad debts. This is an estimate, usually taken as a percentage of the debtors' total. The provision is reviewed each year. Any change since the previous year (increase or decrease) is then adjusted by making the appropriate entries in the provision for bad debts account and the profit and loss account. An *increase* is treated as an *expense* in the profit and loss account, while a *decrease* is treated as *revenue*.
- On a balance sheet, the amount of provision is *deducted* from the debtors' total in order to show a true and fair view of the debtors.

Assignments

19.1
On 1 March 20-7, D. Nelson owes your firm £76.50. He is declared bankrupt and it is decided reluctantly on 30 March 20-7 to write off the debt as a bad

debt. You are required to prepare D. Nelson's account and a bad debts account.

19.2

Alan Senior is a debtor who owes your firm £350. Because of serious financial difficulties he is unable to pay and asks you to agree to a payment of 50 per cent in full settlement of the debt. After consideration, you agree and he pays by cheque on 30 November 20-7. You are required to prepare Alan Senior's account and a bad debts account.

19.3

A. Baxter is declared bankrupt owing your firm £175. On 15 April 20-7, you receive a final settlement payment of 45 pence in the pound, in cash. You are required to prepare A. Baxter's account and a bad debts account.

19.4

John London's debt of £220 was written off some years ago. On 3 August 20-7, you receive a cheque and a note saying he is now in a position to repay his debt. You are required to open the necessary ledger accounts to show how this matter would be dealt with.

19.5

Every business that sells goods on credit wishes to avoid bad debts. You are required to:

(a) Describe the steps you would take before a new customer is allowed credit.
(b) State how you would deal with this customer if his creditworthiness is doubtful.

19.6

(a) What are bad debts? Why is it necessary to write off bad debts?
(b) From the information given below, write up the bad debts account in the books of Jean Wilder for the year 20-7. Debts written off as irrecoverable were:

		£
30 June	A. Noble	160
31 August	P. Jones	120
31 October	R. Scott	250
30 November	L. Skirrow	130

On 1 December 20-7, a final dividend of 5 pence in the pound was received unexpectedly in respect of the debt due from P. Jones. Close off the bad debts account as on 31 December 20-7 and the show the amount to be transferred to the profit and loss account.

19.7

Paul Simpson is a sole trader. During the year ended 31 March 20-8 the following customers were declared bankrupt:

Date	Customer	Amount of debt £	Rate received in final settlement
20-7			
31 July	J. Brown	275.50	20p in the pound
30 September	K. Lawson	350.00	55p in the pound
31 December	B. Nicholas	190.50	40p in the pound
20-8			
28 February	M. Swan	164.00	25p in the pound

You are required to write up the bad debts account in the ledger of Paul Simpson for the year ended 31 March 20-8. Include all relevant dates and show clearly the amount to be transferred to the appropriate final account.

19.8

Nigel Barker runs a small business. He decided to make a provision for bad debts equal to 5 per cent of the total debtors outstanding at the end of each financial year.

	Total debtors £
31 December 20-5	9,000
31 December 20-6	10,000

You are required to:

(a) Prepare the provision for bad debts account for the years ended 31 December 20-5 and 20-6.
(b) Show the entries in the profit and loss account for the years 20-5 and 20-6.
(c) Show the balance sheet entries (extracts) for the years 20-5 and 20-6.

19.9

H. Crawford had a business that adjusted its provision for bad debts at the end of the financial year, at a given percentage of the total debtors. The percentage varied each year, depending on the economic situation. Irrecoverable debts were written off during the year to a bad debts account, as and when they occurred. On 1 January 20-1 the balance on the provision for bad debts account was £500.

	Bad debts written off during year to bad debts account £	Total debtors at year end £	Rate of percentage for provision of doubtful debts %
31 December 20-1	750	14,000	5
31 December 20-2	4,085	10,000	10
31 December 20-3	2,900	15,000	5

From the above information you are required to:

(a) Prepare the bad debts account, showing clearly the transfer to the final accounts, for the financial years 31 December 20-1, 20-2 and 20-3.
(b) Prepare the provision for bad debts account for the years 31 December 20-1, 20-2 and 20-3, showing clearly the balance brought forward each year.
(c) An extract from the balance sheets showing how the provision would affect the total debtors, as at 31 December 20-1, 20-2 and 20-3.

19.10

On 20 September 20-7, Brian Fox's debtors totalled £12,000. He decided to write off the following as bad debts:

	£
G. Green	60
H. Wilson	80

He further decided to make a provision for doubtful debts of 10 per cent on the remaining debtors. On 30 September 20-8 his debtors totalled £10,000 when Brian Fox decided to maintain the provision at 10 per cent. You are required to show for each of the years ended 30 September 20-7 and 20-8:

(a) provision for doubtful debts account:
(b) the appropriate entries in the profit and loss account:
(c) the necessary balance sheet entries.

19.11

(a) What are the differences between bad debts written off and provision for bad debts?
(b) Give two reasons for creating a provision for bad debts.
(c) What is meant by bad debts recovered? How are such items entered in the profit and loss account of a business?
(d) On 1 January 20-4 there was a balance of £500 in the provision for bad debts account, and it was decided to maintain the provision at 5 per cent of the debtors' total at each year-end.

The debtors on 31 December each year were as follows:

	£
20-4	8,000
20-5	8,000
20-6	11,000

You are required to show the necessary entries for the years ended 31 December 20-4, 20-5 and 20-6 in:

(a) the provision for bad debts account; and
(b) the profit and loss account.

■ Ṿ **20** Control accounts

In order to understand control accounts you must first appreciate why they are necessary. In a small business, the accounts can easily and quickly be checked to find any errors. However, in a large business with hundreds of accounts, any errors can be very difficult to find and extremely time-consuming. Firms with large numbers of debtors and creditors often divide a ledger into alphabetical sections, for example: A to F, G to L, M to S, T to Z; they use *control accounts* to check on the accuracy of each ledger or section of the ledger. A control account contains the same information as the individual ledger accounts that it *controls*, but in the form of totals. Because totals are used they are also known as *total accounts*.

A control account can be maintained for any ledger or part of a ledger, but the two most frequently used control accounts are the *sales ledger control account* and the *purchase ledger control account*. They operate on the principle that whatever is entered in an individual account is also entered in the control account, and the balance on the control account must equal the total of the individual balances on the ledger, or section of the ledger, which it controls.

It must be emphasised that control accounts are not necessarily part of the double entry system. They are mathematical proofs performing the same function as a trial balance to a particular ledger or section of a ledger. When individual debtors' and creditors' accounts are kept on the double entry system, then the control account is *not*, otherwise the entries would be duplicated. It is usual to find control accounts in the same format as a normal account.

Control accounts are an excellent test of a student's ability, and for this reason appear regularly as examination questions.

Sales ledger control account

Accounts in the sales ledger will normally have debit balances because they are the personal accounts of debtors. Everyday entries are made in the sales ledger to record sales, sales returns, cash and cheques received from customers, discounts allowed and any bad debts. A sales ledger control account is prepared using the *total* of all the individual items that have been entered in the debtors' accounts. We can now look at a typical example question.

From the following information, prepare a sales ledger control account for the month of May, clearly showing the balance carried forward at 31 May 20-9.

		£
(i)	1 May Sales ledger balances	23,524
(ii)	Sales day book	19,870
(iii)	Sales returns day book	670
(iv)	Cheques received from customers	17,450
(v)	Discount allowed	371
(vi)	Bad debts written off	300

To prepare a sales ledger control account, simply ask, for each item, where this would appear on an ordinary debtor's account. This is because the items appear in exactly the same place in the sales ledger control account.

(i)   This is the total of all the individual debtors' balances, they would appear at the debit side of each debtor's account, so the total is placed at the debit side of the control account, like this:

Sales Ledger Control Account

20-9		£	20-9		£
1 May	Balance b/d	23,524			

(ii)   This is the total of the sales day book for the month of May (or the sales account if day books are not used). Sales are entered at the debit side of each customer's account, so the total sales for the month are placed at the debit side of the control account, like this:

Sales Ledger Control Account

20-9		£	20-9		£
1 May	Balance b/d	23,524			
31 May	Sales	19,870			

(iii)   This is the total of the sales returns day book for the month of May (or the sales returns account if day books are not used). Sales returns are entered at the credit side of each customer's account, so the total for the month is placed at the credit side of the control account, like this:

Sales Ledger Control Account

20-9		£	20-9		£
1 May	Balance b/d	23,524	31 May	Sales returns	670
31 May	Sales	19,870			

(iv) This is the total amount of cheques received from customers during the month of May. Money received is entered at the credit side of each customer's account, so the total for the month is placed at the credit side of the control account, like this:

Sales Ledger Control Account

20-9		£	20-9		£
1 May	Balance b/d	23,524	31 May	Sales returns	670
31 May	Sales	19,870	31 May	Bank	17,450

(v) This is the total discount allowed to customers during the month of May. Discount allowed is entered at the credit side of each customer's account, so the total for the month is placed at the credit side of the control account, like this:

Sales Ledger Control Account

20-9		£	20-9		£
1 May	Balance b/d	23,524	31 May	Sales returns	670
31 May	Sales	19,870	31 May	Bank	17,450
			31 May	Discount allowed	371

(vi) This is the total bad debts written off during the month of May. Bad debts are entered at the credit side of a customer's account, so the total for the month is placed at the credit side of the control account, like this:

Sales Ledger Control Account

20-9		£	20-9		£
1 May	Balance b/d	23,524	31 May	Sales returns	670
31 May	Sales	19,870	31 May	Bank	17,450
			31 May	Discount allowed	371
			31 May	Bad debts	300

Now all we need to do is to balance the account, like this:

Sales Ledger Control Account

20-9		£	20-9		£
1 May	Balance b/d	23,524	31 May	Sales returns	670
31 May	Sales	19,870	31 May	Bank	17,450
			31 May	Discount allowed	371
			31 May	Bad debts	300
			31 May	Balance c/d	24,603
		43,394			43,394
1 Jun	Balance b/d	24,603			

Purchase ledger control account

Accounts in the purchase ledger will normally have credit balances because they are the personal accounts of creditors. Everyday entries are made in the purchase ledger to record purchases, purchase returns, cash and cheques paid to suppliers and discounts received. A purchase ledger control account is prepared using the *total* of all the individual items that have been entered in the creditors' accounts. We can now look at a typical example question.

From the following information, prepare a purchase ledger control account for the month of May, showing clearly the balance carried forward at 31 May 20-9.

		£
(i)	1 May Purchase ledger balances	20,690
(ii)	Purchase day book	8,760
(iii)	Purchase returns day book	490
(iv)	Cheques paid to creditors	9,765
(v)	Discount received	470

When asked to prepare a purchase ledger control account, you must ask yourself, for each item, where this would appear in a normal creditor's account. This is because the items appear in exactly the same place in the purchase ledger control account.

(i) This is the total of all the individual creditors' balances, they would appear at the credit side of each creditor's account, so the total is placed at the credit side of the control account.

(ii) This is the total of the purchases day book for the month of May (or the purchases account if day books are not used). Purchases are entered at the credit side of each supplier's account, so the total for the month is placed at the credit side of the control account.

(iii) This is the total of the purchase returns day book for the month of May (or the purchase returns account if day books are not used). Purchase returns are entered at the debit side of each creditor's account, so the total for the month is placed at the debit side of the control account.

(iv) This is the total amount of cheques paid to creditors during the month of May. Money paid out is entered at the debit side of each creditor's account, so the total for the month is placed at the debit side of the control account.

(v) This is the total discount received during the month of May. Discount received is entered at the debit side of each creditor's account, so the total for the month is placed at the debit side of the control account.

When these entries have been made, the account would be balanced and it would look like this:

Purchase Ledger Control Account

20-9		£	20-9		£
31 May	Purchase returns	490	1 May	Balance b/d	20,690
31 May	Bank	9,765	31 May	Purchases	8,760
31 May	Discount received	470			
31 May	Balance c/d	18,725			
		29,450			29,450
			1 Jun	Balance b/d	18,725

Some examination questions ask for the debtors' or creditors' accounts to be completed as well as the control account. Here is a typical example:

Elaine Mellor has a small business that produces a wide range of educational toys and games. On 1 May 20-6, her sales ledger contained the following debtors:

	£
A. Buckley	208.00
W. Dixon	275.00
L. Gibson	392.00

During the month of May, the following transactions took place:

Sales

May		Goods £	VAT £	Total £
2	W. Dixon	213.64	37.39	251.03
8	A. Buckley	143.64	25.14	168.78
17	L. Gibson	266.36	46.61	312.97

Sales returns

May		Goods £	VAT £	Total £
10	W. Dixon	31.82	5.57	37.39
27	L. Gibson	42.73	7.48	50.21

Payments received by cheque

May		Discount allowed £	Cheque value £
16	A. Buckley	10.00	198.00
20	L. Gibson	18.00	374.00
30	W. Dixon	12.00	228.00

You are required to:

(a) Open ledger accounts for all debtors and enter the balances as at 1 May 20-6.
(b) Enter the transactions that have taken place during the month of May to the appropriate sales ledger accounts and balance the accounts at the end of the month.
(c) Show the entries that would appear in the sales, sales returns and VAT accounts in the nominal ledger.
(d) Prepare a sales ledger control account for May 20-6 and reconcile the balance with the total debtors' balances in the sales ledger.

This is a fully worked solution to this question:

A. Buckley Account

20-6		£	20-6		£
1 May	Balance b/d	208.00	16 May	Bank	198.00
8 May	Sales	168.78	16 May	Discount allowed	10.00
			31 May	Balance c/d	168.78
		376.78			376.78
1 Jun	Balance b/d	168.78			

W. Dixon Account

20-6		£	20-6		£
1 May	Balance b/d	275.00	10 May	Sales returns	37.39
2 May	Sales	251.03	30 May	Bank	228.00
			30 May	Discount allowed	12.00
			31 May	Balance c/d	248.64
		526.03			526.03
1 Jun	Balance b/d	248.64			

L. Gibson Account

20-6		£	20-6		£
1 May	Balance b/d	392.00	20 May	Bank	374.00
17 May	Sales	312.97	20 May	Discount allowed	18.00
			27 May	Sales returns	50.21
			31 May	Balance c/d	262.76
		704.97			704.97
1 Jun	Balance b/d	262.76			

Sales Account

			20-6		£
			31 May	Total SDB	623.64

Sales Returns Account

20-6		£			
31 May	Total SRDB	74.55			

Value Added Tax Account

20-6		£	20-6		£
31 May	Total SRDB	13.05	31 May	Total SDB	109.14

Sales Ledger Control Account

20-6		£	20-6		£
1 May	Balance b/d	875.00	31 May	Sales returns	74.55
31 May	Sales	623.64	31 May	VAT	13.05
31 May	VAT	109.14	31 May	Bank	800.00
			31 May	Discount allowed	40.00
			31 May	Balance c/d	680.18
		1,607.78			1,607.78
1 Jun	Balance b/d	680.18			

Debtors' balances list:

	£
A. Buckley	168.78
W. Dixon	248.64
L. Gibson	262.76
	680.18 = balance on Sales Ledger Control Account

Points to remember

- A control account contains the same information as the individual ledger accounts that it *controls*, but in total. Because totals are used they are also known as *total accounts*.
- Sales and purchase ledger control accounts are prepared using the *total* of all the individual items that have been entered in the debtors' and creditors' accounts.
- When preparing a *control account* simply ask, for each item, where it would appear on a normal debtor's or creditor's account. This is because the items appear in exactly the same place in the control account.
- The balance on the control account *must* equal the total of the individual balances on the ledger, or section of the ledger that it controls.
- Occasionally, there might be a *dishonoured cheque*; this is a cheque returned unpaid by a debtor's bank. This would be entered at the *debit side* of the *sales ledger control account*.
- *Bad debts* are entered at the *credit side* of the *sales ledger control account*.

Assignments

20.1

From the following information, prepare a sales ledger control account for the month of May, showing clearly the balance carried forward at 31 May 20-7.

		£
May 1	Sales ledger balances	4,760
	Sales day book	5,912
	Sales returns day book	423
	Cheques received from customers	3,969
	Discount allowed	179
	Bad debts written off	57

20.2

From the following information, prepare a purchase ledger control account for the month of May, showing clearly the balance carried forward at 31 May 20-7.

		£
May 1	Purchase ledger balances	8,904
	Purchases day book	7,038
	Purchase returns day book	324
	Cheques paid to creditors	6,604
	Discount received	272

20.3

From the following information, prepare a sales ledger control account for the month of June, showing clearly the balance carried forward at 30 June 20-7.

		£
June 1	Sales ledger balances	6,869
	Sales day book	12,762
	Sales returns day book	295
	Cash received from customers	187
	Cheques received from customers	11,230
	Discount allowed	536
	Bad debts written off	552
	Dishonoured cheque	119

20.4

From the following information, prepare a purchase ledger control account for the month of June, showing clearly the balance carried forward at 30 June 20-7.

		£
June 1	Purchase ledger balances	13,561
	Purchases day book	17,614
	Purchase returns day book	232
	Cheques paid to creditors	12,760
	Discount received	101

20.5

Khalid Shah extracted the following balances from his books for the month of January 20-7.

		£
Jan 1	Purchase ledger balances	14,641
Jan 1	Sales ledger balances	17,542
	Totals for January	
	Purchases day book	135,652
	Sales day book	197,961
	Purchase returns day book	2,864
	Sales returns day book	4,231
	Cheques paid to creditors	142,876
	Cash and cheques received from customers	197,580
	Discount allowed	5,180
	Discount received	2,708
	Bad debts written off	342
	Customers' cheques dishonoured	54

You are required to:

(a) Prepare a sales ledger control account for the month of January, clearly showing the balance carried forward at 31 January 20-7.
(b) Prepare a purchase ledger control account for the month of January, clearly showing the balance carried forward at 31 January 20-7.

20.6

The following information relates to the sales ledger control account for ledger number 2, K to R.

	£
Debit balances on 1 May 20-4	3,788
Cash received from customers	2,300
Cheques received from customers	14,568
Sales returns	292
Bad debts written off	172
Discounts allowed	300
Sales	20,580
Debit balances on 31 May 20-4 as extracted from sales ledger	6,781

You are required to:

(a) Write up the sales ledger control account from the information given above.

(b) Comment on the significance of the closing figure as revealed by the control account with the figure for debtors as extracted from the sales ledger.

20.7

Emily McGregor has a small business that produces a range of garden furniture. On 1 May 20-9 her purchase ledger contained the following creditors:

	£
A. Butler	804.62
W. Dyson	472.95
L. Grainger	628.38

During the month of May the following transactions took place:

Purchases on credit

May	Goods £	VAT £	Total £
2 W. Dyson	394.64	69.06	463.70
8 A. Butler	418.83	73.30	492.13
17 L. Grainger	626.90	109.71	736.61

Purchase returns

May	Goods £	VAT £	Total £
10 W. Dyson	62.72	10.98	73.70
27 L. Grainger	48.34	8.46	56.80

Payments made by cheque

May	Discount received £	Cheque value £
16 A. Butler	28.72	574.38
20 L. Grainger	23.65	449.30
30 W. Dyson	19.84	396.96

You are required to:

(a) Open ledger accounts for all creditors and enter the balances as at 1 May 20-9.

(b) Enter the transactions that have taken place during the month of May to the appropriate purchase ledger accounts, and balance the accounts at the end of the month.

(c) Show the entries that would appear in the purchases, purchase returns and VAT accounts in the nominal ledger.

(d) Prepare a purchase ledger control account for May 20-9 and reconcile the balance with the total creditors balances in the purchase ledger.

20.8

Jean Oldridge has a small business that produces an exclusive range of sportswear. On 1 May 20-9 her sales ledger contained the following debtors:

	£
G. Anderson	796.42
M. Driscoll	250.20
V. Ellis	428.78
M. Hariman	873.96

During the month of May the following transactions took place:

Sales on credit

		Goods	VAT	Total
May		£	£	£
2	V. Ellis	593.20	103.81	697.01
8	G. Anderson	847.92	148.39	996.31
17	M. Hariman	735.70	128.75	864.45

Sales returns

		Goods	VAT	Total
May		£	£	£
10	V. Ellis	63.82	11.17	74.99
27	M. Hariman	77.64	13.59	91.23

Payments received by cheque

		Discount allowed	Cheque value
May		£	£
16	G. Anderson	32.83	656.60
20	M. Hariman	26.50	530.26
30	V. Ellis	15.40	307.94

You are required to:

(a) Open ledger accounts for all debtors and enter the balances as at 1 May 20-9.
(b) Enter the transactions that have taken place during the month of May to the appropriate sales ledger accounts.
(c) On 28 May, notification was received that M. Driscoll had been declared bankrupt. The balance on his account should be written off as a bad debt.
(d) Balance the sales ledger accounts at the end of the month.
(e) Show the entries that would appear in the sales, sales returns, bad debts and VAT accounts in the nominal ledger.
(f) Prepare a sales ledger control account for May 20-9 and reconcile the balance with the total debtors' balances in the sales ledger.

■ ⊻ **21** Adjustments for final accounts: prepayments and accruals – ledger accounts

In the accounts we have looked at so far, we have assumed that the expenses and income related exactly to the accounting period for which we were preparing the profit and loss account. At this point in our studies we must now consider what are called *adjustments*. In the preparation of final accounts there are two main principles:

(i) Every trading and profit and loss account must be prepared accurately so that the correct profit or loss for the period is obtained.
(ii) Every balance sheet must give a *true and fair view* of the business, showing the assets and liabilities at their genuine values.

To achieve these aims, the accounts must be prepared in such a way that all the profit that belongs to the accounting period under consideration is included, whether it has been received or not. Set against this profit should be all expenses incurred during that period, even if they have not yet been paid. This principle is known as the *matching rule*, because the incomes and expenditures are matched with each another.

Expense accounts and revenue received accounts may be prepaid at the end of a financial year: that is, a business may have paid for something or received revenue *in advance* of *using up* that item. Alternatively, expenses and revenue received may be *accrued* (the accounting term for owing) at the end of a financial year. This means that a business would have outstanding debts, either owed to it or owed by it. The purpose of adjustments is to produce an accurate set of final accounts.

The main adjustments are:

1 Payments made in advance by the firm.
2 Payments made in advance to a firm.
3 Expenses owed by the firm.
4 Expenses owed to a firm.
5 Unused stocks.

Payments made in advance by the firm

A prepayment means that a business has paid in advance for something before fully using up that item. Some payments are always made in advance: for example, insurance cover does not begin until the premium is paid. Similarly, rent and rates are frequently paid in advance, and these accounts often have an unused portion remaining at the end of the accounting period. This unused portion will require a year-end adjustment in respect of the unexpired part of the year.

Here is a typical example: Nicholas Davidson is a sole trader, and his accounting period runs from 1 January to 31 December each year. Rates of £1,500 per annum are payable by instalments. During the year ended 31 December 20-7, the following payments were made for rates, by cheque:

3 January 20-7	£375 for the three months to 31 March 20-7
1 April 20-7	£750 for the six months to 30 September 20-7
1 October 20-7	£750 for the six months to 31 March 20-8

Each time a payment is made the details are entered (credit side of the bank account and debit side of the rates account), like this:

Rates Account

20-7		£	
3 Jan	Bank	375.00	
1 Apr	Bank	750.00	
1 Oct	Bank	750.00	

As the payment made on 1 October was for the six months to 31 March 20-8, only three months (half of £750) will be used up in this financial year, and £375 will be prepaid. The amount transferred to the profit and loss account must be the actual cost of rates for this accounting period to 31 December 20-7 – that is, £1,500. We need to adjust the figures to get only this year's expenses in the accounts. To make this adjustment, the amount of the prepayment is entered at the credit side of the rates account, like this:

Rates Account

20-7		£	20-7		£
3 Jan	Bank	375.00			
1 Apr	Bank	750.00	31 Dec	Prepaid c/d	375.00
1 Oct	Bank	750.00			

This will create a balance equal to the amount that has been paid in advance. The amount transferred to the profit and loss account is the difference between the two sides of the account. The completed rates account would look like this:

Rates Account

20-7		£	20-7		£
3 Jan	Bank	375.00	31 Dec	Profit and loss	1,500.00
1 Apr	Bank	750.00	31 Dec	Prepaid c/d	375.00
1 Oct	Bank	750.00			
		1,875.00			1,875.00
20-8					
1 Jan	Prepaid b/d	375.00			

This leaves a balance on the rates account to be carried down to the following year. Since this balance is passed on from one year to the next it is one of the assets of the business. On the balance sheet for the year ending 31 December 20-7, the prepayment is shown under *Current assets*, as *rates prepaid £375*.

Here is another example. A new business whose financial year is 1 January to 31 December 20-7 decided to take out fire insurance. The annual premium of £480 was paid, by cheque, on 1 February 20-7, the details are entered (credit side of the bank account and debit side of the insurance account), like this:

Insurance Account

20-7		£		
1 Feb	Bank	480.00		

At the end of the financial year on 31 December 20-7 the business still has one month's value of insurance unexpired: this is a benefit paid for but not used up. It is an asset and needs to be carried forward to the next year. A year-end adjustment is required for the unexpired portion that is prepaid. It is calculated like this: cost for the year is £480, divided by 12 to give the cost of one month (£480 divided by 12 = £40). Eleven months have been *used up*, and one month is prepaid (£40). To make this adjustment, the amount of the prepayment is entered at the credit side of the insurance account, like this:

Insurance Account

20-7		£	20-7		£
1 Feb	Bank	480.00			
			31 Dec	Prepaid c/d	40.00

This will create a balance equal to the amount that has been paid in advance. The amount transferred to the profit and loss account is the difference between the two sides of the account. The completed account would look like this:

Insurance Account

20-7		£	20-7		£
1 Feb	Bank	480.00	31 Dec	Profit and loss	440.00
			31 Dec	Prepaid c/d	40.00
		480.00			480.00
20-8					
1 Jan	Prepaid b/d	40.00			

This leaves a balance on the Insurance account to be carried down to the next year. Since this balance is passed on from one year to the next it is one of the assets of the business. On the balance sheet for the year ending 31 December 20-7, the prepayment is shown under *Current assets*, as *insurance prepaid £40*.

Payments made in advance to the firm

This is income received in advance for services or a benefit that has not yet been given. The final accounts should reflect the *true and accurate* figures of the income actually earned during the financial year under review. Special attention is always required when dealing with revenue received. This usually causes problems for students because they forget that *revenue received* will be a debit entry in the cash book and a credit entry in the revenue received account. Here is a typical example: suppose a business has larger premises than it needs. On 1 March 20-7 it decides to rent part of it to another firm for £1,200 per annum. During the year ended 31 December 20-7, the following amounts were received from the sub-tenant, by cheque:

1 March	£300 for the three months to 31 May 20-7
2 June	£300 for the three months to 31 August 20-7
1 September	£300 for the three months to 30 November 20-7
2 December	£300 for the three months to 28 February 20-8

Each time a payment is received, the details are entered (debit side of the Bank account and credit side of the rent received account), like this:

Rent Received Account

			20-7		£
			1 Mar	Bank	300.00
			2 Jun	Bank	300.00
			1 Sep	Bank	300.00
			2 Dec	Bank	300.00

During the current financial year, the sub-tenant has paid £1,200 but has only received 10 months' benefit: 2 months has been paid in advance. The amount transferred to the profit and loss account must be the actual amount earned during this financial year, which is 10 months. We need to adjust the figures to get *only* this year's income in the accounts. It is calculated like this: cost for the year is £1,200, divided by 12 to give the cost of one month (£1,200 divided by 12 = £100). Ten months have been *used up*, and two months are prepaid (£200). To make this adjustment, the amount of the prepayment is entered at the debit side of the rent received account, like this:

Rent Received Account

20-7		£	20-7		£
			1 Mar	Bank	300.00
31 Dec	Prepaid c/d	200.00	2 Jun	Bank	300.00
			1 Sep	Bank	300.00
			2 Dec	Bank	300.00

This will create a balance equal to the amount that has been paid in advance. The amount transferred to the profit and loss account is the difference between the two sides of the account. The completed rent received account would look like this:

Rent Received Account

20-7		£	20-7		£
31 Dec	Profit and loss	1,000.00	1 Mar	Bank	300.00
31 Dec	Prepaid c/d	200.00	2 Jun	Bank	300.00
			1 Sep	Bank	300.00
			2 Dec	Bank	300.00
		1,200.00			1,200.00
			20-8		
			1 Jan	Prepaid b/d	200.00

This leaves a balance on the rent received account to be carried down to the next year. Since this balance is passed on from one year to the next it is one of the *liabilities* of the business. This is because the firm has the responsibility to provide accommodation for the sub-tenant for which he has already paid. On the balance sheet for the year ending 31 December 20-7 this is shown under the heading *Current liabilities* as *rent received in advance £200*.

Expenses owed by the firm

Invariably, at the end of the financial year there will be some expenses outstanding that will not be paid until the next financial year. These are called *accrued expenses*. Accrued simply means *owing, outstanding* or *in arrears*. Typical examples are: telephone, wages, rent, electricity and advertising. These are expenses that have been incurred during the current financial year, but full payment has not yet been made. Any expenses that are still outstanding at the end of the financial year will require an adjustment. Suppose that rent of £1,800 a year is payable at the end of every three months. During the year 1 January to 31 December 20-7, the following payments were made for rent, by cheque:

20-7	£
1 April	450.00
3 July	450.00
2 October	450.00

Each time a payment is made the details are entered (credit side of the Bank account and debit side of the rent account), like this:

Rent Account

20-7		£	
1 Apr	Bank	450.00	
3 Jul	Bank	450.00	
2 Oct	Bank	450.00	

On 31 December 20-7, three months' rent was owing. This will not be paid until 3 January 20-8. Clearly, the actual cost of rent for the year 20-7 is £1,800. We need to adjust the figures to get all this year's expenses in the accounts. To make this adjustment, the amount owing (£450) is entered at the debit side of the rent account, like this:

Rent Account

20-7		£	
1 Apr	Bank	450.00	
3 Jul	Bank	450.00	
2 Oct	Bank	450.00	
31 Dec	Accrued c/d	450.00	

This will create a balance equal to the amount owing. The amount transferred to the profit and loss account must be the actual cost of rent for this accounting period to 31 December 20-7; that is, £1,800. The completed rent account would look like this:

Rent Account

20-7		£	20-7		£
1 Apr	Bank	450.00	31 Dec	Profit and loss	1,800.00
3 Jul	Bank	450.00			
2 Oct	Bank	450.00			
31 Dec	Accrued c/d	450.00			
		1,800.00			1,800.00
			20-8		
			1 Jan	Accrued b/d	450.00

On the balance sheet for the year ending 31 December 20-7 this is shown under the heading *Current liabilities* as *rent accrued £450.*

Expenses owed to the firm

It is also possible that there may be revenue owing to the firm. Sometimes a business will not have received all the income to which it is entitled by the end of its financial year. This would be income that had been earned during the current year, but at the end of the year was still outstanding.

When this happens, the amount owing must be added to what has been received to show the true income for the year.

Common examples of these are:

- Rent received: a sub-tenant may be late in paying his/her rent.
- Commission received: the firm may have earned commission that it has not yet received.

Here is a typical example. Anne Thomas is a business consultant, she receives commission on a quarterly basis. During the year 1 January to 31 December 20-7 she received the following amounts by cheque:

	£
1 April	650
4 July	730
3 October	690

On 31 December 20-7 there was commission due of £780 that had not been received. Each time a payment is received the details are entered (debit side of the bank account and credit side of the commission received account), like this:

Commission Received Account

20-7		£
1 Apr	Bank	650.00
4 Jul	Bank	730.00
3 Oct	Bank	690.00

The amount transferred to the profit and loss account must be the actual amount earned during this financial year, which is £2,850. We need to adjust the figures in the accounts to show all this year's income. To make this adjustment, the amount still owing (£780) is entered at the credit side of the commission received account, like this:

Commission Received Account

20-7		£
1 Apr	Bank	650.00
4 Jul	Bank	730.00
3 Oct	Bank	690.00
31 Dec	Accrued c/d	780.00

This will create a balance equal to the amount still outstanding. The amount transferred to the profit and loss account must be the actual amount earned during this financial year to 31 December 20-7, that is £2,850. The completed commission received account would look like this:

Commission Received Account

20-7		£	20-7		£
31 Dec	Profit and loss	2,850.00	1 Apr	Bank	650.00
			4 Jul	Bank	730.00
			3 Oct	Bank	690.00
			31 Dec	Accrued c/d	780.00
		2,850.00			2,850.00
20-8					
1 Jan	Accrued b/d	780.00			

On the balance sheet for the year ended 31 December 20-7 this is shown under the heading *Current assets* as *commission due £780*.

Unused stocks

When items such as packing materials and stationery are bought for use in a business there are often unused stocks remaining at the end of the financial year. This stock is a form of prepayment and needs to be carried down to the following year, when it will be used. It is only the *actual cost of the materials used during the current year* that is transferred to the profit and loss account. Here is a typical example: during the financial year ended 31 December 20-7 the following amounts were paid, by cheque, for packing materials:

20-7	£
10 March	386
3 September	464

On 31 December 20-7 there was a stock of packing materials valued at £200. Each time a payment is made the details are entered (credit side of the bank account and at the debit side of the packing materials account), like this:

Packing Materials Account

20-7		£		
10 Mar	Bank	386.00		
3 Sep	Bank	464.00		

The amount transferred to the profit and loss account must be the *actual cost* of packing materials used during this financial year. We need to adjust the figures in the accounts to show only this year's expenses. To make this adjustment, the value of the unused stock of £200 is entered at the credit side of the packing materials account, like this:

Packing Materials Account

20-7		£	20-7		£
10 Mar	Bank	386.00			
3 Sep	Bank	464.00	31 Dec	Balance c/d	200.00

This will create a balance equal to the value of the unused stock. The amount transferred to the profit and loss account is the difference between the two sides of the account. The completed packing materials account would look like this:

Packing Materials Account

20-7		£	20-7		£
10 Mar	Bank	386.00	31 Dec	Profit and loss	650.00
3 Sep	Bank	464.00	31 Dec	Balance c/d	200.00
		850.00			850.00
20-8					
1 Jan	Balance b/d	200.00			

The stock of packing materials is *not* added to the stock of unsold goods on the balance sheet but is shown separately, under the heading *Current assets* as *packing materials stock £200.*

Examination questions are frequently set which require adjustments for prepayments and accruals at *both* the beginning and the end of the year. Students are often apprehensive when asked to prepare these accounts, so we can now see how this is done. Here are some typical questions with illustrated solutions.

Example 1

The following information refers to the electricity account in the ledger of John Woodstock. On 1 January 20-7 there was an unpaid bill for electricity of £246. During the year, the following payments were made for electricity, by cheque.

20-7	£
15 January	246
19 April	356
16 July	242
18 October	274

On 31 December 20-7 there was an electricity bill outstanding of £382.

You are required to prepare the electricity account, clearly showing the amount to be transferred to the profit and loss account for the year ended 31 December 20-7 and the amount to be carried forward to the next financial year.

This is a fully illustrated solution. Numbers in brackets refer to order in which entries should be made.

(i)   Enter amount owing at the beginning of the year (credit side).
(ii) Enter, in date order, details of the four amounts paid during the current year (debit side).
(iii) Enter details of the electricity bill outstanding at the end of the year (debit side).

At this point, the electricity account would look like this:

Electricity Account

20-7		£	20-7		£
15 Jan	Bank	246.00	1 Jan	Accrued b/d *(i)*	246.00
19 Apr	Bank	356.00			
16 Jul	Bank	*(ii)* 242.00			
18 Oct	Bank	274.00			
31 Dec	Accrued c/d	*(iii)* 382.00			

Once the dates and details of all the information given in the question are entered in the account, the amount transferred to the profit and loss account is the difference between the two sides of the account. The completed electricity account would look like this:

Electricity Account

20-7		£	20-7		£
15 Jan	Bank	246.00	1 Jan	Accrued b/d *(i)*	246.00
19 Apr	Bank	356.00	31 Dec	Profit and loss	1,254.00
16 Jul	Bank	*(ii)* 242.00			
18 Oct	Bank	274.00			
31 Dec	Accrued c/d	*(iii)* 382.00			
		1,500.00			1,500.00
			20-8		
			1 Jan	Accrued b/d	382.00

Example 2

From the following information you are required to write up the rates account in the ledger of E. Mellor.

On 1 July 20-2 the rates prepaid were £725. During the year, the following amounts were paid for rates, by cheque:

£

8 October 20-2   1,450 for the six months ending 31 March 20-3
5 April 20-3   1,650 for the six months ending 30 September 20-3.

Your rates account should clearly show the amount to be transferred to the profit and loss account for the year ended 30 June 20-3 and the amount to be carried forward to the next financial year.

This is a fully illustrated solution. Numbers in brackets refer to the order in which entries should be made.

(i)   Enter amount prepaid at the beginning of the year (debit side).
(ii) Enter in date order, details of the amounts paid during the current year (debit side).
(iii) Enter details of prepayment at the end of the year, credit side £1,650 divided by 6 = £275 per month; 3 months are prepaid (3 × £275 = £825).

At this point the rates account would look like this:

Rates Account

20-2		£	20-3		£
1 Jul	Prepaid b/d *(i)*	725.00			
8 Oct	Bank ⎫	1,450.00	30 Jun	Prepaid c/d *(iii)*	825.00
20-3	⎬ *(ii)*				
5 Apr	Bank ⎭	1,650.00			

Once the dates and details of all the information given in the question are entered in the account, the amount transferred to the profit and loss account is the difference between the two sides of the account, and the completed rates account would look like this:

Rates Account

20-2		£	20-3		£
1 Jul	Prepaid b/d *(i)*	725.00	30 Jun	Profit and loss	3,000.00
8 Oct	Bank ⎫	1,450.00	30 Jun	Prepaid c/d *(iii)*	825.00
20-3	⎬ *(ii)*				
5 Apr	Bank ⎭	1,650.00			
		3,825.00			3,825.00
1 Jul	Prepaid b/d	825.00			

Example 3

The following information refers to the stationery account in the ledger of M. Whiteley. On 1 May 20-5 there was a stock of stationery valued at £158. During the year the following amounts were paid for stationery, by cheque:

	£
20-5	
8 August	136
4 December	204
20-6	
9 March	192

On 30 April 20-6 there was a stock of stationery valued at £85.

You are required to write up and balance the stationery account for the year ended 30 April 20-6, showing clearly the amount to be transferred to the final accounts and the amount to be carried forward to the next financial year.

This is a fully illustrated solution. Numbers in brackets refer to the order in which entries should be made.

(i)   Enter amount of prepaid stock at the beginning of the year (debit side).
(ii) Enter, in date order, details of the amounts paid during the current year (debit side).
(iii) Enter details of stock prepaid at the end of the year (credit side).

At this point the stationery account would look like this:

Stationery Account

20-5			£	20-6			£
1 May	Balance b/d	(i)	158.00				
8 Aug	Bank		136.00	30 Apr	Balance c/d	(iii)	85.00
4 Dec	Bank		204.00				
20-6		(ii)					
9 Mar	Bank		192.00				

Once the dates and details of all the information given in the question are entered in the account, the amount transferred to the profit and loss account is the difference between the two sides of the account. The completed stationery account would look like this:

Stationery Account

20-5			£	20-6		£
1 May	Balance b/d	(i)	158.00	30 Apr Profit and loss		605.00
8 Aug	Bank		136.00	30 Apr Balance c/d (iii)		85.00
4 Dec	Bank		204.00			
20-6		(ii)				
9 Mar	Bank		192.00			
			690.00			690.00
1 May	Balance b/d		85.00			

Points to remember

- An *accounting period* is the length of time from one set of final accounts to the next. It is normally one year.
- An important rule in accounting is that revenue earned must be *matched* with the expenses that have been incurred during the same accounting period. *Adjustments* are necessary in order to produce an accurate set of final accounts.
- A *prepayment* means that a business has paid in advance for something before fully *using up* that item, or has received payment before providing the benefit. An *accrual* is the accounting term for owing; this means that a business would have outstanding debts, either owed to it, or owed by it.
- As well as ensuring that income and expenses are correctly calculated in the profit and loss account, all assets and liabilities *must* be shown on the balance sheet.
- In examination questions, all details should be entered in *date order*. When an annual cost is stated in the question, for example '*a firm occupies premises at annual rental of £2,000*' the amount transferred to the profit and loss account is *always* the cost for the year.

Assignments

21.1

James Grant runs a small mail order business. On 1 January 20-7 there was £500 owing for rent in respect of the business premises. During the year the following payments were made for rent, by cheque:

```
                    £
20-7
4 January    500
3 April      500
5 July       500
8 October    500
```

On 31 December 20-7 there was £500 owing for rent.

You are required to write up James Grant's rent account for the year ended 31 December 20-7, showing clearly the amount to be transferred to the profit and loss account and the amount to be carried forward to the next financial year.

21.2

The following information refers to the rates account in the ledger of K. Parker. On 1 January 20-7 the rates prepaid were £525. During the year the following payments were made for rates, by cheque:

30 April   £1,150 for the six months ending 30 September 20-7.
 5 October   £1,150 for the six months ending 31 March 20-8.

You are required to prepare K. Parker's rates account for the year ending 31 December 20-7, showing clearly the amount to be transferred to the profit and loss account and the amount to be carried forward to the next financial year.

21.3

The following information is available in respect of the electricity account in the ledger of M. Summers. On 1 July 20-6 there was an unpaid bill for electricity of £287. During the year the following payments were made for electricity, by cheque.

```
                  £
20-6
15 July          287
 8 October       320
20-7
10 January       543
 6 April         590
```

On 30 June 20-7 there was an electricity account outstanding for £350.

You are required to prepare M. Summers' electricity account for the year ending 30 June 20-7, showing clearly the amount to be transferred to the profit and loss account and the amount to be carried forward to the next financial year.

21.4

The following information refers to the packing materials account in the ledger of David Dyson:

	£
On 1 June 20-4 there was a stock of packing materials valued at:	350
Packing materials purchased by cheque, during the year were:	1,275
On 31 May 20-5 stocks of packing materials were valued at:	580

You are required to write up and balance the packing materials account for the year ended 31 May 20-5, showing clearly the amount to be transferred to the final accounts and the amount to be carried forward to the next financial year.

21.5

During the year ended 31 December 20-4, Nigel Giffard paid the following amounts for rent by cheque.

18 January	£686 for the half year ended 31 March 20-4.
10 July	£890 for the half year ended 30 September 20-4.
5 December	£890 for the half year ended 31 March 20-5.

You are required to:

(a) Enter the above information in the rent account of Nigel Giffard.
(b) Balance the rent account at 31 December 20-4, showing clearly the amount to be transferred to the final accounts.

21.6

James Conway commenced trading on 1 January 20-7, on which date he acquired premises at an annual rental of £2,700. On 1 May 20-7 he sublet a section of the premises at an annual rental of £900.

During the year ended 31 December 20-7 the following payments had been made in respect of rent, by cheque:

	£
20-7	
30 March	675
29 June	675
28 September	675

And the following amounts had been received by cheque from the sub-tenant:

	£
20-7	
3 May	225
1 August	225
4 November	225

You are required to write up separate accounts for rent payable and rent received for the financial year ending 31 December 20-7. Balance the accounts and show the relevant transfers to the profit and loss account.

21.7

(i) L. George rents his premises at an annual rental of £10,200. On 1 June 20-3 George had paid his rent up to the end of July, and during the year ended 31 May 20-4 he made the following payments for rent, by cheque:

	£
20-3	
1 August	2,550
5 November	2,550
20-4	
1 February	2,550

(ii) L. George sublets part of his premises to S. Broke at a rent of £2,496 per annum. On 1 June 20-3, Broke's rent was one month in arrears. During the year ended 31 May 20-4, George received the following amounts in cash from Broke:

	£
20-3	
25 July	208
18 August	624
4 December	676
20-4	
9 April	312

(iii) On 1 June 20-3, L. George owed £274 for electricity supplies up to that date. During the year he made the following payments for electricity, by cheque:

	£
20-3	
1 June	274
10 September	282
5 December	304
20-4	
7 April	380

On 31 May 20-4 there was an unpaid bill for electricity of £296.

You are required to:

(a) Write up L. George's rent payable account, rent received account and electricity account for the year ended 31 May 20-4.

(b) Balance the accounts, showing clearly the relevant transfers to the final accounts and any amounts to be carried forward to the next financial year.

21.8

(i) Kite Sportswear rent their premises at an annual rental of £5,712. On 1 May 20-6 they had paid rent up to the end of June 20-6. During the year ended 30 April 20-7, the following payments were made for rent, by cheque.

	£
3 July for the three months ended 30 September 20-6	1,428
2 October for the three months ended 31 December 20-6	1,428
4 January for the three months ended 31 March 20-7	1,428

(ii) On 1 May 20-6, £498 was owing for sundry expenses. During the year, a total of £2,706 was paid by cheque and on 30 April 20-7 £148 was owing for sundry expenses.

(iii) On 1 May 20-6 the rates prepaid were £1,050. During the year the following payments were made for rates, by cheque.

	£
2 October for the six months ended 31 March 20-7	1,248
3 April for the six months ended 30 September 20-7	1,380

(iv) Kite Sportswear have larger premises than they require, and on 1 July 20-6 part of their premises was sublet to Moorland Textiles for an annual rental of £2,976. During the year ended 30 April 20-7, the following amounts were received from Moorland Textiles, by cheque.

	£
3 July for the six months ended 31 December 20-6	1,488
4 January for the six months ended 30 June 20-7	1,488

You are required to:

(a) Write up the ledger accounts for rent, sundry expenses, rates and rent received for the year ended 30 April 20-7.
(b) Balance the accounts, showing clearly the relevant transfers to the final accounts and any amounts to be carried forward to the next financial year.

■ ⊻ 22 Adjustments in trading, profit and loss account and balance sheet

At the end of a financial year, before the final accounts are prepared, a *trial balance* is taken out. A trial balance is a list of all balances remaining in the ledger accounts, including the cash and bank balances from the cash book.

It is normal accounting practice, as illustrated in Chapter 21, for any year-end adjustments to be made in the relevant ledger accounts *before* a trial balance is taken out.

Examination questions often ask for final accounts; that is, a trading, profit and loss account and a balance sheet to be prepared from a given trial balance with notes as to the adjustments. These notes give details of the adjustments that need to be made to the figures *before* the final accounts are prepared. Each adjustment will have *two* effects: one may be in the trading or profit and loss account, and the other on the balance sheet.

This chapter works through a typical examination question with a comprehensive range of adjustments.

Example question

On 31 December 20-7 the following trial balance was extracted from the books of Michael Silverwood:

	DR	CR
	£	£
Debtors	6,480	
Creditors		2,360
Stock (1 January 20-7)	4,340	
Motor vehicle	11,500	
Equipment	6,350	
Rent	2,180	
Wages	9,178	
Rates	565	
Purchases	19,200	
Sales		36,840
Sales returns	450	
Purchase returns		750
Bad debts	142	
Cash at bank	6,250	
Insurance	458	
Sundry expenses	907	
Capital at 1 January 20-7		31,300
Drawings	3,250	
	71,250	71,250

Notes: At 31 December 20-7 the following adjustments had not been made:

(i)   Rates prepaid were £126.
(ii) Included in *sundry expenses* is the cost of stationery. There was a stock of stationery valued at £72.
(iii) Wages accrued were £450.
(iv) Stock at 31 December 20-7 was valued at £5,328.

You are required to:

(a) Prepare a trading, profit and loss account for the year ended 31 December 20-7.
(b) Prepare a balance sheet as at 31 December 20-7.

Remember, each of the additional notes will have two effects: one may be in the trading or profit and loss account, the other on the balance sheet. At this point, most students find it useful to look down the trial balance and label each item with the letters T, P & L or BS (trading account, profit and loss account or balance sheet), according to its destination.

The next stage is to prepare a set of *workings* to assist you. We can now look at each adjustment, in turn.

(i)   Rates prepaid were £126.
      This needs to be deducted from the rates figure given in the trial balance because it represents a payment made in advance, to be used in the next financial year. The amount shown in the profit and loss

account should be the actual cost of rates for the current financial year. The amount prepaid is an asset and must be included on the balance sheet. Your *workings* would look like this:

Profit and loss account entry		*Balance sheet entry*
Rates	565	under *Current assets*
Less prepaid	126	Rates prepaid £126
	439	

(ii) Included in *sundry expenses* is the cost of stationery. On 31 December 20-7 there was a stock of stationery valued at £72.

This needs to be deducted from the sundry expenses figure given in the trial balance because it is a form of prepayment. This stationery stock will be used in the next financial year. It is an asset and must be included on the balance sheet. Your *workings* would look like this:

Profit and loss account entry		*Balance sheet entry*
Sundry expenses	907	under *Current assets*
Less prepaid	72	Stationery stock £72
	835	

(iii) Wages accrued were £450.

This needs to be added to the wages figure given in the trial balance because the expense was incurred during the current financial year but it will not be paid until next year. Your *workings* would look like this:

Profit and loss account entry		*Balance sheet entry*
Wages	9,178	under *Current liabilities*
Add accrued	450	Wages accrued £450
	9,628	

(iv) Stock at 31 December 20-7 was valued at £5,328.

No calculations are needed here, but it is useful to include the closing stock on your preparation list. It is used in the trading account and shown on the balance sheet.

Trading account entry	*Balance sheet entry*
Closing stock £5,328	under *Current assets*
	Closing stock £5,328

Now we shall look at the completed trading, profit and loss account and balance sheet for the year ended 31 December 20-7, first in the previously used horizontal style and then in the more preferred vertical style.

Horizontal presentation

Michael Silverwood
Trading, Profit and Loss Account for the year ended 31 December 20-7

	£		£
Stock	4,340	Sales	36,840
Purchases	19,200	*Less* sales returns	450
	23,540		36,390
Less purchase returns	750		
	22,790		
Less closing stock	5,328		
Cost of goods sold	17,462		
Gross profit c/d	18,928		
	36,390		36,390
Rent	2,180	Gross profit b/d	18,928
Wages (9,178 + 450)	9,628		
Rates (565 – 126)	439		
Bad debts	142		
Insurance	458		
Sundry expenses (907 – 72)	835		
Net profit	5,246		
	18,928		18,928

Balance sheet as at 31 December 20-7

	£	£		£	£
Fixed assets			Capital	31,300	
Equipment	6,350		*Add* net profit	5,246	
Motor vehicle	11,500	17,850		36,546	
			Less drawings	3,250	33,296
Current assets			*Current liabilities*		
Stock	5,328		Creditors	2,360	
Debtors	6,480		Wages accrued	450	2,810
Rates prepaid	126				
Stationery stock	72				
Bank	6,250	18,256			
		36,106			36,106

Vertical presentation

Michael Silverwood
Trading, Profit and Loss Account for the year ended 31 December 20-7

	£	£	£
Sales			36,840
Less sales returns			450
			36,390
Less cost of goods sold:			
Stock		4,340	
Purchases	19,200		
Less purchase returns	750		
		18,450	
		22,790	
Less closing stock		5,328	
			17,462
Gross profit			18,928
Less expenses:			
Rent		2,180	
Wages (9,178 + 450)		9,628	
Rates (565 – 126)		439	
Bad debts		142	
Insurance		458	
Sundry expenses (907 – 72)		835	
			13,682
Net profit			**5,246**

Balance Sheet as at 31 December 20-7

	£	£	£
Fixed assets			
Equipment			6,350
Motor vehicle			11,500
			17,850
Current assets			
Stock	5,328		
Debtors	6,480		
Rates prepaid	126		
Stationery stock	72		
Bank	6,250	18,256	
Less current liabilities			
Creditors	2,360	2,810	
Wages accrued	450		15,446
			33,296
Financed by:			
Capital at 01.01.20-7			31,300
Add Net profit			5,246
			36,546
Less drawings			3,250
			33,296

It can be seen that the figures used are exactly the same using either the horizontal or the vertical methods of display. The vertical presentation is the more modern method preferred by examiners and would probably be more meaningful to people who knew very little about accounting.

Your *workings* for all adjustments should be clearly shown (this is usually an examination requirement). They are also of considerable assistance if difficulties arise in making the balance sheet totals agree; this is often a result of an adjusted item being overlooked or omitted.

When there are several items prepaid, these are usually added together and shown as one figure on the balance sheet, as *prepaid expenses*. Similarly, when there are several items accrued, these are usually added together and shown as one figure on the balance sheet, as *accrued expenses*.

We now look at other types of year-end adjustments.

Depreciation of fixed assets

Adjustments usually have to be made regarding the decrease in value of fixed assets. In Chapter 18 we established that the amount of depreciation charged to the profit and loss account is an *expense*. On the balance sheet, the value of a fixed asset is usually shown at its original cost, less the total amount of depreciation to date.

This is a typical example of a year-end adjustment note:

(i) Depreciation is to be charged on fixtures and fittings at 20 per cent per annum, at cost. (Assume that the figure given in the trial balance for fixtures and fittings at cost is £4,000.)

First, a calculation is required: 20 per cent of £4,000 is £800. The amount charged for depreciation is an expense and is set against the profits of the business in the profit and loss account. The fixed asset is reduced in value by the amount of depreciation charged in each financial year. Your *workings* would look like this:

Profit and loss account entry	*Balance sheet entry*		
Debit entry	under *Fixed assets*		
Depreciation £800	Fixtures & fittings	4,000	
	Less depreciation	800	3,200

Bad debts

These are another type of year-end adjustment. This is a typical example:

(ii) A debtor has been declared bankrupt, and the amount of £250 owing is to be written off as a bad debt. (Assume the figure given in the trial balance for debtors is £6,750.)

A debtor who cannot pay his debt is called a *bad debtor*, and the amount owing is referred to as a *bad debt*. A bad debt is a business *loss*, and must be treated in the same way as other losses and expenses by charging the amount of the bad debt against the profits of the business. On the balance sheet, in order to show a true and fair view of debtors, the amount of the bad debt is deducted from the total debtors. Your *workings* would look like this:

Profit and loss account entry	*Balance sheet entry*		
Debit entry	under *Current assets*		
Bad debts £250	Debtors	6,750	
	Less bad debt	250	6,500

Provision for bad debts

Increasing the provision

Some businesses set aside a certain sum of money to guard against the likelihood of future bad debts. A *provision* is the name given to the sum of money that is set aside. Usually, the provision for bad debts is reviewed each year, and any change since the previous year is then adjusted.

Frequently, year-end adjustments are required relating to the provision for bad debts. This is a typical example where the provision for bad debts is to be increased:

(iii) The provision for bad debts is to be increased to 10 per cent of debtors. (Assume the following figures are given in the trial balance: provision for bad and doubtful debts £250, and debtors £4,500.)

The amount of the provision that already exists is given in the trial balance; in this example it is £250. The adjustment requires this figure to be increased to 10 per cent of the total debtors. Calculations are now required:

	£
10 per cent of £4,500 is	450
Less the existing provision of	250
making an increase of	200

The profit and loss account should be debited with the amount of the *increase*. On the balance sheet, the amount of the provision for bad debts is deducted from the total debtors. Your *workings* would look like this:

Profit and loss account entry	*Balance sheet entry*		
Debit entry	under *Current assets*		
Provision for bad and	Debtors	4,500	
doubtful debts £200	*Less* provision	450	£4,050

Decreasing the provision

This is a typical example where the provision for bad debts is to be decreased:

(iv) The provision for bad debts is to be adjusted to 10 per cent of total debtors. (Assume the following amounts are given in the trial balance: provision for bad debts £500; debtors £4,000.)

The amount of the provision that already exists is given in the trial balance; in this example it is £500. The adjustment requires this figure to be decreased to 10 per cent of the total debtors. Calculations are now required:

	£
Existing provision is	500
10 per cent of £4,000 is	400
making a decrease of	100

When the provision for bad debts is decreased the profit and loss account should be *credited* with the amount of the *difference* between the existing provision and the new provision. On the balance sheet the amount of the provision for bad debts is deducted from the total debtors. Your *workings* would look like this:

Profit and loss account entry		Balance sheet entry		
Credit entry		under *Current assets*		
Reduction in provision for		Debtors	4,000	
bad and doubtful debts £100		*Less* provision	400	£3,600

Drawings

Frequently, year-end adjustments are required concerning the proprietor (owner of the business) and these can be stated in various ways. You will need to study the information given and consider the twofold effect. This is a typical example:

(v) One third of motor expenses for the year is to be regarded as private use. (Assume the following figures are given in the trial balance, motor expenses £1,050, drawings £2,500.)

Calculations are now required: £1,050 ÷ 3 = £350 (one third). Motor expenses will need to be reduced by £350 and drawings will need to be increased by £350. Your *workings* would look like this:

Profit and loss account entry		Balance sheet entry	
	£		£
Motor expenses	1,050	Drawings	2,500
Less private use	350	*Add* private use	350
Motor expenses adjusted	700	Drawings adjusted	2,850

Labour or wages

Under normal circumstances wages and salaries will appear in the profit and loss account. However, a year-end adjustment may require the cost of wages to be apportioned, perhaps a quarter to the trading account and three-quarters to the profit and loss account. In this situation, calculate the respective amounts, then one quarter should be added in the trading account (after the closing stock has been deducted), the remaining three-quarters should be entered in the profit and loss account. *A specific instruction will be given* if any element of labour, wages or any other item of expense is to be apportioned.

Final accounts of non-traders

When final accounts are being prepared for people who are not trading in goods as such – for example, accountants, hairdressers, business consultants and other providers of services, there *will not* be a trading account. This is because goods are not bought and sold. The final accounts for providers of services will consist of a profit and loss account and balance sheet. The profit and loss account will contain all items of revenue received at the credit side and all items of revenue expense at the debit side. The balance sheet will be exactly the same as for traders.

Most of the assignments that follow are taken from past examination papers; they contain many variations of the different types of year-end adjustments. Practice is essential if you are to gain skill and confidence in these important techniques.

Points to remember

- Trading, profit and loss accounts are usually prepared annually at the end of the financial year. Their purpose is to *calculate the profit or loss of a business.*
- *Trading account* calculates gross profit.
- *Profit and loss account* calculates net profit or net loss.
- *Headings* are essential and must clearly state the period of time concerned, usually in the form: 'Trading, profit and loss account for the year ended . . .'
- A *balance sheet* is a financial statement that lists a firm's assets, capital and liabilities at a given moment in time, usually the end of its financial year. It is prepared after the trading, profit and loss account, using the balances that remain.
- Examination questions generally give a series of year-end notes that will usually include prepaid or accrued items. These notes give details of the adjustments that need to be made to the figures *before* the final accounts are prepared. Each adjustment will have *two* effects: one may be in the trading or profit and loss account, the other on the balance sheet.
- Always *take care* when making calculations for adjustments and set out your *workings* clearly.

Assignments

22.1

On 31 December 20-5 the following trial balance was extracted from the books of Richard Martin:

	DR £	CR £
Capital (at 1 January 20-5)		116,148
Land and buildings	98,000	
Motor van (Cost)	25,600	
Motor van (Depreciation)		14,800
Purchases	35,420	
Sales		81,250
Salaries	19,135	
Discount allowed	782	
Discount received		1,648
Debtors	6,290	
Creditors		2,016
Cash	758	
Bank balance	5,092	
Stock at 1 January 20-5	3,870	
Sales and purchase returns	509	724
Insurances	946	
Telephone	584	
Fixtures and fittings	11,800	
Rates	1,650	
Drawings	6,150	
	216,586	216,586

On 31 December 20-5 the following adjustments had not been made:

(i)   Stock of goods was valued at £6,094.
(ii) There was an outstanding telephone bill of £230.
(iii) The annual fire insurance premium of £408 was paid on the due date 1 May 20-5.
(iv) Depreciation is to be charged at 25 per cent on the reducing balance method for the motor van.

You are required to:

(a) Carry out the necessary year-end adjustments stated under the trial balance.
(b) Prepare, in vertical format, a trading, profit and loss account for the year ended 31 December 20-5 and a balance sheet as at that date.

22.2

Marcus Kline is a business consultant. On 31 July 20-6, the following trial balance was extracted from his books:

	DR £	CR £
Premises	92,750	
Office equipment (Cost)	6,280	
Office equipment (Depreciation)		1,884
Advertising	2,196	
Cash	570	
Bank balance	1,862	
General expenses	1,538	
Loan, at 8 per cent per annum		9,500
Drawings	10,070	
Wages	11,824	
Motor vehicle	8,500	
Rent received		3,960
Loan interest	760	
Motor expenses	592	
Capital at 1 August 20-5		94,804
Debtors	1,830	
Commissions received for professional services		28,624
	138,772	138,772

On 31 July 20-6 the following adjustments had not been made:

(i)   There was an outstanding bill of £104 for cleaning expenses to be charged to general expenses.
(ii) Depreciation for the office equipment is to be charged at 15 per cent, using the straight-line method.
(iii) There was an unpaid bill for motor servicing and repairs of £128.
(iv) Part of the premises are sublet at an annual rental of £4,752. On 31 July 20-6 the sub-tenant was two months in arrears.
(v)   General expenses includes the cost of insurance which was £260 prepaid.

You are required to:

(a) Carry out the necessary year-end adjustments stated under the trial balance.
(b) Prepare, in vertical format, a profit and loss account for the year ended 31 July 20-6 and a balance sheet as at that date.

22.3

Kate Devlin extracted the following trial balance from her books on 31 March 20-6:

	DR £	CR £
Motor vehicles	24,750	
Purchases and sales	25,826	59,574
Rent and rates	8,472	
Sundry expenses	2,830	
Capital at 1 April 20-5		41,434
Salaries	10,510	
Wages	6,500	
Bad debts	274	
Provision for bad debts		602
Bank balance		3,196
Cash	862	
Stock at 1 April 20-5	4,070	
Debtors and creditors	13,650	4,282
Drawings	5,930	
Carriage inwards	414	
Equipment (Cost)	9,620	
Equipment (Depreciation)		3,848
Discount allowed and received	506	1,094
Sales and purchase returns	632	816
	114,846	114,846

On 31 March 20-6 the following adjustments had not been made:

(i) Stock of goods was valued at £5,240.
(ii) Provision for bad debts is to be adjusted to 4 per cent of debtors' total.
(iii) Sundry expenses includes the cost of stationery, of which there remained stock valued at £106 and there was an unpaid bill for printing of £128.
(iv) Depreciation is to be charged at 20 per cent for the equipment, using the straight-line method.
(v) A quarter of the wages are to be charged to the trading account and three-quarters to the profit and loss account.
(vi) Kate Devlin rents her premises at an annual rental of £7,824. On 31 March 20-6 the rent had been paid up to 31 May 20-6.

You are required to:

(a) Carry out the necessary year-end adjustments stated under the trial balance.
(b) Prepare, in vertical format, a trading, profit and loss account for the year ended 31 March 20-6 and a balance sheet as at that date.

22.4

On 30 September 20-6 the following trial balance was extracted from the books of Tobias Ainsworth:

	DR £	CR £
Debtors and creditors	16,780	5,904
Bank balance	15,526	
Equipment (Cost)	16,800	
Equipment (Depreciation)		7,560
Stock at 1 October 20-5	7,028	
Salaries	24,794	
Bad debts	372	
Purchases and sales	29,768	69,976
General expenses	1,520	
Rent and rates	10,136	
Vehicle expenses	948	
Bank loan, 10 per cent per annum		12,700
Carriage inwards	624	
Motor vehicles (Cost)	38,500	
Motor vehicles (Depreciation)		13,860
Loan interest	1,270	
Carriage outwards	1,396	
Sales and purchase returns	482	774
Heat and light	2,460	
Drawings	7,180	
Cash	816	
Fixtures and fittings	6,750	
Capital at 1 October 20-5		72,376
	183,150	183,150

On 30 September 20-6 the following adjustments had not been made:

(i) Stock of goods was valued at £6,928.

(ii) Depreciation is to be charged at 15 per cent for equipment, using the straight-line method, and 20 per cent using the reducing balance method for motor vehicles.

(iii) A quarter of the heat and light is to be charged to the trading account and three-quarters to the profit and loss account.

(iv) There was an outstanding bill of £72 for repairs to the photocopier and a stock of stationery valued at £290; to be charged to general expenses.

(v) Vehicle expenses include the cost of annual vehicle licensing of £504, which was paid on 1 August 20-6.

You are required to:

(a) Carry out the necessary year-end adjustments stated under the trial balance.

(b) Prepare, in vertical format, the trading, profit and loss account for the year ended 30 September 20-6 and a balance sheet at that date.

22.5

On 31 October 20-6 the following trial balance was extracted from the books of Helen Robinson:

	DR £	CR £
Premises	150,750	
Motor vehicles (Cost)	24,000	
Motor vehicles (Depreciation)		10,500
Motor expenses	2,016	
Salaries	27,650	
Stock at 1 November 20-5	8,928	
Purchases and sales	30,962	98,630
Insurance	1,204	
Cash	970	
Provision for bad debts		1,626
Bad debts	534	
Debtors and creditors	25,720	9,502
Sundry expenses	1,508	
Drawings	8,360	
Discount allowed and received	492	874
Machinery	20,150	
Loan, at 12 per cent per annum		10,800
Bank balance		5,738
Sales and purchase returns	684	916
Loan interest	972	
Capital at 1 November 20-5		166,314
	304,900	304,900

On 31 October 20-6 the following adjustments had not been made:

(i) Stock of goods was valued at £12,090.
(ii) Provide for carriage on purchases owing of £142.
(iii) The annual fire insurance premium of £648 was paid on 1 February 20-6.
(iv) The provision for bad debts is to be adjusted to 5 per cent of debtors.
(v) Depreciation is to be charged at 25 per cent for the motor vehicles, using the reducing balance method.
(vi) There was three months' interest on the loan outstanding.

You are required to:

(a) Carry out the necessary year-end adjustments stated under the trial balance.
(b) Prepare, in vertical format, a trading, profit and loss account for the year ended 31 October 20-6 and a balance sheet at that date.

22.6

On 31 May 20-7 the following trial balance was extracted from the books of David Towers:

	DR £	CR £
Debtors and creditors	24,850	7,968
Premises	130,280	
Stock at 1 June 20-6	9,056	
Motor vehicles (Cost)	15,200	
Motor vehicles (Depreciation)		6,080
Bank balance	4,768	
Sundry expenses	3,102	
Purchases and sales	29,026	97,954
Cash	972	
Fixtures and fittings (Cost)	8,000	
Fixtures and fittings (Depreciation)		2,220
Carriage inwards	694	
Bank loan, at 8 per cent per annum		10,250
Discount allowed and received	502	970
Carriage outwards	1,850	
Loan interest	820	
Sales and purchase returns	594	836
Drawings	9,070	
Bad debts	358	
Capital at 1 June 20-6		141,020
Salaries	25,850	
Provision for bad debts		702
Rates	3,008	
	268,000	268,000

On 31 May 20-7 the following adjustments had not been made:

(i)   Stock of goods was valued at £10,540.

(ii) Three-quarters of the rates is to be charged to the trading account and a quarter to the profit and loss account.

(iii) The provision for bad debts is to be adjusted to 4 per cent of the debtors' total.

(iv) A cheque for £752 has been paid to a supplier. This had not been entered in the books at the time the trial balance was extracted.

(v)   Depreciation is to be charged at 20 per cent for the motor vehicles, using the straight-line method, and 15 per cent, using the reducing balance method, for the fixtures and fittings.

(vi) There was a stock of packing materials valued at £250 and an outstanding bill for advertising of £97; to be charged to sundry expenses.

You are required to:

(a) Carry out the necessary year-end adjustments stated under the trial balance.
(b) Prepare, in vertical format, a trading, profit and loss account for the year ended 31 May 20-7 and a balance sheet at that date.

22.7

On 30 June 20-8 the following trial balance was extracted from the books of Douglas Van Owen:

	DR £	CR £
Capital at 1 July 20-7		153,328
Purchases and sales	30,124	98,572
Wages	7,500	
Salaries	23,630	
Bank loan at 9 per cent per annum		8,200
General expenses	2,076	
Cash	852	
Bank balance		1,094
Debtors and creditors	25,880	7,390
Motor expenses	1,086	
Equipment (Cost)	7,500	
Equipment (Depreciation)		2,700
Loan interest	738	
Provision for bad debts		1,470
Stock at 1 July 20-7	8,964	
Carriage inwards	512	
Sales and purchase returns	608	956
Bad debts	230	
Motor vehicles (Cost)	20,800	
Motor vehicles (Depreciation)		9,100
Rates	2,472	
Drawings	8,650	
Rent received		4,560
Discount allowed and received	496	1,028
Machinery	5,530	
Premises	140,750	
	288,398	288,398

On 30 June 20-8 the following adjustments had not been made:

(i) Stock of goods was valued at £9,750.
(ii) A third of motor expenses is to be regarded as the owner's private use.
(iii) Depreciation is to be charged at 18 per cent for equipment, using the straight-line method, and 25 per cent, using the reducing balance method, for motor vehicles.

(iv) Rent received in advance was £1,520.
(v) The provision for bad debts is to be adjusted to 5 per cent of debtors' total.
(vi) A quarter of wages is to be charged to the trading account and three-quarters to the profit and loss account.
(vii) Rates prepaid were £854.

You are required to:

(a) Carry out the necessary year-end adjustments stated under the trial balance.
(b) Prepare, in vertical format, a trading, profit and loss account for the year ended 30 June 20-8 and a balance sheet at that date.

22.8
On 30 September 20-9 the following trial balance was extracted from the books of William McKay:

	DR £	CR £
Premises	138,250	
Capital at 1 October 20-8		140,024
Debtors and creditors	23,272	10,358
Salaries	21,426	
Machinery (Cost)	6,200	
Machinery (Depreciation)		1,860
Wages	5,738	
Purchases and sales	29,694	94,896
Vehicle expenses	1,072	
Carriage inwards	368	
Discount allowed and received	416	926
General expenses	1,115	
Electricity	1,392	
Motor van (Cost)	14,500	
Motor van (Depreciation)		5,220
Stock at 1 October 20-8	7,852	
Loan, at 9 per cent per annum		9,600
Bank balance	2,090	
Loan interest	864	
Cash	716	
Sales and purchase returns	572	814
Equipment	6,930	
Bad debts	225	
Provision for bad debts		1,094
Drawings	7,050	
Rent received		4,950
	269,742	269,742

On 30 September 20-9 the following adjustments had not been made:

(i)   Stock of goods was valued at £6,994.
(ii) James Logan, who owes the firm £372, has been declared bankrupt. £38 has been received by cheque, the remainder is to be written off and, after this has been done, the bad debt provision is to be adjusted to 6 per cent of debtors' total.
(iii) Vehicle expenses include the annual cost of £504 for motor insurance, which was paid on 1 March 20-9.
(iv) Depreciation is to be charged at 20 per cent for the motor van, using the reducing balance method, and 10 per cent, using the straight-line method, for machinery.
(v)   Wages includes £350 taken by the owner. There was an outstanding bill for repairs to the motor van of £294.
(vi) A third of the electricity is to be charged to the trading account and two-thirds to the profit and loss account.

You are required to:

(a) Carry out the necessary year-end adjustments stated under the trial balance.
(b) Prepare, in vertical format, a trading, profit and loss account for the year ended 30 September 20-9 and a balance sheet at that date.

◼ ▼ **23** The journal

This is often known as the *journal proper,* the word *journal* being the French word for day book. As we have already seen in earlier chapters, most transactions are first entered in one of the following books of original entry, before being posted to the ledger:

- Sales day book:
- Purchases day book
- Sales returns day book
- Purchase returns day book
- Cash book

These books have grouped together all similar transactions to reduce the number of entries that need to be made in the ledger. The *cash book* is considered to be a book of original entry because entries are made in it directly from documents such as cheques.

At one time, all business transactions were first entered in the journal proper before being entered in the ledger, but today the journal is used only to record transactions that cannot be entered into any of the other books of original entry. Each entry in the journal will contain:

- The date
- The name of the account(s) to be debited and the amount(s)
- The name of the account(s) to be credited and the amount(s)
- A description of the transaction (this is called the *narration* or *narrative*)

This is an illustration of the standard layout of the journal proper:

The journal

Date	Details	Folio	DR	CR
	Name of account to be debited Name of account to be credited Narration			

These are some of the main uses of the journal proper:

- The purchase and sale of fixed assets on credit
- The correction of errors

- Opening entries – these are needed to open a new set of books
- Transfers between accounts
- Writing off bad debts

It is important to remember that the journal is *not* a double entry account. It is a type of diary where a record is kept of special transactions that are not everyday occurrences and will require an explanation. Details are recorded in the journal *before* being posted to the double entry accounts.

All that is necessary to do a journal entry is to think of the *double entry*. You must determine what entries need to be made on the basis of the information provided. When you have considered the information and decided which accounts to debit and credit you record them in the journal and write a short explanation called a *narration*. We can now look at some uses of the journal.

Purchase and sale of fixed assets on credit

This is a typical example. On 1 March 20-9, Daniel Mason purchased new office furniture costing £680 on credit from Jenkins Supplies.

What will the journal entry be? Clearly, the account that has received value is the office furniture account (debit the receiver). Jenkins Supplies, which has not yet been paid, will be credited (credit the giver), and the journal entry would look like this:

The journal

Date	Details	Folio	DR	CR
1 Mar	Office furniture account Jenkins Supplies account *Purchase on credit of new office furniture*	NL1 PL8	680.00	680.00

Journal entries cover many different types of transactions. To separate each entry, a line is drawn underneath. When we post this entry to the ledger accounts we use the folio numbers as a reminder where to find the entry if we need to check it. The double entry accounts would look like this:

Office Furniture Account   NL1

20-9			£	
1 Mar	Jenkins Supplies	NL1	680.00	

Jenkins Supplies Account PL8

	20-9		£
	1 Mar Office furniture	J1	680.00

Now we can look at the sale of a fixed asset on credit. On 15 May 20-9 the old delivery van was sold for £2,200 on credit to B. Robson.

What will the journal entry be? Clearly, B. Robson has received the value (debit the receiver). The delivery van account will be credited (credit the giver), and the journal entry would look like this:

The journal

Date	Details	Folio	DR	CR
15 May	B. Robson account		2,200.00	
	Delivery van account			2,200.00
	Sale on credit of used delivery van			
	Registration No. MDN 34			

As part of the narration, it is good practice to record identification numbers, such as the serial number or registration number. This additional information is very useful for reference purposes.

Correction of errors

It is inevitable that errors will occur, but alterations and erasures should not be made in the ledger. When an error is discovered, the correction is made first by preparing a journal entry, then by posting to the double entry accounts. When correcting errors there is no simple rule; you will need to consider the error and then decide what action is required to make the correction. Let us look at some typical examples.

On 1 June 20-9 we discover that goods sold on credit to M. Cook costing £236.50 had been entered in error in M. Cookson's account.

To correct this error we must remove the £236.50 from M Cookson's account and enter it where it really belongs, in M. Cook's account. The journal entry would look like this:

The journal

Date	Details	Folio	DR	CR
1 June	M. Cook account		236.50	
	M. Cookson account			236.50
	Correction of error, posted to			
	incorrect personal account			

And the ledger accounts would look like this:

M. Cook Account

20-9		£			
1 Jun	Sales	236.50			

M. Cookson Account

20-9		£	20-9		£
1 Jun	Sales	236.50	1 Jun	M. Cook	236.50

Now look at another example of an error in posting. On 15 June 20-9 a payment of £250 for rent had been entered in error in the rates account.

To correct this error we must remove the £250.00 from the rates account and enter it where it really belongs, in the rent account. The journal entry would look like this:

The journal

Date	Details	Folio	DR	CR
15 June	Rent account		250.00	
	Rates account			250.00
	Correction of error, posted to incorrect expense account			

Opening entries

An *opening journal entry* is required when a business is first established or when opening a new set of books using the double entry system. Here is a typical example:

John Clayton has been in business for some time without keeping proper records. On 1 March 20-7 he establishes that his assets and liabilities are as follows:

Assets	Cash in hand £325, cash at bank £3,862, office equipment £750, motor van £4,600, stock of goods £3,500 Debtors: J. Lister £763, K. Turner £450.
Liabilities	Creditors: B. Freeman £670, F. Brooks £580.

To prepare an opening journal entry we must always calculate the capital. The formula is:

Assets *less* Liabilities = Capital

Assets   £325 + £3,862 + £750 + £4,600 + £3,500 + £763 + £450 = £14,250

Liabilities   £670 + £580 = £1,250

	£
Assets total	14,250
Less Liabilities	1,250
Capital =	13,000

We can now prepare the opening journal entry:

The journal

Date	Details	Folio	DR	CR
20-7 1 Mar	Cash in hand	CB	325.00	
	Cash at bank	CB	3,862.00	
	Office equipment	NL	750.00	
	Motor van	NL	4,600.00	
	Stock	NL	3,500.00	
	Debtors: J. Lister	SL	763.00	
	K. Turner	SL	450.00	
	Creditors: B. Freeman	PL		670.00
	F. Brooks	PL		580.00
	Capital			13,000.00
			14,250.00	14,250.00
	Being the assets and liabilities at this date, entered to open the books			

An opening journal entry is a summary of the financial position. It is a permanent record to which reference can be made at any time. The next stage is to open the double entry accounts in the ledgers. Each asset is shown as a debit balance, and each liability and capital is shown as a credit balance. When the opening journal entry is posted, the ledger accounts would look like this:

Cash book

Date	Particulars	F	Cash	Bank	Date	Particulars	F	Cash	Bank
20-7 1 Mar	Balance b/d	J	325.00						
1 Mar	Balance b/d	J		3,862.00					

Nominal ledger

Office Equipment Account

20-7			£			
1 Mar	Balance b/d	J	750.00			

Motor Van Account

20-7			£			
1 Mar	Balance b/d	J	4,600.00			

Stock Account

20-7			£			
1 Mar	Balance b/d	J	3,500.00			

Capital Account

				20-7			£
				1 Mar	Balance b/d	J	13,000.00

Sales ledger

J. Lister Account

20-7			£			
1 Mar	Balance b/d	J	763.00			

K. Turner Account

20-7			£			
1 Mar	Balance b/d	J	450.00			

Purchase ledger

B. Freeman Account

				20-7			£
				1 Mar	Balance b/d	J	670.00

F. Brooks Account

	20-7			£
	1 Mar Balance b/d	J		580.00

As each item is entered in the ledger the folio column is completed. All the accounts are then ready for future transactions to be recorded.

Transfers between accounts

There are many types of transfers between accounts and it is impossible to give a complete list. Whenever a transfer is necessary, a preliminary record is first made in the journal, with a narration explaining the reasons, and then posted to the ledger accounts. This is a typical example. On 17 June 20-7 it was discovered that a garage bill of £250 for stereo equipment fitted to the owner's private car had been entered in the motor expenses account, but should have been charged to drawings. What will the journal entry be? Clearly, we must make a debit entry of £250.00 in the drawings account, where it really belongs, and remove £250.00 from the motor expenses account by making a credit entry. The journal entry would look like this:

The journal

Date	Details	Folio	DR	CR
20-7 17 June	Drawings account Motor expenses account *Owner's private motor expenses* *transferred to drawings account*		250.00	250.00

Bad debts written off

A debtor who cannot or will not pay his debts is known as a *bad debtor*, and the amount owing is referred to as a *bad debt*. Once it is discovered that a debt is never going to be collected, the account can no longer be regarded as an asset to the business.

Usually, many attempts will have been made to recover the outstanding amount. However, regardless of the circumstances, if a debtor cannot pay what is owed it is treated as a business loss.

Here is a typical example: Charles Bentley is a debtor for the sum of £295. On 31 July 20-7 he is declared bankrupt and the amount owing is written off as a bad debt. To write off this debt, a debit entry is made in the bad debts account, and a credit entry in Charles Bentley's account. A preliminary record is first made in the journal, like this:

The journal

Date	Details	Folio	DR	CR
20-7 31 July	Bad debts account Charles Bentley account *Irrecoverable debt written off*		295.00	295.00

A debt that is partially bad

Sometimes, a debtor comes to an arrangement to repay only part of the debt. In these circumstances the money received would be debited in the bank or cash account, and the unpaid portion would be written off to the bad debts account. Here is a typical example of a debt that is partially bad: Brian Forbes, who owes the firm £268, has been declared bankrupt. On 20 August 20-7 a cheque for 50 pence in the pound of the amount owed is received, in full settlement of the debt. The remainder is to be written off as a bad debt.

A preliminary record is first made in the journal, like this:

The journal

Date	Details	Folio	DR	CR
20-7 20 Aug	Bank account Bad debts account Brian Forbes account *Fifty pence in the pound received* *in final settlement of debt, balance* *irrecoverable*		134.00 134.00	268.00

Points to remember

- Today the *journal proper* is used only to record transactions that cannot be entered into any of the other books of original entry. Details are recorded in the journal *before* being posted to the double entry accounts.
- To prepare a journal entry, you need to think of the *double entry*. First decide what entries need to be made on the basis of the information provided; then make the journal entry and write a short explanation, which is known as a *narration*.

Assignments

23.1

A. Teagle owns a hardware shop. During February 20-3, the following transactions took place:

Feb   4   A. Teagle purchased some new shop fittings costing £8,600 on credit from Arthur Blake

      15   Peter Payne bought some old shop fittings from A. Teagle at an agreed price of £400, payable on 1 April 20-3

      18   Simon Bates owed A. Teagle £51. The debt had been outstanding for ten months and Teagle decided to treat this as a bad debt

      29   Goods purchased on credit from Henry Jones costing £210 had been incorrectly posted to the account of Harry Albert Jones

You are required to prepare journal entries, including narrations to record the above items.

23.2

Elaine Patterson owns a small business. During the month of June 20-3 the following transactions took place:

Jun   3   Purchased on credit new office furniture costing £4,500 from Crescent Furniture Ltd

      7   Philip Richards' account of £470 was written off as a bad debt

      9   Goods sold on credit to John Belling costing £150 had been posted to John Bell's account

      10   Sold old motor van for £70 on credit to Car Trader

You are required to prepare journal entries, including narrations, to record the above items.

23.3

(a) Percy Green had been in business for several years and had not kept proper records. His new financial year began on 1 May 20-7 and he decided to convert his accounts to a full double entry system. He establishes that his assets and liabilities are as follows:

	£
Freehold premises	32,000
Motor van	2,600
Fixtures	1,800
Stock	6,400
Bank and cash	2,965
Debtors: T. Ross	90
A. Baker	64
T. Bone	128
Long term loan at 10 per cent per annum	10,000
Creditors: T. Black	271
D. Bacon	194
Rates prepaid	42
Interest on loan outstanding	1,100

You are required to prepare the journal entry necessary to open the books, clearly showing the amount of his capital.

(b) During the month of May 20-7 the following transactions took place.

May 6 Purchased on credit new fixtures costing £950 from Micawber & Sons

8 Some of the fittings, costing £60, were returned to Micawber & Sons because they were unsuitable

12 Percy Green was notified that A. Baker had been declared bankrupt; his account of £64 was written off as a bad debt

22 Some of the fixtures that had been purchased from Micawber & Sons, costing £90, were found to be surplus to requirements and were sold to Gatt & Co. on credit

29 Goods sold on credit to T. Davies, costing £130, had been posted to T. Davis's account

You are required to prepare journal entries, with narrations, to record the above transactions.

23.4
George Jones is the owner of a small business. During the month of May 20-6 the following transactions took place:

May 7 £40 paid for rent had been entered in error in the rates account

16 A motor van costing £2,400, bought for use in the business, had been entered in the purchases account

18 An amount of £250 received from John Boon had been credited to Tom Boon's account

22 Cash sales of £205 had been entered in the cash book and posted to the ledger as £250

You are required to prepare journal entries, with narrations, to record the above transactions.

23.5

(a) David Robson runs a small business. He has not previously kept a correct set of books but now wishes to start a double entry system from 1 February 20-7. On 1 February 20-7 he had the following assets and liabilities:

	£
Stock	5,950
Equipment	7,350
Bank overdraft	2,738
Insurance prepaid	962
Motor vehicles	18,500
Rent owing	358
Debtors	6,898
Creditors	3,094
Cash	160

You are required to write up David Robson's opening journal entry showing clearly the amount of his capital.

(b) At the end of February the following matters were discovered:
  (i) Goods costing £350 purchased on credit from T. Marsland had been posted to T. Marsden's account.
  (ii) F. Ryder, who owes the firm £475, has been declared bankrupt. A cheque for 20 per cent of the amount owed has been received in full and final settlement of the debt. The remainder is to be written off as a bad debt.
  (iii) David Robson had taken goods costing £176 and £150 in cash for his own use, but no entry had been made in the books.
  (iv) B. Clifton had taken £65 cash discount to which he was not entitled. This had been entered in both the customer's and the discount account.
  (v) A payment made to D. Anderson of £395 had been entered at the debit side of the bank account and the credit side of D. Anderson's account.

You are required to draft the journal entries, including narrations, to record items (i)–(v).

23.6

(a) On 1 May 20-7, Tony Simms had the following assets and liabilities:

	£
Freehold land and buildings	125,000
Fixtures and fittings	4,250
Motor vehicle	2,000
Stock	7,640
Bank and cash	3,580
Debtors	4,500
Long term loan	11,200
Creditors	2,390
Electricity account outstanding	460

You are required to prepare an opening journal entry for Tony Simms showing his capital as at 1 May 20-7.

(b) During the month of May the following transactions took place.

May 7 Tony Simms purchased a new van costing £14,750 from Better Motors, paying £2,000 cash and being given credit for the remainder

14 Tony Simms sold on credit to A. Baker fixtures and fittings that the business no longer required, value £250

18 Notification was received that J. Smith, a debtor for £194, had been declared bankrupt. It was decided to write off this account as a bad debt

21 It was discovered that a purchase of goods on credit from T. Murphy, value £125, had been debited to Murphy's account and credited to sales

You are required to prepare journal entries, including narrations, to record the above transactions.

23.7

(a) John Jennings is the owner of a small engineering firm. During October the following transactions took place:

Oct 3 New office equipment was purchased from Mega Systems, consisting of 2 computers at £1,950 each, 2 printers at £395 each and a photocopier at £2,470, all less 12.5% trade discount. Twenty-five per cent was paid by cheque, with the remainder on credit.

10 I. Hardrup, who owes the firm £603.50, has been declared bankrupt. A cheque for 20p in the pound of the amount owed has been received in full and final settlement of the debt. The remainder is to be written off as a bad debt.

15 A delivery van has been sold for book value of £1,950 to R. Groves on credit. A cheque for one third of the cost has been received, and the balance is to be paid on 15 December 20-1.

You are required to show journal entries, with narrations, to record the above transactions.

(b) His accounts were reviewed on 31 October and the following errors were discovered:

    (i) A cash payment of £143 to M. Dyson had been entered in the cash book and posted to the ledger as £341.

    (ii) Goods bought on credit from T. Clark costing £390 had been entered in J. Clarkson's account.

You are required to show journal entries, with narrations, to record items (i) and (ii).

(c) John Jennings' financial year ends on 31 October. From the balances given below prepare the closing journal entries to transfer the figures to the final accounts.

General expenses   £2,074
Carriage inwards   £652
Discount allowed   £890

■ ☑ **24** Errors not affecting trial balance agreement

Taking out a *trial balance* is a way of checking the bookkeeping. A trial balance that agrees indicates that for every debit entry there has been a corresponding credit entry, but it does *not* prove that no errors have been made. A trial balance has limitations, and for this reason it is only considered to be a prima facie proof of accuracy. Prima facie means 'at first sight'. There are six types of error that will not affect the agreement of the trial balance:

1 Original errors
2 Errors of omission
3 Errors of commission
4 Errors of principle
5 Compensating errors
6 Complete reversal of entries.

Original errors

These happen when the original document is incorrect, therefore the bookkeeping entries made from that document will also be incorrect: for example, if an error was made in the calculation of a sales invoice and double entry was carried out using the incorrect figure.

More often, these errors occur when copying figures from original documents, such as invoices or credit notes, into the day books. For example, if an invoice for £459 received from James Cartwright, a supplier, is entered in the supplier's account and the purchases account as £495, the trial balance would still agree, and would not show that this error has been made.

When correcting errors, there is no simple rule; you will need to consider the error and then decide what action is required to make the correction.

When an error is discovered, the correction is made, first by preparing a journal entry, then by posting to the double entry accounts.

We can now look at this example: the amount posted to the double entry accounts was greater than the correct amount, the original invoice of £459 was entered in the accounts as £495. First, we must calculate the amount involved (£495 – £459 = £36). This is the amount needed to correct the error. A debit entry of £36 in the supplier's account will make the necessary reduction, with a corresponding credit entry in the purchases account. The journal entry would look like this:

The journal

Date	Details	Folio	DR	CR
8 Mar	James Cartwright account Purchases account *Correction of error, purchase invoice of £459 posted as £495*		36.00	36.00

Errors of omission

As the name suggests, these are transactions that have been omitted completely from the books. Sometimes a document is mislaid before it is even entered into the books, and neither the debit or credit entry is made in the ledger so the trial balance would still agree. This is a typical example: an invoice dated 4 April for £499 received from Office Supplies for a new printer had been mislaid and not entered in the accounts. These types of errors are probably the easiest to correct, because all you need to consider is the double entry. Clearly, the account that has received value is the office equipment account (debit the receiver), and Office Supplies, who has not yet been paid, will be credited (credit the giver). When an error is discovered, the correction is made, first by preparing a journal entry then by posting to the double entry accounts. The journal entry for this example would look like this:

The journal

Date	Details	Folio	DR	CR
4 Apr	Office equipment account Office Supplies account *Correction of omission, invoice for new printer omitted from the books*		499.00	499.00

Errors of commission

The word *commission* means *authority to take action*, so an error of commission is one where the action taken is incorrect. *Errors of commission* happen when both the debit and credit entries are made but a wrong account is used. Frequently, this type of error occurs when two debtors or creditors have the same or similar names. It is quite easy to post a debt to the wrong account. This is a typical example: on 7 May, goods sold on credit to C. Green costing £285.60 had been posted to C. Greenway's account. The trial balance would still agree because the total debtors would be correct, and it cannot distinguish between these two debtors. The error would probably be discovered when C. Greenway was asked to pay for goods he had neither ordered nor received.

When an error is discovered, the correction is made first by preparing a journal entry, then by posting to the double entry accounts.

To correct this error, a debit entry is needed in C. Green's account (debit the receiver). C. Greenway's account will be credited to remove the amount posted in error. The journal entry would look like this:

The journal

Date	Details	Folio	DR	CR
7 May	C. Green account		285.60	
	C. Greenway account			285.60
	Correction of error, posted to incorrect personal account			

Errors of principle

This type of error occurs when a transaction is entered in the wrong type of account. It is a common mistake when purchasing assets to treat them as purchases of goods and include them in the purchases account. However, this type of error has a serious effect on the profits of a business. The trial balance would still agree, but the assets figure would be less than it should be and the purchases figure would be too large. This is a typical example: on 17 June, some new office furniture costing £950 was purchased on credit from New Systems Ltd, and this had been debited in error to the purchases account. One of the entries is wrong in principle but the trial balance would still agree and would not reveal the error.

When an error is discovered, the correction is made first by preparing a journal entry, then by posting to the double entry accounts. To correct this error, a debit entry is needed in the office furniture account, and a credit entry in the purchases account will remove the amount posted in error. The journal entry would look like this:

The journal

Date	Details	Folio	DR	CR
17 Jun	Office furniture account		950.00	
	Purchases account			950.00
	Correction of error, new office furniture posted to purchases account			

Compensating errors

These are errors that cancel each other out. They happen when two separate errors of the same amount have been made, one affecting the debit column and the other affecting the credit column. The trial balance would still agree, the debit column and the credit column would be incorrect by the same amount, but the errors would cancel each other out.

These are often addition errors; for example, if the sales day book is overcast by £100 and the purchases day book is overcast by the same amount, the trial balance would still agree. The extra £100 in the sales account (credit column) will have been compensated by the extra £100 in the purchases account (debit column). Details of the correction would first be entered in the journal and then posted to the double entry accounts. To correct this error, we need a debit entry to reduce the sales account by £100 and a credit entry to reduce the purchases account by £100. The journal entry would look like this:

The journal

Date	Details	Folio	DR	CR
30 Jun	Sales account Purchases account *Correction of compensating errors,* *totals of sales and purchases day* *books incorrectly totalled*		100.00	100.00

Complete reversal of entries

These errors occur when the entries for a transaction are reversed, and the account that should have been debited is credited and vice versa. The correct amounts are entered in the correct accounts, but the entries are made at the wrong side of each account.

This is a typical example: a cheque of £450 paid to D. Mason, a supplier, was entered at the debit side of the bank account and the credit side of the supplier's account; the trial balance would still agree, because a debit and credit entry for the same amount had been made.

These errors are more difficult to correct, as it is not simply a matter of reversing the incorrect entries. To correct these errors, *double* the amount is needed. Entering only the original amount would merely cancel out the error, leaving no entry of the transaction.

To correct this error, we need a debit entry of £900 in D. Mason's account and a credit entry of £900 in the bank account. The journal entry would look like this:

The journal

Date	Details	Folio	DR	CR
3 Aug	D. Mason account		900.00	
	Bank account			900.00
	Correction of error, payment by cheque of £450 was entered at debit side of bank and credit side of D. Mason's account			

Points to remember

- Errors can occur in many different ways, and *correcting errors* depends on a clear understanding of the double entry system. You will need to *consider the error* and then decide what action is required to make the correction.
- When an error is discovered, the correction is made first by *preparing a journal entry*, then by *posting to the double entry accounts*.
- *Casting* is a term that is often used, to cast means to add up.
- *Overcasting* means adding up a column of figures incorrectly to give an answer that is *greater* than it should be.
- *Undercasting* means adding up a column of figures incorrectly to give an answer that is *less* than it should be.

Assignments

24.1
(a) Explain why a trial balance which agrees is not conclusive proof of the complete accuracy of the accounts.
(b) State three types of errors that will not affect the trial balance agreement.

24.2
(a) To what extent is the agreement of the trial balance proof of accuracy of the books? How would the omission of:

　(i)　the opening stock; and
　(ii)　the closing stock

　affect the trial balance?
(b) State the initial steps you would take to locate the error if the trial balance disagreed.

24.3

On 31 March 20-4 the following balances appeared in the ledger of Terry Dennis:

	£
Drawings	1,600
Rent and rates	350
Stock, 1 April 20-3	5,500
Bank overdraft	750
Wages	8,000
Petty cash	60
Creditor for office equipment	1,600
Selling expenses	3,100
Purchases	11,206
Trade creditors	2,746
Carriage outwards	410
Sales	26,532
Office expenses	4,730
Trade debtors	2,650
Commission received	520
Furniture and equipment	19,600
Discount allowed	428
Capital	?

You are required to:

(a) Prepare a trial balance as at 31 March 20-4 and calculate the capital account balance.
(b) State the procedures you would adopt if the trial balance does not agree.
(c) Certain types of error can occur even though the trial balance agrees. Name and describe *three* types of such errors.

24.4

Andrew Scott is a retailer selling newspapers and confectionery. On 28 February 20-8 the following trial balance was extracted from his books:

	£	£
Capital		40,100
Drawings	5,000	
Rent and rates	2,500	
Lighting and heating	2,400	
Advertising	220	
Motor expenses	1,200	
Wages and salaries	8,500	
Insurance	500	
Purchases	26,100	
Sales		55,320
Creditors		2,500
Motor vehicles	15,000	
Equipment	20,000	
Stock of goods: 1 March 20-7	12,000	
Cash in hand	100	
Cash at bank	4,400	
	97,920	97,920

After preparation of the trial balance the following errors were discovered.

(i) 15 Jun A payment of £200 by cheque to D. Smith, a creditor, had been debited to the account of D. Smithson.

(ii) 13 Aug An invoice for the purchase of sweets and confectionery for £340 from R. Wallis and Co. had not been entered in the books.

(iii) 24 Sep A payment for repairs to the motor vehicles of £500 had been entered in the motor vehicles account.

(iv) 30 Oct Andrew Scott had bought petrol for his own use costing £200. This had been entered in the motor expenses account.

You are required to:

(a) Prepare journal entries to correct these errors.
(b) Rewrite the trial balance *after* the errors have been corrected.

24.5

After a year's trading, the following balances appeared in the ledger of Nicholas Davidson on 31 May 20-6.

	£
Stock	2,025
Drawings	1,396
Carriage outwards	194
Wages and salaries	16,830
Discount allowed	103
Creditors	2,405
General expenses	810
Purchases	10,092
Bad debts	158
Sales	14,580
Sales returns	175
Debtors	3,890
Discount received	369
Premises	38,500
Purchase returns	238
Petty cash	82
Cash at bank	1,837
Capital	?

A short time later the following information was discovered:

(i)   Nicholas Davidson's private motor expenses had been entered in general expenses. These are estimated to be 20 per cent of the general expenses.

(ii) A. Slowman, who owes the firm £240, has been declared bankrupt. A cheque for 15 per cent of the amount owed is received in full and final settlement of the debt. The remainder is to be written off as a bad debt.

(iii) An invoice for £158 received from M. Ramsden, a supplier, had not been entered in the books.

(iv) Goods bought on credit from F. Greenwood costing £350 had been posted incorrectly to the account of T. Greenfield.

You are required to:

(a)   Prepare journal entries to record items (i) to (iv). Full narrations are required.

(b)   After considering the above information, prepare a trial balance as at 31 May 20-6 and calculate the capital account balance.

(c)   Show clearly the correct date against the stock item in your trial balance.

24.6

You work in the accounts department of Moortown Enterprises. On 30 April 20-9, the following balances appeared in the ledger:

	£
Stock	3,095
Carriage outwards	249
Drawings	2,586
Discount allowed	403
Creditors	5,409
Sundry expenses	1,608
Purchases	11,928
Bad debts	685
Sales	18,470
Sales returns	430
Debtors	8,750
Discount received	682
Rates	1,206
Premises	68,500
Purchase returns	964
Bank overdraft	3,145
Petty cash	220
Wages and salaries	16,260
Capital	?

A short time later the following information was discovered:

(i) The bank statement showed that a payment for rates of £850 had been made by direct debit, but no entry had been made in the accounts.

(ii) D. Myers, who owes the firm £480, has been declared bankrupt. A cheque for 15 per cent of the amount owed is received, in full and final settlement of the debt. The remainder is to be written off as a bad debt.

(iii) Goods bought on credit from K. Williams costing £578 had been posted incorrectly to K. Williamson's account.

(iv) An invoice for £202 received from A. Oldridge had not been entered in the books.

(v) A payment of £253 for repairs to the owner's private car had been entered in sundry expenses.

You are required to:

(a) Show journal entries to record items (i) to (v). Full narrations are required.

(b) After considering the above information, prepare a trial balance as at 30 April 20-9 and calculate the capital account balance.

24.7

You work in the accounts department of Weetwood Enterprises. On 31 May 20-9, the following balances appeared in the ledger:

	£
Purchases	11,026
Creditors	3,862
Stock	3,252
Purchase returns	493
Discount received	495
Sales returns	364
Bad debts	315
Petty cash	183
Debtors	6,396
Commission received	780
Carriage outwards	574
Discount allowed	402
Equipment	18,750
Carriage inwards	369
Drawings	2,040
Wages and salaries	16,865
General expenses	840
Sales	15,480
Bank balance	1,364
Capital	?

A short time later the following information was discovered:

(i) A credit note for £76 received from R. Foxwood had not been entered in the books.

(ii) Goods bought on credit from M. Kellerman costing £485 had been posted incorrectly to the account of M. Keller.

(iii) C. Gulliver, who owes the firm £360, has been declared bankrupt. A cheque for 15 per cent of the amount owed is received, in full and final settlement of the debt. The remainder is to be written off as a bad debt.

(iv) The owner's private motor expenses had been entered in general expenses. These are estimated to be 12.5 per cent.

(v) A customer, G. Sanderson, had deducted £18 discount to which he was not entitled. This had been entered in the customer's account and the discount account.

You are required to:

(a) Prepare journal entries to record items (i) to (v). Full narrations are required.

(b) After considering the above information, prepare a trial balance as at 31 May 20-9 and calculate the capital account balance.

◼ ᴍ **25** Suspense accounts

Errors in the trial balance

In the previous chapter we looked at errors that did not affect the agreement of the trial balance. However, there are some errors that will mean that the trial balance totals will not be the same.

We should always try to find errors immediately when the trial balance totals do not agree with each other. When we are unable to find the errors, the trial balance totals are made to agree with each other by inserting the amount of the difference between the two sides in a *suspense account*. As the name implies, this is an account that is in suspense, a temporary measure waiting until we decide what to do with it. The suspense account is a constant reminder that there are some undiscovered errors in the books.

A suspense account can have a balance on either side – whatever is necessary to make the trial balance totals agree with each other. This is a typical example:

Trial Balance as at 30 September 20–5

	DR	CR
	£	£
Totals when all accounts have been listed	95,000	94,800
Suspense account		200
	95,000	95,000

To make the two totals agree, a figure of £200 for the suspense account has been shown on the credit side. A suspense account is opened and the £200 difference is entered at the credit side, like this:

Suspense Account

		20–5		£
		30 Sep	Difference in trial balance	200

Correction of errors

When errors are found they must be corrected, observing the rules of double entry. Each correction must first have an entry in the journal describing what has happened; it is then posted to the accounts concerned.

Now assume that the error of £200 shown on the 30 September 20–5 trial balance is found at the end of October. It was discovered that the sales account was incorrectly calculated, being undercast by £200. The action to be taken is:

(i) prepare the journal entry:

The journal

Date	Details	Folio	DR	CR
30 Oct	Suspense account		200.00	
	Sales account			200.00
	Correction of error, sales account was undercast by £200 in September 20–5			

(ii) Post to the relevant accounts. The suspense account is debited, like this:

Suspense Account

20–5		£	20–5		£
31 Oct	Sales	200	30 Sep	Difference in trial balance	200

And the sales account is credited, like this:

Sales Account

			20–5		£
			31 Oct	Suspense	200

We can now look at an example where the suspense account difference was caused by more than one error.

Trial Balance as at 31 October 20–5

	DR £	CR £
Totals when all accounts have been listed	89,104	89,500
Suspense account	396	
	89,500	89,500

To make the totals agree, a figure of £396 for the suspense account has been entered at the debit side, a suspense account opened and the £396 difference is entered at the debit side, like this:

Suspense Account

20–5		£	
31 Oct	Difference in trial balance	396	

During the month of November the following errors were discovered:

(a) A cheque of £346 paid to T. McCarthy had been correctly entered in the cash book but had not been entered in T. McCarthy's account.
(b) In October, the purchase returns day book had been totalled incorrectly, being overcast by £50.

First we need to prepare the journal entries:

The journal

Date	Details	Folio	DR	CR
30 Nov (a)	T. McCarthy account		346.00	
	Suspense account			346.00
	Correction of error, payment omitted from T. McCarthy's account			
30 Nov (b)	Purchase returns account		50.00	
	Suspense Account			50.00
	Correction of £50 overcast in purchase returns day book in October			

Now we need to post to the accounts concerned. A debit entry in T. McCarthy's account, like this:

(a)

T. McCarthy Account

20–5		£	20–5		£
30 Nov	Bank	346	30 Nov	Balance b/d	346

And a credit entry in the Suspense account, like this:

Suspense Account

20–5		£	20–5		£
31 Oct	Difference in trial balance	396	30 Nov	T. McCarthy	346

Now we need a debit entry in the purchase returns account:

(b)

Purchase Returns Account

20–5		£			
30 Nov	Suspense	50			

And a credit entry in the suspense account:

Suspense Account

20–5		£	20–5		£
31 Oct	Difference in trial balance	396	30 Nov	T. McCarthy	346
			30 Nov	Purchase returns	50
		396			396

The two errors from October have been corrected and the suspense account has now been cleared. A suspense account will only stay on the books temporarily. When the errors are discovered, the suspense account can be cleared. Only those errors that make the trial balance totals different from each other need to be corrected using the suspense account.

Questions involving the use of a suspense account appear regularly in examinations. Always consider carefully the information given in the question because there may be some errors that do not affect the suspense account.

Here is a fully worked example of this type of question.

On 30 June 20–6, the following balances were extracted from the books of George Williams:

	£
Premises	69,500
Sales	36,542
Purchases	17,124
Wages	27,846
Bank overdraft	4,072
Discount allowed	614
Discount received	1,026
Cash	753
Equipment	2,950
Sundry expenses	2,518
Drawings	5,720
Creditors	3,622
Debtors	8,300
Bank loan, 5 years at 10 per cent per annum	19,250
Stock	6,984
Sales returns	508
Loan interest	1,925
Capital	89,868
Purchase returns	692
Motor vehicles	10,950

You are required to:

(a) Prepare a trial balance from the above figures; and total the trial balance.
(b) Enter the amount of any difference between the two columns of the trial balance into a suspense account.

After further inspection of the ledgers and information recently received, the following errors have been discovered:

(i) A cheque for £392 received from R. Malik had been entered correctly in the cash book, but had not been entered in R. Malik's account.
(ii) Goods sold on credit to Joseph Walker for £204 had been entered correctly in the personal account but had been entered in the sales day book as £240.

(iii) The purchases day book for June had been overcast by £100.

(iv) An invoice for £164 received from Johnson Ltd had been correctly entered in the purchases day book but had been omitted in the personal account.

(c) Prepare journal entries with suitable narratives to record and correct items (i)–(iv).

(d) Write up the suspense account to include any entries arising from the correction of errors.

(e) Balance the suspense account.

(f) Calculate adjustments and correct ledger balances.

(g) Prepare and total the revised trial balance.

This is a fully worked solution.

George Williams
Trial Balance as at 30 June 20–6

	DR	CR
Premises	69,500	
Sales		36,542
Purchases	17,124	
Wages	27,846	
Bank overdraft		4,072
Discount allowed	614	
Discount received		1,026
Cash	753	
Equipment	2,950	
Sundry expenses	2,518	
Drawings	5,720	
Creditors		3,622
Debtors	8,300	
Bank loan, 5 years at 10 per cent per annum		19,250
Stock	6,984	
Sales returns	508	
Loan interest	1,925	
Capital		89,868
Purchase returns		692
Motor vehicles	10,950	
	155,692	155,072
Suspense account		620
	155,692	155,692

The journal

Date	Details	Folio	DR	CR
30 Jun (i)	Suspense account R. Malik account *Correction of error, cheque received from R. Malik omitted from his account*		392.00	392.00
30 Jun (ii)	Sales account Suspense account *Sales invoice of £204 entered in sales day book as £240*		36.00	36.00
30 Jun (iii)	Suspense account Purchases account *Correction of £100 overcast in purchases day book*		100.00	100.00
30 Jun (iv)	Suspense account Johnson Ltd *Correction of error, invoice omitted from personal account*		164.00	164.00

Suspense Account

20–6		£	20–6		£
30 Jun	R. Malik	392	30 Jun	Difference in	
30 Jun	Purchases	100		trial balance	620
30 Jun	Johnson Ltd	164	30 Jun	Sales	36
		656			656

George Williams
Revised Trial Balance as at 30 June 20–6

	DR	CR
Premises	69,500	
Sales (36,542 – 36)		36,506
Purchases (17,124 – 100)	17,024	
Wages	27,846	
Bank overdraft		4,072
Discount allowed	614	
Discount received		1,026
Cash	753	
Equipment	2,950	
Sundry expenses	2,518	
Drawings	5,720	
Creditors (3,622 + 164)		3,786
Debtors (8,300 – 392)	7,908	
Bank loan, 5 years at 10 per cent per annum		19,250
Stock	6,984	
Sales returns	508	
Loan interest	1,925	
Capital		89,868
Purchase returns		692
Motor vehicles	10,950	
	155,200	155,200

Points to remember

- Every attempt should be made to find *errors*. When we are unable to find the errors, the trial balance totals are made to agree with each other by inserting the amount of the difference between the two sides in a suspense account. A *suspense account* should be opened only when all other efforts to find errors have failed.
- When a trial balance has been made to agree by creating a suspense account it is a *temporary* measure. This account will stay on the books for as short a time as possible. When the errors are discovered, the suspense account can be cleared.
- A suspense account can have *a balance on either side*, whatever is necessary to make the trial balance totals agree with each other.
- When errors are found they must be corrected, *observing the rules of double entry*. Each correction must first have an entry in the *journal* describing what has happened, and is then posted to the accounts concerned.

Continued

- Questions requiring the use of a suspense account regularly appear in *examinations*. This type of question often involves preparing journal entries, calculating the effect of each error on the original figures and then preparing a revised trial balance.
- Only those errors that make the trial balance totals different from each other need to be corrected using the suspense account.
- Always consider the information given in the question carefully because there may be some errors to correct that do not affect the suspense account.

Assignments

25.1

On 31 March 20–5 the following balances were extracted from the books of Ruth Sampson:

	£
Rent and rates	5,740
Motor vehicles	12,390
Purchases	24,058
Bank loan, 10 years at 8 per cent per annum	12,750
Drawings	6,925
Bad debts	185
Sales	63,294
Bank	1,736
Cash	282
Purchase returns	856
Wages	25,018
Sales returns	604
Loan interest	1,020
Sundry expenses	2,596
Capital	14,350
Discount allowed	218
Fixtures and fittings	2,094
Creditors	2,638
Debtors	7,024
Discount received	742
Equipment	3,620

You are required to:

(a) Prepare a trial balance from the above figures and total the trial balance.
(b) Enter the amount of any difference between the two columns of the trial balance into a suspense account.

After further inspection of the ledgers and information recently received, the following errors and omissions have been discovered:

(i) A direct debit of £210 for rates had been paid but no entry had been made in the nominal account.
(ii) A credit note for £98 received from S. Hanif had been correctly entered in the nominal account but had been posted to the personal account twice.
(iii) The debit balance of £895 on D. Cooper's account in the sales ledger had been brought down as £89.
(iv) The cash book total of £202 for discount allowed in March had not been posted to the nominal account.

(c) Prepare journal entries with suitable narratives to record and correct items (i)–(iv).
(d) Write up the suspense account to include any entries arising from the correction of errors.
(e) Balance the suspense account.
(f) Calculate adjustments and correct ledger balances.
(g) Prepare and total a revised trial balance.

25.2
On 31 May 20–5, the following balances were extracted from the books of Richard Vincento:

	£
Equipment	15,780
Debtors	6,847
Salaries	27,506
Creditors	1,216
Motor vehicles	14,394
Purchases	21,072
Rent and rates	6,530
Bank loan, 10 years at 8 per cent per annum	15,000
Commission received	1,750
General expenses	3,854
Purchase returns	613
Loan interest	1,200
Bad debts	192
Sales	65,613
Drawings	9,296
Bank	2,104
Capital	24,450
Sales returns	726
Discount allowed	208
Discount received	590
Cash	436

You are required to:

(a) Prepare a trial balance from the above figures; and total the trial balance.
(b) Enter the amount of any difference between the two columns of the trial balance into a suspense account.

After further inspection of the ledgers and information recently received, the following errors and omissions have been discovered:

(i)   The credit balance of £680 on Tee Jays' account in the Purchase ledger had been brought down as £68.
(ii) A payment of £204 for repairs to the owner's private car had been entered in general expenses.
(iii) Goods sold on credit to M. King amounting to £105 had been correctly entered in the sales day book but had not been posted to the personal account.
(iv) The purchase returns day book for May had been incorrectly totalled as £209; it should have been £290.
(v)   A sales invoice for £325 had been correctly entered in the personal account but had been omitted in the sales day book.

(c) Prepare journal entries with suitable narratives to record and correct items (i)–(v).
(d) Write up the suspense account to include any entries arising from the correction of errors.
(e) Balance the suspense account.
(f) Calculate adjustments and correct ledger balances.
(g) Prepare and total a revised trial balance.

25.3

On 31 October 20–5, the following balances were extracted from the books of Andrew Montague:

	£
Motor vehicles	8,250.48
Purchases	15,912.16
Bank overdraft	3,312.72
Sales	59,410.38
General expenses	1,324.56
Drawings	8,596.30
Discount allowed	725.92
Discount received	1,608.34
Machinery	6,954.20
Wages	30,782.58
Cash	905.82
Bank loan, 5 years at 8 per cent per annum	8,500.00
Insurance	1,059.88
Sales returns	603.72
Creditors	2,741.86
Loan interest	680.00
Premises	97,520.00
Purchase returns	904.26
Debtors	8,018.18
Rent received	3,760.00
Carriage outwards	2,426.08
Stock	6,478.24
Capital	112,018.36

You are required to:

(a) Prepare a trial balance from the above figures; and total the trial balance.
(b) Enter the amount of any difference between the two columns of the trial balance into a suspense account.

After further inspection of the ledgers and information recently received, the following errors and omissions have been discovered:

(i)   Purchases day book total for October of £1,872.60 had been posted to the nominal account as £187.26.
(ii) A cheque of £450.00 received from the sub-tenant had not been entered in the books.
(iii) The balance of £174.68 owed to J. Singh had been omitted from the trial balance.
(iv) An invoice of £196.20 for general expenses had been posted as £19.62 in the insurance account.
(v)   The discount allowed column in the cash book was overcast by £10.00.

(vi) Goods sold on credit to Aspin Bros amounting to £340.56 had been correctly entered in the sales day book but had been omitted in the personal account.

(c) Prepare journal entries with suitable narratives to record and correct items (i)–(vi).
(d) Write up the suspense account to include any entries arising from the correction of errors.
(e) Balance the suspense account.
(f) Calculate adjustments and correct ledger balances.
(g) Prepare and total a revised trial balance.

25.4
On 30 June 20–5, the following balances were extracted from the books of William Winrose:

	£
Premises	90,750.00
Salaries	30,028.56
Sales	57,135.48
Stock	6,482.38
Equipment	5,750.60
Bank loan, 5 years at 12 per cent per annum	16,500.00
Electricity	1,346.20
Drawings	8,625.00
Discount allowed	716.08
Discount received	1,038.42
Loan interest	1,980.00
Bank overdraft	2,418.08
Purchases	18,056.38
Carriage inwards	594.16
Purchase returns	1,012.58
Debtors	8,530.24
Cash	709.90
Rent received	4,650.00
Motor vehicles	10,340.60
Sales returns	652.82
Creditors	2,706.38
Sundry expenses	2,150.48
Capital	99,713.20

You are required to:

(a) Prepare a trial balance from the above figures; and total the trial balance.
(b) Enter the amount of any difference between the two columns of the trial balance into a suspense account.

After further inspection of the ledgers and information recently received, the following errors and omissions have been discovered:

(i)   An invoice amounting to £590.80 received from J. Mills had been correctly entered in the purchases day book but had been posted as £59.08 in the personal account.
(ii) A credit note amounting to £42.50 sent to D. Chang had been correctly entered in D. Chang's account but had not been posted to the nominal account.
(iii) A sale on credit to M. Lister amounting to £399.20 had been correctly entered in the personal account but was entered in the sales day book as £39.92.
(iv) A direct debit of £74.60 for electricity had been paid but no entries had been made in the accounts.
(v)   Two credit balances of £410.26 and £280.50 had been omitted from the list extracted from the purchase ledger.

(c) Prepare journal entries with suitable narratives to record and correct items (i)–(v).
(d) Write up the suspense account to include any entries arising from the correction of errors.
(e) Balance the suspense account.
(f) Calculate adjustments and correct ledger balances.
(g) Prepare and total a revised trial balance.

25.5

On 30 September 20–5, the following balances were extracted from the books of Nicholas Barraclough.

	£
Capital	74,182.60
Bad debts	308.54
Cash	512.78
Creditors	1,671.34
Carriage inwards	383.64
Bank	2,095.36
Debtors	7,077.68
Commission received	3,430.00
Drawings	12,121.26
Sundry expenses	3,532.28
Discount allowed	327.96
Discount received	409.58
Bank loan, 10 years at 9 per cent per annum	15,000.00
Equipment	3,690.62
Premises	72,105.00
Purchases	21,964.36
Loan interest	1,350.00
Purchase returns	782.74
Rates	1,048.92
Sales	66,700.96
Salaries	34,268.48
Sales returns	617.24

You are required to:

(a) Prepare a trial balance from the above figures; and total the trial balance.
(b) Enter the amount of any difference between the two columns of the trial balance into a suspense account.

After further inspection of the ledgers and information recently received, the following errors and omissions have been discovered:

(i)   The debit balance of £250.96 on the account of J. Myers, a customer, had been included twice in the list of balances.
(ii) A credit note received from D. Stanley, amounting to £70.36, had been correctly entered in the nominal account but had been posted to the credit side of the personal account.
(iii) Sundry expenses includes £428.74 for repairs to the owner's private car.
(iv) The sales day book for September had been overcast by £950.00.
(v)   An invoice of £92.60 for carriage inwards had been posted as £9.26 in the sundry expenses account.

(vi) A cheque received of £150.00 for commission received had been correctly entered in the cash book but had not been posted to the nominal account.

(c) Prepare journal entries with suitable narratives to record and correct items (i)–(vi).

(d) Write up the suspense account to include any entries arising from the correction of errors.

(e) Balance the suspense account.

(f) Calculate adjustments and correct ledger balances.

(g) Prepare and total a revised trial balance.

■ Ṿ 26 Capital and revenue expenditure and receipts

Whenever a firm spends money it receives some form of *value in goods or services*. However, the value received from the money spent varies in the length of time it is of benefit to the business. For example, if a firm buys a filing cabinet it may last ten years, but if a firm buys petrol it will last a much shorter time. The contrast between these two types of expense is the difference between *capital* and *revenue expenditure*.

Capital expenditure

Capital expenditure is when a firm spends money to buy fixed assets or when money is spent to increase the value of an existing fixed asset. The assets will usually last a long time (more than a year) and provide the framework within which the business activities are carried out.

Capital expenditure includes:

- Buying fixed assets
- Increasing the value of an existing fixed asset. This could be an extension to an existing building
- Legal costs incurred in buying or extending buildings
- Cost of carriage and installation of new machinery
- Any other cost needed to get a fixed asset ready for use.

Revenue expenditure

Money spent on the day-to-day running of a business is known as *revenue expenditure*. This includes goods purchased for resale, or materials that are purchased for manufacture before being sold, also expenses such as salaries, wages, lighting and heating, rent, rates and so on. Generally, these costs are used up in one year or less and do not add to the value of fixed assets.

Differences between capital and revenue expenditure

Basically, the difference between these two types of expenditure is the *length of time* the expenditure is of benefit to the business. A good general guideline is:

- *longer than one year* – **capital expenditure**
- *one year or less* – **revenue expenditure**

Difficulty is sometimes experienced in what is generally referred to as *capitalisation* of revenue expenditure. This happens when a business incurs revenue expenditure on an item that is a fixed asset. This is best illustrated in the following example:

Wages paid to the firm's workmen engaged in building a new office extension.

Normally, wages are revenue expenditure, but in this example the wages are paid to workmen employed on building a new office extension. The new building would be capital expenditure and because these wages costs are directly involved with *increasing the value of an existing fixed asset*, they would be capitalised and treated as capital expenditure.

Legal expenses are normally revenue expenditure. However, the legal charges incurred for conveyancing in the purchase of land or buildings, or an extension to an existing building, would be capital expenditure, because these costs would be directly related to the purchase of a fixed asset.

Dealing with borderline cases

In some situations it is difficult to decide whether the expenditure is capital or revenue. For example, if a firm redecorates its premises every three years, is this capital or revenue expenditure? Generally, it will last more than a year, but the expenditure has not provided a new asset, it has only ensured that the premises do not deteriorate. This type of expense is considered to be part of the *normal maintenance running costs* and is regarded as *revenue expenditure*. A few examples will illustrate the difference.

Types of Expenditure

Expenditure	Type of expenditure
Purchase of new motor van	Capital
Petrol costs for motor van	Revenue
Insurance for motor van	Revenue
Repairs to motor van	Revenue
Cost of building extension to factory	Capital
Cost of painting new extension	Capital
Cost of repainting extension three years later	Revenue

Revenue expenditure is charged to the *trading or profit and loss account*, while capital expenditure will result in increased figures for fixed assets on the *balance sheet.*

Joint expenditure

Sometimes, an item of expenditure will be *part capital* and *part revenue expenditure*. A typical example would be the purchase of a motor van.

- *Buying* the motor van would be the purchase of a fixed asset, probably useful for a number of years, so this would be capital expenditure.
- However, *paying for insurance* to use the motor van would be revenue expenditure, because it would be used up in a short time and does not add to the value of fixed assets.

Capital receipts

Capital receipts consist of the money received from the sale of fixed assets. For example, if a plot of land was sold, the money received would be a *capital receipt*. Similarly, if the owner of a business invested a further sum of money for use in the business, this would be treated as a capital receipt.

Revenue receipts

Revenue receipts consist of money received from sales, commission received for services supplied and all other *revenue received items* such as, rent received and discount received.

At the end of the financial year, all items of revenue received are transferred to the profit and loss account to be set against the revenue expenses.

Points to remember

- *Capital expenditure* is the money spent to buy fixed assets or to increase the value of an existing fixed asset.
- *Revenue expenditure* is money spent on the daily running costs of a business.
- The difference between these two types of expenditure is the *length of time* the expenditure is of benefit to the business.
- *Capital receipts*: the money received when a fixed asset is sold is called a capital receipt.
- *Revenue receipts* are money received from sales and all other revenue received items.

Assignments

26.1

Classify the following items under the heading of capital expenditure or revenue expenditure:

(a) Purchase of a new machine for use in the business.
(b) Quarterly account for electricity.
(c) Purchase of a new motor van.
(d) Cost of road tax for new van.
(e) Cost of repairs to photocopier.
(f) Fire insurance premium.

26.2

John Conway has a retail food business. Classify the following items under the heading of capital or revenue expenditure:

(a) Purchase of a refrigerated display counter.
(b) Repainting shop door.
(c) Repairs to meat slicer.
(d) Purchase of new cash register.
(e) Replacement of a broken window.
(f) New tyres for the delivery van.
(g) Installation of burglar alarm system.
(h) Insurance premium for delivery van.
(i) Wages of shop assistant.

26.3

Angus Scott is in business as an estate agent. Some of his transactions are given below:

(a) Rent.
(b) Purchase of photocopying machine.
(c) Commission received from builder.
(d) Fees received from clients for professional services.
(e) Wages of secretary.
(f) Cost of new display equipment.
(g) Cost of installing new display equipment.
(h) Redecoration of shop front.
(i) Proceeds from sale of old computer.

You are required to:

(a) Explain the meaning of the following accounting terms:

Capital expenditure   *Revenue expenditure*
Capital receipts   *Revenue receipts*

(b) Rule up four columns headed: Capital expenditure, Revenue expenditure, Capital receipt and Revenue receipt and list the items in the appropriate columns.

26.4

The Pier View Garage paid for the items given below:

(a) Breakdown truck.
(b) Paper for photocopier.
(c) Sweets for sale in forecourt kiosk.
(d) Insurance for breakdown truck.
(e) New petrol pumps.
(f) Repairs to forecourt lighting.
(g) A secondhand car for resale.
(h) Wages of forecourt cashier.

You are required to:

(a) Briefly explain the term *revenue expenditure*.
(b) List the items as appropriate under the headings of capital or revenue expenditure.

26.5

A. Rogers opened his own business as a newsagent and paid the following:

(a) Wages of shop assistant.
(b) Purchase of a new cash register.
(c) Repairs to leaking shop window.
(d) Fire insurance premium.
(e) A new extension to the rear of the premises to provide more storage space.
(f) Purchase of floor cleaning materials for use in the shop.
(g) Legal fees paid in connection with the building of the extension.
(h) Purchase of stock for resale.

You are required to:

(a) For each item, state whether it is capital or revenue expenditure.
(b) Explain briefly the difference between these two types of expenditure.

26.6

Mr Brown has recently started a new business and is puzzled by the terms *capital expenditure* and *revenue expenditure*.

(a) Explain to him what capital expenditure is.

(b) Mr Brown has purchased a new van; the details of the account were as follows:

	£
Van	13,000
Seat belts	124
Delivery charges	242
Number plates	15
Road tax	150
Insurance	320
	13,851

He has also received an account from his local builder, details of which are as follows:

	£
Redecorate shop front	400
Erect shelves in stock room	90
	490

You are required to list the items from both invoices under their respective headings of capital and revenue expenditure.

26.7

State whether the following transactions of Salford Engineering Company are *capital* or *revenue* expenditure.

(a) Purchase of motor van.
(b) Yearly premium to insure motor van.
(c) Cost of rebuilding factory wall damaged by frost.
(d) Purchase of freehold land.
(e) Cost of building extension to factory.
(f) Cost of painting new extension.
(g) Legal costs on acquiring land for the extension.
(h) Repainting extension four years after completion.
(i) Cost of repairs to motor van.

26.8

(a) Explain briefly the difference between capital and revenue expenditure.
(b) Identify each of the following items of expenditure as capital or revenue.
(c) State which items will be charged to the trading account, profit and loss account or balance sheet.

(i) £200 paid to hauliers for carriage inwards.

(ii) £125 paid to Better Garages for fitting seat belts to new van.

(iii) £300 for replacement of broken window.

(iv) £450 to Unicold for supply and installation of refrigerated shop counter.

26.9

During the month of February, Thomas Wilding paid for the following items:

(i) Fire insurance premium for factory.

(ii) Cost of building new extension to factory.

(iii) Legal fees paid in connection with new extension.

(iv) Carriage costs on purchases.

(v) Cost of painting new extension.

(vi) Cost of repairing photocopier.

You are required to:

(a) List the items as appropriate, under the headings of capital or revenue expenditure.

(b) State which items will be charged to the trading account, the profit and loss account or the balance sheet.

◼ ꙮ **27** Receipts and payments accounts, income and expenditure accounts and balance sheets

Most people run a business primarily to make a profit, but clubs, societies and other non-profit-making organisations are run for the benefit of their members. These types of organisations are not concerned in trading as such or in profit-making, they are established by people who have joined together to pursue a common interest. Their main purpose is to promote activities that interest them. The final accounts for these types of organisations are different from those prepared for businesses.

In most cases, a committee elected by the members manages the financial affairs of a club or similar organisation. The committee consists of elected officers, such as a chairperson, treasurer and secretary. The *treasurer* is the committee member responsible for collecting subscriptions from the members and paying the bills. The treasurer must also prepare suitable final accounts to submit to the committee at the Annual General Meeting (AGM). In the case of a small club these final accounts are called *receipts and payment accounts*. Larger organisations, particularly those with substantial assets, present their final accounts in the form of *income and expenditure accounts*, together with a balance sheet.

Cash book of a club

Many clubs use an analysed cash book. With this type of cash book, the money received and the payments that occur most frequently will be given a separate analysis column. Obviously, the number of analysis columns will depend on what each club finds useful. At the end of the year, all the analysis columns are totalled to show the entire amount received and spent under each heading.

Receipts and payments account

A receipts and payments account is the simplest way that a treasurer can present the final accounts. It is prepared using the totals of the analysis columns from the club's cash book. A receipts and payments account begins with the balance of cash/bank in hand, then lists all money received and all payments made during the year, ending with the closing balance; this represents the amount of cash remaining at the end of the year. Here is a typical example:

For the year ended 31 December 20-9, the following information is available for the Queensway Cricket Club:

	£
Bank balance at 1 January 20-9	872
Light and heat	820
Ground maintenance	358
Members' subscriptions	2,920
Travelling expenses	752
Purchase of new equipment	395
Insurance	295
Rent	1,450
Proceeds of jumble sale	382
Sundry expenses	168
Bar sales	4,972
Bar purchases	1,856
Bar staff wages	650

You are required to prepare a receipts and payments account for the year ended 31 December 20-9.

Solution

Queensway Cricket Club
Receipts and Payments Account for the year ended 31 December 20-9

20-9		£	20-9		£
1 Jan	Balance b/d	872		Light and heat	820
	Subscriptions	2,920		Ground	
	Jumble sale	382		maintenance	358
	Bar sales	4,972		Travelling expenses	752
				New equipment	395
				Insurance	295
				Rent	1,450
				Sundry expenses	168
				Bar purchases	1,856
				Bar staff wages	650
			31 Dec	Balance c/d	2,402
		9,146			9,146

Only very small organisations would produce their final accounts in the form of a receipts and payments account, for the following reasons:

- A receipts and payments account simply lists all money received and all payments made during the year. It gives no details of any existing assets already owned by the club, other than the cash balance and any assets purchased during the current year.
- There is no mention of any outstanding liabilities, but there may be some unpaid bills at the end of the year.
- Members cannot see if a profit or loss was made on any particular activity.

For these important reasons it is more usual for a club or organisation to present their final accounts in much greater detail, in the form of an income and expenditure account and a balance sheet.

Bar trading accounts

Although the main purpose of a club is to pursue a common interest, they often carry out some activities to provide additional income: for example, running a bar, a dance, a raffle or a jumble sale. These types of activities are intended to make a profit, and in order to find out if a profit has been made a separate trading account may be prepared for each activity.

Particularly when a club provides a bar for its members it is usual to prepare a bar trading account, as this information will tell them whether the prices they charge for drinks are too high or too low.

Bar trading accounts for clubs are no different from the normal trading accounts of a business and are prepared in exactly the same way. When additional expenses are incurred, such as bar staff wages, these would be charged to the bar trading account because these costs are related directly to running the bar.

To illustrate this we can now prepare a bar trading account for the Queensway Cricket Club. There was an opening bar stock of £674, and on 31 December 20-9 there was a stock of drinks valued at £720. We also need to use some items from the receipts and payments account:

Queensway Cricket Club
Receipts and Payments Account for the year ended 31 December 20-9

20-9		£	20-9		£
1 Jan	Balance b/d	872		Light and heat	820
	Subscriptions	2,920		Ground	
	Jumble sale	382		maintenance	358
	Bar sales ✓	4,972		Travelling expenses	752
				New equipment	395
				Insurance	295
				Rent	1,450
				Sundry expenses	168
				Bar purchases ✓	1,856
				Bar staff wages ✓	650
			31 Dec	Balance c/d	2,402
		9,146			9,146

First, we shall see the bar trading account prepared in horizontal style and then in the more popular vertical format.

Horizontal style

Queensway Cricket Club
Bar Trading Account for the year ended 31 December 20-9

	£		£
Opening stock	674	Bar sales	4,972
Add Bar purchases	1,856		
	2,530		
Less closing stock	720		
Cost of goods sold	1,810		
Add Bar staff wages	650		
	2,460		
Profit on bar *to income and expenditure account*	2,512		
	4,972		4,972

Queensway Cricket Club
Bar Trading Account for the year ended 31 December 20-9

	£	£
Bar sales		4,972
Less cost of goods sold:		
Stock	674	
Bar purchases	1,856	
	2,530	
Less closing stock	720	
	1,810	
Bar staff wages	650	
		2,460
Profit on bar, *to income and expenditure account*		2,512

Income and expenditure account

Because clubs do not exist primarily to make profits, but rather for the benefit of their members, these types of organisations do not calculate a *profit* or *loss*. Instead, they produce an income and expenditure account that results in the calculation of a *surplus* or a *deficit*. An income and expenditure account follows exactly the same principles as a profit and loss account. Year-end *adjustments* may have to be made in club accounts just as they are in an ordinary business.

Adjustments

Once again, the rule is that final accounts must be prepared in such a way that all the income that belongs to the accounting period under consideration is included, whether it has actually been received or not. Set against this should be all expenses incurred during that period, even if they have not actually been paid. This principle is known as the *matching rule*, because the incomes and expenditures are matched with one another. Examination questions will often include notes giving details of any adjustments that need to be made for prepayments and accruals.

Subscriptions

People who wish to join a club or society usually pay membership fees; these funds are in the form of subscriptions collected from members during the year. Adjustments may have to be made for subscriptions paid in advance or in arrears.

Subscriptions in advance

Subscriptions that have been paid in advance for the following year are deducted from the subscriptions figure for the current year. Subscriptions paid in advance are a liability, because the club has received payment before providing the benefit of the facilities. On the balance sheet, the amount of subscriptions paid in advance are shown under *current liabilities*.

Subscriptions in arrears

These relate to members who have not paid their subscriptions for the current year. Most clubs observe the prudence concept and do not adjust for subscriptions in arrears at the year-end. This is because some members leave without notice and no attempt is made to collect their outstanding subscriptions. However, in examination questions, unless an instruction is given to the contrary, you will be expected to include subscriptions in arrears in your calculations. Subscriptions in arrears at the year-end are added to the subscriptions total for the current year. On the balance sheet the amount of subscriptions in arrears are shown under *current assets*.

Prepare a set of workings to assist you *before* you start the income and expenditure account. You may need to revise the procedure; adjustments are fully detailed in Chapter 22.

An income and expenditure account, like the profit and loss account, is a revenue account and follows the same rules. Any capital expenditure, such as the purchase of new equipment is *never* entered in the income and expenditure account. Any new equipment purchased during the current year would be added to the existing equipment and shown under fixed assets on the balance sheet. When no previous equipment exists, the new equipment would be entered, under fixed assets on the balance sheet.

Accumulated fund

A sole trader would have a capital account, while a non-profit-making organisation has an *accumulated fund*. A *surplus* is added to the accumulated fund in the same way that a net profit increases a sole trader's capital. A *deficit* is deducted and would decrease the accumulated fund.

In effect, the accumulated fund represents the same as capital and is calculated in the same way: it is the difference between assets and liabilities. To illustrate this, if we list the assets and liabilities of the Queensway Cricket Club at the start of the year we can calculate the accumulated fund:

Assets	£
Bar stock	674
Equipment	950
Cash at bank	872
	2,496

Less liabilities	
Unpaid bill for travelling expenses	56
Accumulated fund at 1 January 20-9 =	2,440

When final accounts are prepared for the first year a club has been in existence, there can be no accumulated fund at the beginning of the year. At the end of the first year, any surplus is entered as the accumulated fund on the balance sheet.

Balance sheet

Balance sheets for non-profit-making organisations follow the same principles and layout as those prepared for sole traders. The accumulated fund occupies the same position as the capital of a sole trader.

Now we can look at the preparation of an income and expenditure account and a balance sheet for the Queensway Cricket Club.

On 1 January 20-9 the Queensway Cricket Club had the following assets and liabilities: bar stock £674, equipment £950, cash at bank £872, unpaid bill for travelling expenses £56.

During the year ended 31 December 20-9, the following receipts and payments were made.

	£	
Bank balance at 1 January 20-9	872	
Light and heat	820	
Ground maintenance	358	
Members' subscriptions	2,920	
Travelling expenses	752	
Purchase of new equipment	395	
Insurance	295	
Rent	1,450	
Proceeds of jumble sale	382	
Sundry expenses	168	
Bar sales	4,972	✓
Bar purchases	1,856	✓
Bar staff wages	650	✓

On 31 December 20-9 the following adjustments had not been made:

(i) There was an unpaid bill for travelling expenses of £72.
(ii) Insurance prepaid was £75.
(iii) Closing bar stock was valued at £720.

You are required to:

(a) Prepare an income and expenditure account for the year ended 31 December 20-9.
(b) Calculate the accumulated fund as at 1 January 20-9.
(c) Prepare a balance sheet as at 31 December 20-9.

To prepare the income and expenditure account we must use the remaining items in the above list, include the profit on the bar, and make the necessary adjustments. (Items ticked have already been used to prepare the bar trading account.)

Adjustments at 31 December 20-9

(i) There was an unpaid bill for travelling expenses of £72.
Your *workings* would look like this:

Income and expenditure entry		*Balance sheet entry*
Travelling expenses	752	under *Current liabilities*
Less owing on 1 Jan 20-9	56	Travelling
	696	expenses owing £72
Add owing on 31 Dec 20-9	72	
	768	

(ii) Insurance prepaid was £75.
Your *workings* would look like this:

Income and expenditure entry		*Balance sheet entry*
Insurance	295	under *Current assets*
Less prepaid	75	Insurance prepaid £75
	220	

First, we shall see the income and expenditure account and balance sheet prepared in horizontal style and then in the more preferred vertical format.

Queensway Cricket Club
Income and Expenditure Account for the year ended 31 December 20-9

	£		£
Light and heat	820	Profit on bar	2,512
Ground maintenance	358	Subscriptions	2,920
Travelling expenses		Proceeds of jumble sale	382
(752 – 56 + 72)	768		
Insurance (295 – 75)	220		
Rent	1,450		
Sundry expenses	168		
Surplus	2,030		
	5,814		5,814

Note: Calculation of surplus: total income less total expenditure:

	£
Total income	5,814
Less total expenditure	3,784
Surplus	2,030

Queensway Cricket Club Balance sheet as at 31 December 20-9

	£	£		£	£
Fixed assets			***Accumulated fund***		
Equipment	950		at 1 Jan 20-9	2,440	
Add new			Add surplus	2,030	4,470
equipment	395	1,345			
Current assets			***Current liabilities***		
Bar stock	720		Travelling expenses		
Insurance prepaid	75		accrued		72
Bank balance	2,402	3,197			
		4,542			4,542

Vertical format

Queensway Cricket Club Income and Expenditure Account for year ended 31 December 20-9

	£	£
Profit on bar		2,512
Subscriptions		2,920
Proceeds of jumble sale		382
		5,814
Less expenses:		
Light and heat	820	
Ground maintenance	358	
Travelling expenses (752 − 56 + 72)	768	
Insurance (295 − 75)	220	
Rent	1,450	
Sundry expenses	168	
		3,784
Surplus		2,030

Queensway Cricket Club Balance sheet as at 31 December 20-9

	£	£	£
Fixed Assets			
Equipment		950	
Add new equipment		395	1,345
Current Assets			
Bar stock	720		
Insurance prepaid	75		
Bank	2,402		
		3,197	
Less Current Liabilities			
Travelling expenses accrued		72	
			3,125
			4,470
Financed by:			
Accumulated fund at 01.01.20-9			2,440
Add Surplus			2,030
			4,470

You can see that the figures used are exactly the same using either the horizontal or vertical method of display. The vertical presentation is the more modern method usually preferred by examiners and would probably be more meaningful to people who knew very little about accounting.

Points to remember

- A *receipts and payments account* is prepared using the totals of the analysis columns from a club's cash book. It begins with the balance of cash/bank in hand, then lists all money received and all payments made during the year, ending with the closing balance, which represents the amount of cash remaining at the end of the year.
- An *income and expenditure account,* like the profit and loss account, is a *revenue account* and follows the same rules. Any capital expenditure, such as the purchase of new equipment, is *never* entered in the income and expenditure account. Any new equipment purchased during the current year is added to the existing equipment and shown under fixed assets on the balance sheet.

Continued

- *Adjustments* for final accounts follow the principle known as the *matching rule*. They must be prepared in such a way that all income that belongs to the accounting period under consideration is included, whether it has actually been received or not. Set against this should be all expenses incurred during that period, even if they have not actually been paid. Examination questions generally include notes giving details of any *adjustments* that need to be made. It is the adjusted figure that is used in the income and expenditure account, and the amount of the prepayment or accrual that will appear on the balance sheet.
- The accumulated fund occupies the same position as the capital on a balance sheet: a *surplus* will *increase* it, and a *deficit* will *decrease* it.
- The figures used are exactly the same using either the horizontal or vertical method of display.

This unit provides the underpinning knowledge you will need to prepare club accounts. Now you should attempt the assignments, which are all recent examination questions, to gain practice in the method and procedures.

Assignments

27.1

On 1 January 20-9 the Oakdale Youth Club had the following assets. Furniture and fittings £1,500, games equipment £640, motor van £5,000, cash at bank £460. There were no liabilities.

During the year ended 31 December 20-9 the following receipts and payments were made:

	£
Subscriptions: 284 members at £6 each	
Electricity	905
Repairs to equipment	138
Proceeds of annual fete	852
Motor expenses	496
New games equipment	420
Postage and stationery	184
Insurance	375
General expenses	118

On 31 December 20-9 the following information was also available.

(i) There was an electricity bill outstanding of £107.
(ii) Insurance prepaid was £115.

You are required to:

(a) Prepare a receipts and payments account for the year ended 31 December 20-9.
(b) Prepare an income and expenditure account for the year ended 31 December 20-9.
(c) Calculate the accumulated fund at 1 January 20-9.
(d) Prepare a balance sheet as at 31 December 20-9.

27.2

On 1 June 20-8 the Northside Sports Club had the following assets and liabilities: sports equipment £1,580, furniture £1,090, cash at bank £692, sundry expenses owing £76, stock of drinks £708.

The following is a summary of the receipts and payments of the club for the year ended 31 May 20-9:

Receipts	£	Payments	£
Subscriptions	3,750	Expenses of annual dance	432
Annual dance	974	Rent	1,595
Locker rents	548	New tables	360
Competition fees	396	Prizes for competitions	158
Bar sales	2,836	Sundry expenses	612
		Bar purchases	1,574
		Insurance	495

On 31 May 20-9 the following adjustments had not been made:

(i)   Bar stock was valued at £692.
(ii) Insurance prepaid was £78.
(iii) There was £145 owing for rent.

You are required to:

(a) Calculate the club's bank balance at 31 May 20-9.
(b) Prepare a bar trading account for the year ended 31 May 20-9.
(c) Prepare an income and expenditure account for the year ended 31 May 20-9.
(d) Calculate the accumulated fund at 1 June 20-8.
(e) Prepare a balance sheet as at 31 May 20-9.

27.3

On 1 June 20-4, the assets and liabilities of the Ambrose Cricket Club were as follows:

	£
Club premises	65,000
Equipment	12,500
Cash at bank	7,370
Unpaid bill for travelling expenses	55

During the year ended 31 May 20-5 the following receipts and payments were made:

	£
Members' subscriptions	7,500
Purchase of new grass cutting machine	1,695
Insurance premium	830
Travelling expenses to away matches	1,315
Rates	920
Stationery and postage	163
Purchases of refreshments	738
Payment of league entry fees	250
Wages of groundsman	1,400
Printing expenses	97
Refreshment bar takings	1,576
Lighting and heating	410
Interest received from bank	74

The following adjustments have not yet been made:

(i) On 31 May 20-5 there was an invoice for printing of £49 that had not been paid.
(ii) There was an unused stock of stationery valued at £35 and unused postage stamps valued at £18.

You are required to:

(a) Prepare a receipts and payments account for the year ending 31 May 20-5.
(b) Prepare an income and expenditure account for the year ending 31 May 20-5.
(c) Calculate the accumulated fund at 1 June 20-4.
(d) Prepare a balance sheet as at 31 May 20-5.

The profit or loss on the refreshment bar should be shown. You should show clearly how you have dealt with the adjustments.

27.4
On 1 January 20-2, the Adelmead Tennis Club had the following assets and liabilities: equipment £9,000, cash at bank £850, cash in hand £270, unpaid electricity bill £45.

During the year, receipts and payments were:

	£
Subscriptions	4,250
Postage and stationery	45
Fees received for tournament	660
Prizes for tournament	215
Electricity	150
Wages of groundsman	1,450

Rent	935
Purchase of new equipment	411
Insurance	387

On 31 December 20-2 the following information is available.

	£
Tournament fees not paid	40
Rent owing	85
Insurance prepaid	67
Cash in hand	237

You are required to:

(a) Prepare a receipts and payments account for the year ended 31 December 20-2.
(b) Prepare an income and expenditure account for the year ended 31 December 20-2.
(c) Prepare a balance sheet as at 31 December 20-2.

27.5
On 1 June 20-6, the Woodside Sports Club had the following assets and liabilities: equipment £450, cash in hand £173, cash at bank £1,690, rent due but unpaid £75.

During the year receipts and payments were as follows:

	£
Subscriptions from 96 full members, each paying	65
Subscriptions from 34 part-time members, each paying	35
Fees received for competitions	492
Insurance	385
Lighting and heating	1,463
General expenses	472
Rent paid	1,296
Prizes for competitions	284
Deposit paid on new equipment costing £690	150

On 31 May 20-7, the following adjustments had not been made:

		£
(i)	Insurance was prepaid	35
(ii)	Rent owing was	108
(iii)	Cash in hand	96
(iv)	There was an unpaid bill for general expenses	152

You are required to:

(a) Prepare a receipts and payments account for the year ending 31 May 20-7.
(b) Prepare an income and expenditure account for the year ending 31 May 20-7.
(c) Prepare a balance sheet as at 31 May 20-7.

Show clearly how you have dealt with the adjustments. Full and part-time members are listed and accounted for separately.

27.6
On 1 November 20-6, the Lawnswood Tennis Club had the following assets and liabilities: club premises £45,500, equipment £12,750, bar stock £980, bank balance £5,220, cash £326, creditor for bar supplies £450.

The following receipts and payments were made during the year ended 31 October 20-7:

	£
Subscriptions: 98 full-time members, each paying	250
45 part-time members, each paying	125
Travelling expenses to away matches	1,454
Payments to suppliers for bar purchases	8,428
Lighting and heating	2,962
Payment of league entry fees	545
Rent received from private functions	1,485
General expenses	3,835
Rates	3,180
Insurance premium	2,472
Bar staff wages	5,950
Purchase of new equipment	5,790
Stationery and postage	508
Bar sales	16,592

On 31 October 20-7, the following information was available:

(i) Rent of £395 was owing to the club for private functions.
(ii) Insurance prepaid was £1,854.
(iii) There was a stock of stationery valued at £96 and a stock of drinks valued at £1,080. There were no bar creditors.

You are required to:

(a) Prepare a bar trading account for the year ended 31 October 20-7.
(b) Prepare a receipts and payments account for the year ended 31 October 20-7.
(c) Prepare an income and expenditure account for the year ended 31 October 20-7.

Note: A balance sheet is *not* required. Show clearly how you have dealt with the adjustments. Full and part-time members are listed and accounted for separately.

■ ⌄ 28   Accounting ratios

So far we have concentrated on the mechanics of accounting and the way in which accounts are prepared and presented. It is vital that the information contained in accounts is understood and used. In this final chapter we shall consider the people who may want to use the accounts, and the tools of analysis used to help them make sense of the figures in those accounts. This is an important part of your studies as it begins to show how accounts are used in the business world and how it is possible to understand what they mean.

The final accounts of any business are capable of providing a considerable amount of useful information. Much of this information is provided by the use of *ratio analysis* that involves the *calculation of ratios or percentages*. Although ratios are used extensively in the interpretation of accounts it is a mistake to believe that simply calculating and producing a list of accounting ratios can interpret accounts. The skill of interpretation is in choosing a suitable ratio for a particular task, making appropriate comparisons and reaching the correct conclusion.

Many people may be interested in information regarding a business. In particular, the *owner* would wish to learn all he can about his own business. Other interested people will include the firm's *bank*; a request for overdraft facilities or a loan would probably result in the banker requiring quite detailed information. *Trade creditors* would also need assurance that a firm has the ability to pay its debts promptly.

To provide this information we use a number of *accounting ratios*. These are statistics derived from the figures provided in the final accounts. We shall now look at the ratios in common use, and the formula and method of calculation. To do this we need a set of final accounts, starting with the trading account section:

Michael Silverwood
Trading account for the year ended 31 December 20-7

	£	£	£
Sales			36,840
Less sales returns			450
			36,390
Less cost of goods sold:			
Stock		4,340	
Purchases	19,200		
Less purchase returns	750		
		18,450	
		22,790	
Less closing stock		5,328	
			17,462
Gross profit			18,928

Analysing the trading account

From the trading account we can calculate the following ratios:

- Gross profit ratio
- Rate of stock turnover

Gross profit ratio

The basic formula is:

$$\frac{\text{Gross profit}}{\text{Net sales}} \times 100 = gross\ profit\ ratio$$

Using the figures in Michael Silverwood's trading account we can now calculate the gross profit ratio:

Gross profit
Net sales
$$\frac{18,928}{36,390} \times 100 = 52.01\%\ gross\ profit\ ratio$$

   At first sight this may seem to be a very good percentage rate of profit, but a firm will need a reasonably high rate of gross profit percentage if it is going to make sufficient profit to cover all the overheads of a business. The major cause of bankruptcies among small businesses is a low gross profit percentage. The main use of the gross profit percentage figure is to compare the current year with the previous year. This is because the gross profit percentage should be approximately the same from year to year.

Rate of stock turnover ratio

The basic formula is:

$$\frac{\text{Cost of goods sold}}{\text{Average stock}}$$

Average stock is taken as:

$$\frac{\text{Opening stock} + \text{closing stock}}{2}$$

We have the figures we need in the trading account: opening stock 4,340 plus the closing stock 5,328 = 9,668.

$$\frac{9,668}{2} = 4,834 \; \textit{average stock}$$

We can now calculate the rate of stock turnover ratio:

Cost of goods sold:
Average stock:
$$\frac{17,462}{4,834} = 3.61 \; \textit{rate of stock turnover}$$

This represents the number of times the stock is turned over in a year. Whether this is an acceptable rate of stock turnover will depend upon the type of goods in which the business deals. It would not be good for a newsagent where stock is moving daily, but it would be adequate for lawnmowers and other types of mechanical equipment, say. There are several ways of improving the rate of stock turnover: for example, extending opening hours, media advertisements, competitive pricing and tightening stock control. Stocks may be piling up and not being sold, and this could mean that money is being taken out of the bank simply to buy increased stocks of slow-moving items.

Analysing the profit and loss account

- Net profit ratio
- Expense ratio

To consider these ratios we shall need the profit and loss section of the final accounts.

Profit and loss account for the year ended 31 December 20-7

	£	£	£
Gross profit			18,928
Less expenses:			
Rent		2,180	
Wages (9,178 + 450)		9,628	
Rates (565 − 126)		439	
Bad debts		142	
Insurance		458	
Sundry expenses (907 − 72)		835	
			13,682
Net profit			5,246

Net profit ratio

The basic formula is:

$$\frac{\text{Net profit}}{\text{Net sales}} \times 100 = net\ profit\ ratio$$

We have all the figures we need in the trading and profit and loss account:

Net profit
Net sales
$$\frac{5,246}{36,390} \times 100 = 14.42\%\ net\ profit\ ratio$$

Is this a reasonable net profit percentage? It may be, but it must be compared with that of the previous year. (About 15% is considered reasonable.) As with the gross profit ratio, the net profit ratio tends to be constant from year to year. Even if the turnover increases or decreases the ratio should stay constant. A business always strives to make as much net profit as possible by charging competitive prices to its customers and keeping expenses as low as possible.

Expense ratio

This ratio is used to discover if any particular item of expense has increased. The basic formula is:

$$\frac{\text{Expense item}}{\text{Net sales}} \times 100 = expense\ ratio$$

We can now calculate this ratio by using the wages expense:

$$\frac{\text{Wages}}{\text{Net sales}} \qquad \frac{9,628}{36,390} \times 100 = 26.46\% \; \textit{wages expense ratio}$$

This would be compared with the wages expense ratio for the previous year. If the wages expense ratio was 20% last year, this would be a serious increase. If staff asked for a pay rise this year it is likely they would be refused.

Analysing the balance sheet

The balance sheet is a snapshot of the affairs of a business at a given moment in time. Using the balance sheet, we can calculate the following ratios:

- Return on capital employed (ROCE)
- Current ratio (also known as working capital ratio)
- Acid test ratio
- Debtors' collection period, in days
- Creditors' payment period, in days

Balance sheet as at 31 December 20-7

	£	£	£
Fixed assets			
Equipment			6,350
Motor vehicle			11,500
			17,850
Current assets			
Stock	5,328		
Debtors	6,480		
Rates prepaid	126		
Stationery stock	72		
Bank	6,250	18,256	
Less **Current liabilities**			
Creditors	2,360		
Wages accrued	450	2,810	
			15,446
			33,296
Financed by:			
Capital at 01.01.20-7			31,300
Add Net profit			5,246
			36,546
Less drawings			3,250
			33,296

Return on capital employed (ROCE)

The basic formula is:

$$\frac{\text{Net profit}}{\text{Capital employed}} \times 100 = return\ on\ capital\ employed$$

Capital employed is generally regarded as the difference between total assets and current liabilities. In this example, fixed assets are 17,850 plus current assets 18,256 = 36,106, less current liabilities of 2,810 = 33,296. We now have the figures we need:

$$\frac{\text{Net profit}}{\text{Capital employed}} \qquad \frac{5,246}{33,296} \times 100 = 15.76\%\ return\ on\ capital\ employed$$

Using this ratio, we are able to compare the profits earned with the capital employed to earn them, to discover if the return is adequate. It expresses the net profit as a percentage of the capital invested in the business and is mainly used by bankers. In this case, 15.76 per cent is quite good, probably better than the same amount of money would earn if it was invested in a safe investment such as a building society, but then, the risk is also higher.

Current ratio

The basic formula is:

$$\frac{\text{Current assets}}{\text{Current liabilities}} = current\ ratio$$

using the figures on the balance sheet:

$$\frac{\text{Current assets}}{\text{Current liabilities}} \qquad \frac{18,256}{2,810} = 6.50\ current\ ratio$$

This ratio tells us how easily the business can pay its debts. This means that, with the present level of current assets, this business can pay its current liabilities (its debts) more than six times over. This is a good, sound position.

Acid test ratio

The basic formula is:

$$\frac{\text{Current assets less closing stock}}{\text{Current liabilities}} = current\ ratio$$

Using the figures on the balance sheet:

$$\frac{\text{(Current assets – closing stock)}}{\text{Current liabilities}} \qquad \frac{12{,}928}{2{,}810} = 4.60 \; \textit{current ratio}$$

This ratio is used to test the liquidity of a business; that is, its ability to pay its debts. The ratio here suggests a good state of affairs; the essential figure is at least 1:1, so the business can pay its debts in full without any difficulty. This business can pay its debts more than four times over.

Debtors' collection period, in days

The basic formula is:

$$\frac{\text{Debtors}}{\text{Net sales}} \times 365 = \textit{debtors' collection period, in days}$$

using the figures in the final accounts:

$$\frac{\text{Debtors}}{\text{Net sales}} \qquad \frac{6{,}480}{36{,}390} \times 365 = 65 \; \textit{days debtors' collection period}$$

This means that it takes the average debtor 65 days (approximately 2 months) to pay their debt, which is unsatisfactory. Money tied up in debtors is unproductive money. It might be that this business has no proper credit control system. Alternatively, it might have offered extended credit to its customers to encourage sales.

An important concern in any business is the ability of its debtors to pay their debts promptly. If they fail to pay within the agreed time it places the business in a difficult position because the business has debts to pay. It is very important to monitor and control debtors to ensure sufficient money flows into the business.

Creditors' payment period, in days

The basic formula is:

$$\frac{\text{Creditors}}{\text{Net purchases}} \times 365 = \textit{creditors' collection period, in days}$$

using the figures in the final accounts:

$$\frac{\text{Creditors}}{\text{Net purchases}} \qquad \frac{2{,}360}{18{,}450} \times 365 = 46 \; \textit{days creditors' collection period}$$

This translates into the length of time a business takes to pay its creditors. This business takes an average of 46 days to pay its creditors. Generally, 30 days' credit is considered to be normal business practice, so 46 days is not ideal but is acceptable. An increase may indicate that the firm is overtrading, which could be rather risky. A sudden fall could indicate a withdrawal of credit facilities by suppliers.

How to use ratios

Ratio analysis is the most widely used technique for interpreting and comparing financial information. Ratios are useful because they can be used as indicators of the efficiency of a business; for the purpose of comparing financial performance from year to year, they also assist in predicting the future.

It is only sensible to compare like with like, and figures are only comparable if they have been constructed on a similar basis. There are a considerable number of other ratios that can be used, far more than can be mentioned in this textbook. Exactly which ratios are considered to be the most important will always depend on the type of business.

Points to remember

- *Practice* is essential if you are to gain skill and confidence in calculating these important ratios.
- Net sales are frequently referred to as the *turnover* of a business.
- In the trading account, it is extremely important to list all the items in the correct sequence. The *cost of goods sold* is the figure after the closing stock has been deducted.
- *Ratios* are used extensively in the interpretation of accounts but it is a mistake to believe that simply calculating and producing a list of accounting ratios can interpret accounts.
- Always *compare like with like*, and figures are only comparable if they have been constructed on a similar basis.

Assignments

Practice is essential if you are to gain skill and confidence in calculating accounting ratios. In the following assignments, give your answers correct to *two decimal places* except where the number of days is requested.

28.1
Tony Simms' trading account shows net sales of £40,850 and a gross profit of £20,620.

You are required to enter a correct formula and calculate his gross profit ratio.

28.2
Ruth Sampson's final accounts show a net profit of £10,158 and net sales of £38,726. Two of the expenses in the profit and loss account are: rent and

rates £6,250 and salaries £10,430. You are required to enter correct formulae and calculate:

(i) Net profit ratio.
(ii) Rent and rates expense ratio.
(iii) Salaries expense ratio.

28.3
John King's final accounts show a gross profit of £50,126, a net profit of £20,852 and net sales of £84,734. Two of the expenses in the profit and loss account are advertising £2,208, and heat and light £3,250. You are required to enter correct formulae and calculate:

(i) Gross profit ratio.
(ii) Net profit ratio.
(iii) Advertising expense ratio.
(iv) Heat and light expense ratio.

28.4
Use the figures in the trading, profit and loss account and balance sheet you prepared for Richard Martin in Assignment 22.1 on page 281, enter correct figures and formulae, and calculate the following accounting ratios:

(i)   Gross profit ratio.
(ii)   Rate of stock turnover.
(iii)   Net profit ratio.
(iv)   Expense ratio – salaries
(v)   Return on capital employed ratio.
(vi)   Current ratio.
(vii)   Acid test ratio.
(viii)   Debtors' collection period, in days.
(ix)   Creditors' payment period, in days.

28.5
Use the figures in the trading, profit and loss account and balance sheet you prepared for Kate Devlin in Assignment 22.3 on page 283, enter correct figures and formulae, and calculate the following accounting ratios:

(i)   Gross profit ratio.
(ii)   Rate of stock turnover.
(iii)   Net profit ratio.
(iv)   Expense ratio – rent and rates
(v)   Return on capital employed ratio.
(vi)   Current ratio.
(vii)   Acid test ratio.
(viii)   Debtors' collection period in days.
(ix)   Creditors' payment period in days.

28.6

Use the figures in the trading, profit and loss account and balance sheet you prepared for Helen Robinson in Assignment 22.5 on page 285, enter correct figures and formulae, and calculate the following accounting ratios:

(i)   Gross profit ratio.
(ii)   Rate of stock turnover.
(iii)   Net profit ratio.
(iv)   Return on capital employed ratio.
(v)   Current ratio.
(vi)   Acid test ratio.
(vii) Debtors' collection period, in days.
(viii) Creditors' payment period, in days.

28.7

Use the figures in the trading, profit and loss account and balance sheet you prepared for David Towers in Assignment 22.6 on page 286, enter correct figures and formulae, and calculate the following accounting ratios:

(i)   Gross profit ratio.
(ii)   Rate of stock turnover.
(iii)   Net profit ratio.
(iv)   Return on capital employed ratio.
(v)   Current ratio.
(vi)   Acid test ratio.
(vii) Debtors' collection period, in days.
(viii) Creditors' payment period, in days.

28.8

Use the figures in the trading, profit and loss account and balance sheet you prepared for Douglas Van Owen in Assignment 22.7 on page 287, enter correct figures and formulae, and calculate the following accounting ratios:

(i)   Gross profit ratio.
(ii)   Rate of stock turnover.
(iii)   Net profit ratio.
(iv)   Return on capital employed ratio.
(v)   Current ratio.
(vi)   Acid test ratio.
(vii) Debtors' collection period in days.
(viii) Creditors' payment period in days.

28.9

Use the figures in the trading, profit and loss account and balance sheet you prepared for William McKay in Assignment 22.8 on page 288, enter correct figures, formula and calculate the following accounting ratios.

(i)   Gross profit ratio.
(ii)   Rate of stock turnover.
(iii)   Net profit ratio.
(iv)   Return on capital employed ratio.
(v)   Current ratio.
(vi)   Acid test ratio.
(vii)   Debtors' collection period, in days.
(viii) Creditors' payment period, in days.

▮▼ Answers to assignments

Unit 1

1.1 *Assets*   *Liabilities*
     Motor van   Creditors
     Cash at bank
     Office equipment
     Stock of goods

1.2 *Assets*   *Liabilities*
     Premises   Creditors
     Debtors   Capital
     Motor vehicle
     Office furniture
     Cash in hand

1.3 Total assets £25,000

1.4 Total liabilities £20,500

1.5 Total assets £21,000

1.6 (a) £24,700 (b) £26,500 (c) £59,750 (d) £48,700 (e) £25,000

1.7 (a) £31,800 (b) £92,200 (c) £18,950 (d) £48,830 (e) £81,000

1.8 (a) £32,750 (b) £44,650 (c) £59,450 (d) £31,100 (e) £24,800

1.9 (a) £28,950 (b) £35,050 (c) £56,700 (d) £13,900 (e) £22,100

1.10 Balance sheet totals: £25,600

1.11 Balance sheet totals: £32,400

1.12 Balance sheet totals: £30,250

Unit 2

2.1 *Account to be debited*   *Account to be credited*
     (a) Machinery   Mitchells Ltd
     (b) Cash   Motor van
     (c) M. Fieldhouse   Bank
     (d) Cash   D. Nelson (Loan)
     (e) Office equipment   Bank
     (f) Cash   B. Dixon

2.2 *Account to be debited*   *Account to be credited*
     (a) Motor van   Cash

(b) B. Groves   Bank
(c) Office furniture   Modern Offices Ltd
(d) Bank   K. Williams (Loan)
(e) Machinery   Cash
(f) Cash   W. Preston

2.3 K. Chippendale

Capital Account

			1 May	Cash	2,000

Cash Account

| 1 May | Capital | 2,000 | 12 May | Office furniture | 500 |
| 24 May | L. Gibson (Loan) | 500 | 30 May | Crossways Garage | 950 |

Motor Van Account

3 May	Crossways Garage	950

Crossways Garage Account

30 May	Cash	950	3 May	Motor van	950

Office Furniture Account

12 May	Cash	500

L. Gibson (Loan) Account

			24 May	Cash	500

2.4 S. Curtis

Capital Account

			1 Apr	Bank	5,000

Bank Account

1 Apr	Capital	5,000	10 Apr	Motor van	1,500
20 Apr	D. Lester (Loan)	2,000	23 Apr	Machinery	500
			29 Apr	Design Centre	450

Office Furniture Account

4 Apr	Design Centre	450

Design Centre Account

29 Apr	Bank	450	4 Apr	Office furniture	450

Motor Van Account

10 Apr	Bank	1,500

D. Lester (Loan) Account

			20 Apr	Bank	2,000

Machinery Account

23 Apr	Bank	500

2.5 J. Patel

Capital Account

			1 Jun	Cash	7,000

Cash Account

| 1 Jun | Capital | 7,000 | 3 Jun | Bank | 6,500 |
| 14 Jun | P. Wilson (Loan) | 1,000 | | | |

Bank Account

3 Jun	Cash	6,500	6 Jun	Motor van	1,950
			23 Jun	Machinery	750
			30 Jun	Elite Supplies	350

Motor Van Account

6 Jun	Bank	1,950			

Office Furniture Account

9 Jun	Elite Supplies	500	20 Jun	Elite Supplies	150

Elite Supplies Account

20 Jun	Office furniture	150	9 Jun	Office furniture	500
30 Jun	Bank	350			

P. Wilson (Loan) Account

			14 Jun	Cash	1,000

Machinery Account

23 Jun	Bank	750			

2.6 M. Sanchez

Capital Account

			1 Oct	Bank	5,000

Bank Account

1 Oct	Capital	5,000	5 Oct	Cash	250
12 Oct	S. Ramsden (Loan)	2,000	10 Oct	Motor van	1,750
			20 Oct	Machinery	250
			26 Oct	Systems Ltd	694

Office Equipment Account

3 Oct	Systems Ltd	750	15 Oct	Systems Ltd	56

Systems Ltd Account

15 Oct	Office equipment	56	3 Oct	Office equipment	750
26 Oct	Bank	694			

Cash Account

5 Oct	Bank	250	23 Oct	Shop fittings	175
31 Oct	Shop fittings	60			

Motor Van Account

10 Oct	Bank	1,750			

S. Ramsden (Loan) Account

			12 Oct	Bank	2,000

Machinery Account

20 Oct	Bank	250			

Shop Fittings Account

23 Oct	Cash	175	31 Oct	Cash	60

Unit 3

3.1 J. Singh

Cash Account

1 May	Capital	5,000.00	4 May	Bank	3,000.00
			30 May	Kilroy Ingram	100.00

Capital Account

			1 May	Cash	5,000.00

Purchases Account

2 May	G. Moore	258.00			
8 May	Kilroy Ingram	175.20			
20 May	Kilroy Ingram	204.76			

Value Added Tax Account

2 May	G. Moore	45.15	15 May	G. Moore	10.92
8 May	Kilroy Ingram	30.66	28 May	Kilroy Ingram	10.28
20 May	Kilroy Ingram	35.83			

G. Moore Account

15 May	Purchase returns	73.32	2 May	Purchases	303.15
24 May	Bank	229.83			

Bank Account

4 May	Cash	3,000.00	24 May	G. Moore	229.83

Kilroy Ingram Account

28 May	Purchase returns	69.04	8 May	Purchases	205.86
30 May	Cash	100.00	20 May	Purchases	240.59

Purchase Returns Account

			15 May	G. Moore	62.40
			28 May	Kilroy Ingram	58.76

3.2 S. Munro

Bank Account

1 Jul	Capital	8,000.00	5 Jul	Cash	500.00
			31 Jul	E. Mason	747.25

Capital Account

			1 Jul	Bank	8,000.00

Purchases Account

2 Jul	M. Clifton	362.40			
8 Jul	E. Mason	273.50			
19 Jul	E. Mason	420.76			

Value Added Tax Account

2 Jul	M. Clifton	63.42	14 Jul	M. Clifton	11.97
8 Jul	E. Mason	47.86	27 Jul	E. Mason	10.20
19 Jul	E. Mason	73.63			

M. Clifton Account

14 Jul	Purchase returns	80.37	2 Jul	Purchases	425.82
25 Jul	Cash	250.00			

Cash Account

5 Jul	Bank	500.00	25 Jul	M. Clifton	250.00

E. Mason Account

27 Jul	Purchase returns	68.50	8 Jul	Purchases	321.36
31 Jul	Bank	747.25	19 Jul	Purchases	494.39

Purchase Returns Account

			14 Jul	M. Clifton	68.40
			27 Jul	E. Mason	58.30

3.3 C. Gulliver

Cash Account

1 Sep	Capital	7,000.00	5 Sep	Bank	5,500.00
			30 Sep	F. Armitage	50.00

Capital Account

			1 Sep	Capital	7,000.00

Purchases Account

3 Sep	G. Stewart	386.76
10 Sep	W. Rycroft	294.24
18 Sep	F. Armitage	196.58

Value Added Tax Account

3 Sep	G. Stewart	67.68	15 Sep	G. Stewart	10.99
10 Sep	W. Rycroft	51.49	26 Sep	W. Rycroft	9.58
18 Sep	F. Armitage	34.40			

G. Stewart Account

15 Sep	Purchase returns	73.79	3 Sep	Purchases	454.44
24 Sep	Bank	380.65			

Bank Account

5 Sep	Cash	5,500.00	24 Sep	G. Stewart	380.65

W. Rycroft Account

26 Sep	Purchase returns	64.34	10 Sep	Purchases	345.73

Purchase Returns Account

			15 Sep	G. Stewart	62.80
			26 Sep	W. Rycroft	54.76

F. Armitage Account

30 Sep	Cash	50.00	18 Sep	Purchases	230.98

3.4 M Gonzalas

Bank Account

1 Oct	Capital	9,000.00	4 Oct	Cash	750.00
			31 Oct	Tee-Jay Products	311.48

Capital Account

			1 Oct	Bank	9,000.00

Purchases Account

2 Oct	Tee-Jay Products	392.75
8 Oct	Demland Supplies	268.92

12 Oct	W. Jackson	302.99			
23 Oct	W. Jackson	374.80			

Value Added Tax Account

2 Oct	Tee-Jay Products	68.73	16 Oct	Demland Supplies	8.40
8 Oct	Demland Supplies	47.06	26 Oct	W. Jackson	9.80
12 Oct	W. Jackson	53.02			
23 Oct	W. Jackson	65.59			

Tee-Jay Products Account

20 Oct	Cash	150.00	2 Oct	Purchases	461.48
31 Oct	Bank	311.48			

Cash Account

4 Oct	Bank	750.00	20 Oct	Tee-Jay Products	150.00

Demland Supplies Account

16 Oct	Purchase returns	56.40	8 Oct	Purchases	315.98

W. Jackson Account

26 Oct	Purchase returns	65.80	12 Oct	Purchases	356.01
			23 Oct	Purchases	440.39

Purchase Returns Account

			16 Oct	Demland Supplies	48.00
			26 Oct	W. Jackson	56.00

Unit 4

4.1 Dean Sayer

Cash Account

1 May	Capital	7,000.00	6 May	Bank	5,000.00
26 May	V. Reedman	226.07			

Capital Account

			1 May	Capital	7,000.00

K. Bradshaw Account

3 May	Sales	353.44	15 May	Sales returns	56.40

Sales Account

			3 May	K. Bradshaw	300.80
			10 May	V. Reedman	192.40
			20 May	James Seymore	286.20

Value Added Tax Account

15 May	K. Bradshaw	8.40	3 May	K. Bradshaw	52.64
28 May	James Seymore	6.22	10 May	V. Reedman	33.67
			20 May	James Seymore	50.08

Bank Account

| 6 May | Cash | 5,000.00 | | | |

V. Reedman Account

| 10 May | Sales | 226.07 | 26 May | Cash | 226.07 |

Sales Returns Account

| 15 May | K. Bradshaw | 48.00 | | | |
| 28 May | James Seymore | 35.56 | | | |

James Seymore Account

| 20 May | Sales | 336.28 | 28 May | Sales returns | 41.78 |

4.2 M. Daswani

Bank Account

| 1 Jun | Capital | 10,000.00 | 8 Jun | Cash | 850.00 |
| 28 Jun | T. Ross | 377.06 | | | |

Capital Account

| | | | 1 Jun | Bank | 10,000.00 |

T. Ross Account

| 2 Jun | Sales | 433.81 | 4 Jun | Sales returns | 56.75 |
| | | | 28 Jun | Bank | 377.06 |

Sales Account

			2 Jun	T. Ross	369.20
			4 Jun	Aztec Sportswear	604.00
			18 Jun	Classic Casuals	530.40

Value Added Tax Account

14 Jun	T. Ross	8.45	2 Jun	T. Ross	64.61
24 Jun	Aztec Sportswear	13.19	4 Jun	Aztec Sportswear	105.70
			18 Jun	Classic Casuals	92.82

Aztec Sportswear Account

| 4 Jun | Sales | 709.70 | 24 Jun | Sales returns | 88.57 |

Cash Account

| 8 Jun | Bank | 850.00 | | | |

Sales Returns Account

| 14 Jun | T. Ross | 48.30 | | | |
| 24 Jun | Aztec Sportswear | 75.38 | | | |

Classic Casuals Account

| 18 Jun | Sales | 623.22 | | | |

4.3 Thomas Wagner

Cash Account

| 1 Jul | Capital | 8,000.00 | 7 Jul | Bank | 7,500.00 |
| 24 Jul | M. Shah | 250.00 | | | |

Capital Account

| | | | 1 Jul | Cash | 8,000.00 |

Oakwood Stores Account

| 3 Jul | Sales | 346.93 | 18 Jul | Sales returns | 42.59 |

Sales Account

			3 Jul	Oakwood Stores	295.26
			10 Jul	M. Shah	408.70
			14 Jul	J. Courtway	197.50

Value Added Tax Account

18 Jul	Oakwood Stores	6.34	3 Jul	Oakwood Stores	51.67
30 Jul	J. Courtway	5.03	10 Jul	M. Shah	71.52
			14 Jul	J. Courtway	34.56

Bank Account

7 Jul	Cash	7,500.00	

M. Shah Account

10 Jul	Sales	480.22	24 Jul	Cash	250.00

J. Courtway Account

14 Jul	Sales	232.06	30 Jul	Sales returns	33.78

Sales Returns Account

18 Jul	Oakwood Stores	36.25	
30 Jul	J. Courtway	28.75	

4.4 Joseph McKenzie

Bank Account

1 Aug	Capital	7,000.00	8 Aug	Cash	750.00
31 Aug	Montague Giles	294.50			

Capital Account

			1 Aug	Bank	7,000.00

Montague Giles Account

3 Aug	Sales	294.50	31 Aug	Bank	294.50
24 Aug	Sales	458.86			

Sales Account

			3 Aug	Montague Giles	250.64
			12 Aug	D. Towers	402.80
			15 Aug	Buywise	268.24
			24 Aug	Montague Giles	390.52

Value Added Tax Account

20 Aug	D. Towers	6.23	3 Aug	Montague Giles	43.86
26 Aug	Buywise	8.53	12 Aug	D. Towers	70.49
			15 Aug	Buywise	46.94
			24 Aug	Montague Giles	68.34

Cash Account

8 Aug	Bank	750.00	

D. Towers Account

12 Aug	Sales	473.29	20 Aug	Sales returns	41.83

Buywise Account

15 Aug	Sales	315.18	26 Aug	Sales returns	57.28

Sales Returns Account

20 Aug	D. Towers	35.60
26 Aug	Buywise	48.75

Unit 5

5.1 Account to be debited — Account to be credited
  (a) Motor expenses — Cash
  (b) Rent — Bank
  (c) Drawings — Cash
  (d) Rates — Bank
  (e) Cash — Commission received
  (f) Insurance — Bank

5.2 Account to be debited — Account to be credited
  (a) Purchases — Cash
  (b) Bank — Rent received
  (c) Motor expenses — Bank
  (d) J. Kendall — Sales
  (e) Motor van — Leaders Garages
  (f) Wages — Cash

5.3 Account to be debited — Account to be credited
  (a) Electricity — Bank
  (b) Cash — Sales
  (c) Bank — Commission received
  (d) Sales returns — J. Kilburn
  (e) Office furniture — Bank
  (f) Drawings — Cash

5.4 Account to be debited — Account to be credited
  (a) R. Bright — Purchase returns
  (b) Rates — Bank
  (c) K. Williams — Sales
  (d) Drawings — Purchases
  (e) Sales returns — K. Williams
  (f) Cash — Rates

5.5 A. Oldridge

Bank Account

1 May	Capital	5,000.00	4 May	Cash	500.00
16 May	Rent received	230.00	12 May	Rent	275.50
24 May	K. Stead	148.05	30 May	Drawings	150.00

Capital Account

			1 May	Bank	5,000.00

Purchases Account

2 May	J. Richardson	750.00
19 May	S. Ramsden	720.80

Value Added Tax Account

2 May	J. Richardson	131.25	6 May	J. Richardson	7.00
14 May	K. Stead	4.20	11 May	K. Stead	26.25
15 May	Cash	26.00	26 May	T. Barnett	21.35
19 May	S. Ramsden	126.14	27 May	S. Ramsden	12.06

J. Richardson Account

6 May	Purchase returns	47.00	2 May	Purchases	881.25

Cash Account

4 May	Bank	500.00	7 May	Drawings	100.00
			15 May	Motor expenses	174.60
			22 May	Wages	150.00

Purchase Returns Account

		6 May	J. Richardson	40.00
		27 May	S. Ramsden	68.94

Drawings Account

7 May	Cash	100.00
30 May	Bank	150.00

K. Stead Account

11 May	Sales	176.25	14 May	Sales returns	28.20
			24 May	Bank	148.05

Sales Account

		11 May	K. Stead	150.00
		26 May	T. Barnett	122.00

Rent Account

12 May	Bank	275.50

Sales Returns Account

14 May	K. Stead	24.00

Motor Expenses Account

15 May	Cash	148.60

Rent Received Account

		16 May	Bank	230.00

S. Ramsden Account

27 May	Purchase returns	81.00	19 May	Purchases	846.94

Wages Account

22 May	Cash	150.00

T. Barnett Account

26 May	Sales	143.35

5.6 Keith Wilson

Cash Account

1 Jun	Capital	10,000.00	3 Jun	Rent	250.00
			6 Jun	Bank	9,000.00
			12 Jun	Drawings	175.00

Capital Account

		1 Jun	Cash	10,000.00

Purchases Account

2 Jun	Kruger Imports	502.54
10 Jun	A. Dawson	329.50
20 Jun	A. Dawson	650.70

Value Added Tax Account

2 Jun	Kruger Imports	87.94	8 Jun	J. Stevens	43.91
10 Jun	A. Dawson	57.66	16 Jun	Kruger Imports	6.74
14 Jun	J. Stevens	4.53	23 Jun	G. Blackman	86.73
20 Jun	A. Dawson	113.87			
29 Jun	G. Blackman	10.15			

Kruger Imports Account

16 Jun	Purchase returns	45.26	2 Jun	Purchases	590.48
30 Jun	Bank	250.00			

Rent Account

3 Jun	Cash	250.00

Bank Account

6 Jun	Cash	9,000.00	18 Jun	Rates	150.00
28 Jun	J. Stevens	264.40	26 Jun	Drawings	120.00
			30 Jun	Kruger Imports	250.00

J. Stevens Account

8 Jun	Sales	294.83	14 Jun	Sales returns	30.43
			28 Jun	Bank	264.40

Sales Account

			8 Jun	J. Stevens	250.92
			23 Jun	G. Blackman	495.60

A. Dawson Account

			10 Jun	Purchases	387.16
			20 Jun	Purchases	764.57

Drawings Account

12 Jun	Cash	175.00
26 Jun	Bank	120.00

Sales Returns Account

14 Jun	J. Stevens	25.90
29 Jun	G. Blackman	58.00

Purchase Returns Account

			16 Jun	Kruger Imports	38.52

Rates Account

18 Jun	Bank	150.00

G. Blackman Account

23 Jun	Sales	582.33	29 Jun	Sales returns	68.15

5.7 Denise Shelley

Bank Account

1 Aug	Capital	5,000.00	10 Aug	Cash	300.00
			12 Aug	Drawings	150.00
			31 Aug	Smith & Weston	250.00

Capital Account

					1 Aug	Bank	5,000.00

Purchases Account

2 Aug	Smith & Weston	359.20			
23 Aug	Dale Supplies	620.54			

Value Added Tax Account

2 Aug	Smith & Weston	62.86	5 Aug	H. Gibson	49.12
19 Aug	H. Gibson	7.00	7 Aug	Smith & Weston	6.78
23 Aug	Dale Supplies	108.59	24 Aug	J. Youngman	48.74
			27 Aug	Dale Supplies	10.06

Smith & Weston Account

7 Aug	Purchase returns	45.53	2 Aug	Purchases	422.06
31 Aug	Bank	250.00			

H. Gibson Account

5 Aug	Sales	329.81	19 Aug	Sales returns	47.00
			21 Aug	Cash	200.00

Sales Account

			5 Aug	H. Gibson	280.69
			24 Aug	J. Youngman	278.54

Purchase Returns Account

			7 Aug	Smith & Weston	38.75
			27 Aug	Dale Supplies	57.50

Cash Account

10 Aug	Bank	300.00	15 Aug	Rent	280.00
21 Aug	H. Gibson	200.00	22 Aug	Wages	175.00
28 Aug	Rent received	50.00			

Drawings Account

12 Aug	Bank	150.00			

Rent Account

15 Aug	Cash	280.00			

Sales Returns Account

19 Aug	H. Gibson	40.00			

Wages Account

22 Aug	Cash	175.00			

Dale Supplies Account

27 Aug	Purchase returns	67.56	23 Aug	Purchases	729.13

J. Youngman Account

24 Aug	Sales	327.28			

Rent Received Account

			28 Aug	Cash	50.00

5.8 Thomas Garside

Bank Account

1 Oct	Capital	7,000.00	3 Oct	Cash	750.00

12 Oct	Commission received	75.00	24 Oct	T. Richie	807.77
29 Oct	D. Jenkins	301.48			

Capital Account

			1 Oct	Bank	7,000.00

Purchases Account

2 Oct	T. Richie	750.00
14 Oct	R. Kemp	267.96
22 Oct	R. Kemp	360.80

Value Added Tax Account

2 Oct	T. Richie	131.25	5 Oct	D. Jenkins	51.71
14 Oct	R. Kemp	46.89	10 Oct	T. Richie	10.94
15 Oct	D. Jenkins	6.81	18 Oct	J. Patel	26.25
22 Oct	R. Kemp	63.14	26 Oct	R. Kemp	9.78
			27 Oct	D. Jenkins	22.87

T. Richie Account

10 Oct	Purchase returns	73.48	2 Oct	Purchases	881.25
24 Oct	Bank	807.77			

Cash Account

3 Oct	Bank	750.00	7 Oct	Rent	195.00
28 Oct	Commission received	165.00	20 Oct	Wages	250.00
			30 Oct	Drawings	150.00
			31 Oct	Wages	275.50

D. Jenkins Account

5 Oct	Sales	347.21	15 Oct	Sales returns	45.73
27 Oct	Sales	153.57	29 Oct	Bank	301.48

Sales Account

			5 Oct	D. Jenkins	295.50
			18 Oct	J. Patel	150.00
			27 Oct	D. Jenkins	130.70

Rent Account

7 Oct	Cash	195.00

Purchase Returns Account

			10 Oct	T. Richie	62.54
			26 Oct	R. Kemp	55.90

Commission Received Account

			12 Oct	Bank	75.00
			28 Oct	Cash	165.00

R. Kemp Account

26 Oct	Purchase returns	65.68	14 Oct	Purchases	314.85
			22 Oct	Purchases	423.94

Sales Returns Account

15 Oct	D. Jenkins	38.92

J. Patel Account

18 Oct	Sales	176.25

Value Added Tax Account

3 Feb	Premier Imports	71.62	1 Feb	Balance b/d	582.98
5 Feb	Keswick Timber	65.78	10 Feb	Premier Imports	6.74
22 Feb	Morris Parks	7.64	16 Feb	Morris Parks	69.12
24 Feb	Bank	582.98	20 Feb	Decking Centre	87.94
28 Feb	Balance c/d	18.76			
		746.78			746.78
			1 Mar	Balance b/d	18.76

6.4 Moorland Textiles

Giles Murray Account

16 Nov	Bank	184.60	1 Nov	Balance b/d	369.20
30 Nov	Balance c/d	801.12	7 Nov	Purchases	616.52
		985.72			985.72
			1 Dec	Balance b/d	801.12

Four Star Supplies Account

10 Nov	Purchase returns	38.42	1 Nov	Balance b/d	502.84
15 Nov	Bank	251.42	2 Nov	Purchases	360.64
30 Nov	Balance c/d	573.64			
		863.48			863.48
			1 Dec	Balance b/d	573.64

Escape Hotels Account

1 Nov	Balance b/d	703.92	28 Nov	Bank	352.96
20 Nov	Sales	827.62	30 Nov	Balance c/d	1,178.58
		1,531.54			1,531.54
1 Dec	Balance b/d	1,178.58			

Myers Group Account

1 Nov	Balance b/d	850.38	26 Nov	Sales returns	47.94
18 Nov	Sales	658.82	30 Nov	Bank	426.50
			30 Nov	Balance c/d	1,034.76
		1,509.20			1,509.20
1 Dec	Balance b/d	1,034.76			

Bank Account

1 Nov	Balance b/d	6,729.76	12 Nov	Machinery	690.90
26 Nov	Escape Hotels	352.96	15 Nov	Four Star Supplies	251.42
30 Nov	Myers Group	426.50	16 Nov	Giles Murray	184.60
			30 Nov	Balance c/d	6,382.30
		7,509.22			7,509.22
1 Dec	Balance b/d	6,382.30			

Machinery Account

1 Nov	Balance b/d	9,650.50	30 Nov	Balance c/d	10,238.50
12 Nov	Bank	588.00			
		10,238.50			10,238.50
1 Dec	Balance b/d	10,238.50			

Purchases Account

1 Nov	Balance b/d	2,804.40	30 Nov	Balance c/d	3,636.03
2 Nov	Four Star Supplies	306.93			
7 Nov	Giles Murray	524.70			
		3,636.03			3,636.03
1 Dec	Balance b/d	3,636.03			

Purchase Returns Account

30 Nov	Balance c/d	338.60	1 Nov	Balance b/d	305.90
			10 Nov	Four Star Supplies	32.70
		338.60			338.60
			1 Dec	Balance b/d	338.60

Sales Account

30 Nov	Balance c/d	12,013.38	1 Nov	Balance b/d	10,748.32
			18 Nov	Myers Group	560.70
			20 Nov	Escape Hotels	704.36
		12,013.38			12,013.38
			1 Dec	Balance b/d	12,013.38

Sales Returns Account

1 Nov	Balance b/d	267.04	30 Nov	Balance c/d	307.84
26 Nov	Myers Group	40.80			
		307.84			307.84
1 Dec	Balance c/d	307.84			

Capital Account

30 Nov	Balance c/d	8,587.00	1 Nov	Balance b/d	8,587.00
			1 Dec	Balance b/d	8,587.00

Value Added Tax Account

2 Nov	Four Star Supplies	53.71	1 Nov	Balance b/d	492.74
7 Nov	Giles Murray	91.82	10 Nov	Four Star Supplies	5.72
12 Nov	Bank	102.90	18 Nov	Myers Group	98.12
26 Nov	Myers Group	7.14	20 Nov	Escape Hotels	123.26
30 Nov	Balance c/d	464.27			
		719.84			719.84
			1 Dec	Balance b/d	464.27

7.4 Paramont Designs

Trial Balance as at 31 May 20–7

	Dr	Cr
Springfields		1,556.08
Moonstones	1,128.14	
Owen & Robins	3,656.74	
Vandervilles	1,478.12	
Bank		1,942.36
Capital		5,231.54
General expenses	941.78	
Machinery	12,334.11	
Purchases	11,032.90	
Purchase returns		388.54
Sales		21,736.56
Sales returns	389.82	
Value Added Tax		106.53
	30,961.61	30,961.61

7.5 Focus Lighting

Trial Balance as at 30 November 20–7

	Dr	Cr
Court Fabrics		851.82
Walkers Ltd		471.91
Aladdin Lamps	1,007.07	
Supreme Deco	1,297.90	
Bank	2,931.10	
Capital		11,667.50
Fixtures & Fittings	17,342.20	
Purchases	9,471.58	
Purchase returns		669.90
Sales		19,778.34
Sales returns	483.74	
Sundry expenses	1,598.64	
Value Added Tax		692.76
	34,132.23	34,132.23

Unit 8

8.1 (a) 14.80 (b) 164.30 (c) 175.30 (d) 50.75 (e) 150.00

8.2 (a) 100.00 (b) 15.17 (c) 14.47 (d) 92.05 (e) 84.50 (f) 92.05 (g) 3.72 (h) 85.53

8.3 Pudsey Electronics

Petty Cash Book

RECEIPTS	DATE	DETAILS	VOUCHER NO	TOTAL PAYMENTS	VAT	Postage	Stationery	Refreshments	Sundry Expenses	Ledger
38.42	1-Sep	Balance b/d								
161.58	1-Sep	Cash								
	2-Sep	Kettle, tea, coffee	38	27.25	2.75			8.75	15.75	
	6-Sep	Envelopes, batteries	39	11.71	1.74		5.72		4.25	
6.78	7-Sep	J. Martinez (use of telephone)	101							
	10-Sep	Postage stamps, parcel post	40	22.18		22.18				
	12-Sep	Petrol	41	18.50	2.75				15.75	
	15-Sep	Milk, teabags	42	3.54				3.54		
	15-Sep	Special delivery parcel	43	16.80		16.80				
7.50	19-Sep	M. Readings (use of photocopier)	102							
	24-Sep	G. Van Owen (PL14)	44	20.98						20.98
	24-Sep	Eight beakers, marker pens	45	23.64	3.52		5.52		14.60	
	26-Sep	Printer ribbon, parcel post	46	21.70	1.12	14.20	6.38			
	27-Sep	D. Chippendale (PL19)	47	18.26						18.26
				184.56	11.88	53.18	17.62	12.29	50.35	39.24
	30-Sep	Balance c/d		29.72						
214.28				214.28						
29.72	1-Oct	Balance b/d								

Amount to restore imprest on 1 October £170.28.

9.7

The three parties in a cheque: *drawee* – name of the bank

payee – to whom the cheque is made payable

drawer – person who signs the cheque.

9.8

Details of transfers are made electronically rather than providing individual bank giro credit forms.

9.9

(a) The holder of the account.

(b) Date, payee, amount in figures, amount in words, signature.

Unit 10

10.1 Robert Hurford

Cash Book										
Date	Particulars	F		Cash	Bank	Date	Particulars	F	Cash	Bank
01-May	Balances b/d			262.00	2,756.00	05-May	Cash purchases		134.00	
02-May	R. Douglas				368.00	08-May	Insurance			48.00
10-May	Cash sales			120.00		12-May	Motor expenses		97.00	
19-May	S. Myers				594.00	21-May	D. Nicholas			368.00
20-May	Cash sales			350.00		25-May	Cash purchases		173.00	
23-May	Bancroft Ltd				469.00	26-May	Giles Murray			502.00
30-May	J. Singh				375.00	28-May	Premier Imports			436.00
						31-May	Balances c/d		328.00	3,208.00
				732.00	4,562.00				732.00	4,562.00
01-Jun	Balances b/d			328.00	3,208.00					

10.2 Ann Bannister

Date	Particulars	F		Cash	Bank	Date	Particulars	F		Cash	Bank
							Cash Book				
01-Sep	Balances b/d			308.00	1,062.00	03-Sep	Motor expenses				104.00
04-Sep	Cash sales			158.00		12-Sep	Drawings			170.00	
08-Sep	C. M. Lupton				304.00	14-Sep	J. Oldridge				620.00
18-Sep	Rent received			250.00		16-Sep	T. Wilson Ltd				136.00
20-Sep	Marcus Ltd				498.00	24-Sep	Rates				290.00
22-Sep	Cash sales			320.00		25-Sep	Cash purchases			84.00	
27-Sep	R. Mills				376.00	28-Sep	Office supplies				52.00
29-Sep	M. Shah			94.00		30-Sep	Cash purchases			168.00	
30-Sep	Groves & Son				520.00	30-Sep	Balances c/d			708.00	1,558.00
				1,130.00	2,760.00					1,130.00	2,760.00
01-Oct	Balances b/d			708.00	1,558.00						

10.3 James Chang
  Totals: Cash 842.00   Bank 2,508.00
  Balances b/d: Cash debit 284.00 Bank debit 1,460.00
10.4 William Dyson
  Totals: Cash 1,302.00   Bank 5,693.00
  Balances b/d: Cash debit 310.00 Bank debit 2,724.00
10.5 Alison De Klerk
  Totals: Cash 1,350.00   Bank 4,518.00
  Balances b/d: Cash debit 812.00 Bank credit £2,210.00
10.6 Douglas Lockwood
  Totals: Cash 1,764.00   Bank 3,660.00
  Balances b/d: Cash debit 620.00 Bank debit 868.00

Unit 11

11.1 Morley Enterprises

Cash Book

Date	Particulars	F	Discount Allowed	Cash	Bank	Date	Particulars	F	Cheque Number	Discount Received	Cash	Bank
01-Sep	Balances b/d			406.72	724.98	03-Sep	H Schwartz		30126	10.74		492.78
04-Sep	Cash sales			169.76		04-Sep	Contract Blinds		30127			295.50
06-Sep	Curtis Ltd		18.64		286.90	06-Sep	Garside Holmes		30128	19.80		508.26
08-Sep	Kinsell & Co				680.34	15-Sep	Cash purchases				60.76	
12-Sep	T. Edmondson			125.82		18-Sep	Hudson Chase & Co		30129	27.78		672.84
18-Sep	Aztec Sportswear		28.62		576.28	20-Sep	Briggs & Booth		30130	10.52		315.28
20-Sep	De Wan Textiles				604.32	24-Sep	Cash purchases				120.58	
23-Sep	B. Chandler		14.80	94.38		28-Sep	T. G. Munro		30131	12.50		237.50
24-Sep	Apex Casuals				281.20	30-Sep	Balances c/d				720.54	1,070.62
27-Sep	Cash sales			105.20								
30-Sep	Kilroy & Ross		20.40		438.76							
			82.46	901.88	3,592.78					81.34	901.88	3,592.78
01-Oct	Balances b/d			720.54	1,070.62							

11.2 Andrews & Fox

Cash Book

Date	Particulars	F	Discount Allowed	Cash	Bank	Date	Particulars	F	Cheque Number	Discount Received	Cash	Bank
01-Oct	Balances b/d			168.52	998.20	04-Oct	Cash purchases				102.50	
02-Oct	S. Driver		18.39		357.30	08-Oct	Motor expenses		34612			76.32
06-Oct	Gladstone Bros		10.48		209.70	10-Oct	Delta Designs		34613	22.53		428.07
12-Oct	Lucas Sykes			120.38		17-Oct	Romana Products		34614	14.74		280.06
14-Oct	Chervilles Ltd				592.94	19-Sep	Sureguard Security		34615			195.50
15-Oct	Cash sales			350.76		21-Oct	Cash purchases				176.92	
20-Oct	W. Dyson Ltd		14.54		290.80	23-Oct	Evana Ltd		34616	19.52		370.88
24-Oct	J. Hussain			173.94		27-Oct	Montague Miles		34617			250.24
26-Oct	Cusack & Son		17.51		350.28	29-Oct	Insurance		34618			203.65
28-Oct	Cash sales			164.86		30-Oct	Star Plastics		34619	18.78		356.82
30-Oct	Adam Bates				182.42	31-Oct	Balances c/d				699.04	820.10
			60.92	978.46	2,981.64					75.57	978.46	2,981.64
01-Nov	Balances b/d			699.04	820.10							

11.3 Madhur Daswani
    Totals: Cash 1,014.12   Bank 2,894.19
    Totals: Discount allowed 65.86   Discount received 38.38
    Balances b/d: Cash debit 743.48   Bank debit 1,248.32

11.4 Harry Bairstow
    Totals: Cash 914.16   Bank 3,036.86
    Totals: Discount allowed 102.84   Discount received 49.23
    Balances b/d: Cash debit 649.88   Bank credit 559.58

11.5 Wilson Singer
    Totals: Cash 953.80   Bank 3,176.00
    Totals: Discount allowed 55.40   Discount received 82.31
    Balances b/d: Cash debit 569.86   Bank credit 361.28

11.6 Gina Howard
    Totals: Cash 989.70   Bank 3,474.08
    Totals: Discount allowed 119.22   Discount received 39.12
    Balances b/d: Cash debit 728.96   Bank debit 483.56

Unit 12

12.1 Morley Enterprises

Cash Book (Bank columns)

30 Sep	Balance b/d	1,070.62		30 Sep	L. D. Council (DD)	137.20
30 Sep	Roberts Ltd (BGC)	497.76		30 Sep	T. Kay Group (SO)	104.94
				30 Sep	Bank charges	13.04
				30 Sep	Balance c/d	1,313.20
		1,568.38				1,568.38
1 Oct	Balance b/d	1,313.20				

Bank Reconciliation Statement as at 30 September 20-9

Balance as per cash book		1,313.20
Add: Unpresented cheques:	508.26	
	237.50	745.76
		2,058.96
Less deposits not yet banked		438.76
Balance as per Bank statement		1,620.20

12.2 Andrew & Fox

Cash Book (Bank columns)

31 Oct	Balance b/d	820.10	31 Oct	Medleys (DD)	114.50
31 Oct	Catlow Ltd (BGC)	607.25	31 Oct	Y D C (SO)	213.76
			31 Oct	Bank charges	10.50
			31 Oct	Balance c/d	1,088.59
		1,427.35			1,427.35
1 Nov	Balance b/d	1,088.59			

Bank Reconciliation Statement as at 31 October 20-9

Balance as per cash book		1,088.59
Add: Unpresented cheques:	280.06	
	203.65	
	356.82	840.53
		1,929.12
Less deposits not yet banked		182.42
Balance as per Bank statement		1,746.70

12.3 Madhur Daswani

Cash Book (Bank columns)

31 May	Balance b/d	1,248.32	31 May	AOW Group (SO)	136.72
31 May	Lock Ltd (BGC)	592.58	31 May	Bank charges	12.65
31 May	Smythe Group (BACS)	436.94	31 May	Balance c/d	2,128.47
		2,277.84			2,277.84
1 Jun	Balance b/d	2,128.47			

Bank Reconciliation Statement as at 31 May 20-9

Balance as per cash book		2,128.47
Add: Unpresented cheques:	351.31	
	288.99	
	132.62	772.92
		2,901.39
Less deposits not yet banked		400.49
Balance as per Bank statement		2,500.90

12.4 Harry Bairstow

Cash Book, updated Bank total 1,249.24   Balance b/d debit 625.90

Bank Reconciliation Statement as at 30 June 20-9

Balance as per cash book		625.90
Add: Unpresented cheques:	409.89	
	279.63	689.52
		1,315.42
Less deposits not yet banked		305.82
Balance as per Bank statement		1,009.60

12.5 Wilson Singer

Cash Book, updated Bank total 825.95   Balance b/d debit 100.43

Bank Reconciliation Statement as at 30 September 20-8

Balance as per cash book		100.43
Add: Unpresented cheques:	618.26	
	260.75	879.01
		979.44
Less deposits not yet banked		138.98
Balance as per Bank statement		840.46

12.6 Gina Howard

Cash Book, updated Bank total 1,582.32   Balance b/d debit 1,417.58

Bank Reconciliation Statement as at 31 October 20-8

Balance as per cash book		1,417.58
Add: Unpresented cheques:	127.53	
	292.79	420.32
		1,837.90
Less deposits not yet banked		872.74
Balance as per Bank statement		965.16

12.7 Simms Enterprises

Totals:	Cash 784.32	Bank 2,979.86
Totals:	Discount allowed 88.00	Discount received 48.74
Updated total:	Bank 2,005.18	Balance b/d debit 1,758.99

Bank Reconciliation Statement as at 31 May 20-8

Balance as per cash book		1,758.99
Add: Unpresented cheques:	350.46	
	237.88	588.34
		2,347.33
Less deposits not yet banked		585.25
Balance as per Bank statement		1,762.08

Unit 13

13.1 West Park Centre

Purchases Day Book

Date 20-5	Details	Camping	Gardening	VAT	Total
2 Feb	Dalesman Products	435.60		76.23	511.83
7 Feb	Stanley Engineering	409.90	536.50	165.62	1,112.02
15 Feb	Earltex Supplies	349.82	247.05	104.45	701.32
20 Feb	Dalesman Products	875.20		153.16	1,028.36
24 Feb	Earltex Supplies	207.92	494.10	122.85	824.87
28 Feb		2,278.44	1,277.65	622.31	4,178.40

Purchases Returns Day Book

Date 20-5	Details	Camping	Gardening	VAT	Total
14 Feb	Dalesman Products	63.16		11.05	74.21
17 Feb	Stanley Engineering	79.96	29.50	19.16	128.62
28 Feb		143.12	29.50	30.21	202.83

Purchase Ledger

Dalesman Products Account

14 Feb	Purchase returns	74.21	2 Feb	Purchases	511.83
28 Feb	Balance c/d	1,465.98	20 Feb	Purchases	1,028.36
		1,540.19			1,540.19
			1 Mar	Balance b/d	1,465.98

Stanley Engineering Account

17 Feb	Purchase returns	128.62	7 Feb	Purchases	1,112.02
28 Feb	Balance c/d	983.40			
		1,112.02			1,112.02
			1 Mar	Balance b/d	983.40

Earltex Supplies Account

28 Feb	Balance c/d	1,526.19	15 Feb	Purchases	701.32
			24 Feb	Purchases	824.87
		1,526.19			1,526.19
			1 Mar	Balance b/d	1,526.19

Nominal Ledger

Purchases Account – Camping

28 Feb	Total P D B	2,278.44

Purchases Account – Gardening

28 Feb	Total P D B	1,277.65

Purchase returns Account – Camping

28 Feb	Total P R D B	143.12

Purchase returns Account – Gardening

28 Feb	Total P R D B	29.50

Value Added Tax Account

28 Feb	Total P D B	622.31	28 Feb	Total P R D B	30.21

13.2 Pick-up Parts

Purchases Day Book

Date 20-5	Details	Tyres	Exhausts	VAT	Total
2 May	Auto Factors	309.86	274.90	102.33	687.09
7 May	Mitchells Ltd	672.50		117.69	790.19
16 May	Euro Universal	407.60	318.58	127.08	853.26
20 May	Auto Factors	494.80	205.76	122.60	823.16
24 May	Mitchells Ltd	392.75		68.73	461.48
31 May		2,277.51	799.24	538.43	3,615.18

Purchases Returns Day Book

Date 20-5	Details	Tyres	Exhausts	VAT	Total
14 May	Auto Factors	59.65	47.28	18.71	125.64
18 May	Mitchells Ltd	94.50		16.54	111.04
28 May	Euro Universal	62.49	79.50	24.85	166.84
31 May		216.64	126.78	60.10	403.52

Purchase Ledger

Auto Factors Account

14 May	Purchase returns	125.64	2 May	Purchases	687.09
31 May	Balance c/d	1,384.61	20 May	Purchases	823.16
		1,510.25			1,510.25
			1 Jun	Balance b/d	1,384.61

Mitchells Ltd Account

18 May	Purchase returns	111.04	7 May	Purchases	790.19
31 May	Balance c/d	1,140.63	24 May	Purchases	461.48
		1,251.67			1,251.67
			1 Jun	Balance b/d	1,140.63

Euro Universal Account

28 May	Purchase returns	166.84		16 May	Purchases	853.26
31 May	Balance c/d	686.42				
		853.26				853.26
				1 Jun	Balance b/d	686.42

Nominal Ledger

Purchases Account – Tyres

31 May	Total P D B	2,277.51	

Purchases Account – Exhausts

31 May	Total P D B	799.24	

Purchase returns Account – Tyres

		31 May	Total P R D B	216.64

Purchase returns Account – Exhausts

		31 May	Total P R D B	126.78

Value Added Tax Account

31 May	Total P D B	538.43	31 May	Total P R D B	60.10

13.3 Europas Fashions

Purchases Day Book

Date 20-5	Details	Jackets	Jeans	VAT	Total
2 Nov	Hongtai Imports	374.90	460.58	146.21	981.69
5 Nov	James Wyatt Ltd	502.76	296.38	139.85	938.99
14 Nov	Focus Marketing		407.32	71.28	478.60
17 Nov	James Wyatt Ltd	364.20	590.75	167.12	1,122.07
25 Nov	Hongtai Imports	278.50	205.20	84.65	568.35
30 Nov		1,520.36	1,960.23	609.11	4,089.70

Purchases Returns Day Book

Date 20-5	Details	Jackets	Jeans	VAT	Total
10 Nov	Hongtai Imports	39.45	48.50	15.39	103.34
23 Nov	Focus Marketing		39.95	6.99	46.94
27 Nov	James Wyatt Ltd	49.92	38.78	15.52	104.22
30 Nov		89.37	127.23	37.90	254.50

13.4 Marcus Cavendish

Purchases Day Book

Date 20-6	Details	China	Cutlery	VAT	Total
2 Feb	Ainsley Sykes	208.76	519.50	127.45	855.71
4 Feb	Ultimate Designs	326.48	290.20	107.92	724.60
6 Feb	Kilncroft Ltd	450.42		78.82	529.24
18 Feb	Ainsley Sykes	375.56	462.90	146.73	985.19
24 Feb	Ultimate Designs	128.90	509.74	111.76	750.40
28 Feb		1,490.12	1,782.34	572.68	3,845.14

Purchases Returns Day Book

Date 20-6	Details	China	Cutlery	VAT	Total
15 Feb	Ultimate Designs	73.56	40.38	19.94	133.88
20 Feb	Kilncroft Ltd	32.78		5.74	38.52
26 Feb	Ainsley Sykes	39.20	84.36	21.62	145.18
28 Feb		145.54	124.74	47.30	317.58

13.5 Kerterama Ltd

Purchases Day Book

Date 20-6	Details	Curtains	Cushions	VAT	Invoice Total
3 May	Yorkshire Fabrics	420.76	89.50	89.30	599.56
7 May	Kirk Mills Ltd	704.20		123.24	827.44
15 May	Venture Textiles	498.62	186.30	119.86	804.78
20 May	Yorkshire Fabrics	394.78	138.26	93.28	626.32
28 May	Kirk Mills Ltd	409.50	115.78	91.92	617.20
31 May		2,427.86	529.84	517.60	3,475.30

Purchases Returns Day Book

Date 20-6	Details	Curtains	Cushions	VAT	Total
12 May	Yorkshire Fabrics	58.26	20.50	13.78	92.54
18 May	Kirk Mills Ltd	92.70		16.22	108.92
25 May	Venture Textiles	69.30	28.52	17.12	114.94
31 May		220.26	49.02	47.12	316.40

Unit 14

14.1 Otterman Supplies

Sales Day Book

Date 20-6	Details	Quilts	Pillows	VAT	Invoice Total
2 May	Homecraft Ltd	384.50	130.00	90.04	604.54
4 May	Tradeways		812.00	142.10	954.10
7 May	Windsor Stores	172.50	712.50	154.88	1,039.88
14 May	Tradeways	698.00	260.00	167.65	1,125.65
21 May	Windsor Stores	724.40		126.77	851.17
31 May		1,979.40	1,914.50	681.44	4,575.34

Sales Returns Day Book

Date 20-6	Details	Quilts	Pillows	VAT	Total
12 May	Homecraft Ltd	57.40	15.00	12.67	85.07
18 May	Windsor Stores	9.75	60.00	12.21	81.96
26 May	Tradeways		47.45	8.30	55.75
31 May		67.15	122.45	33.18	222.78

Sales Ledger

Homecraft Ltd Account

2 May	Sales	604.54		12 May	Sales returns	85.07
				31 May	Balance c/d	519.47
		604.54				604.54
1 Jun	Balance b/d	519.47				

Tradeways Account

4 May	Sales	954.10		26 May	Sales returns	55.75
14 May	Sales	1,125.65		31 May	Balance c/d	2,024.00
		2,079.75				2,079.75
1 Jun	Balance b/d	2,024.00				

Windsor Stores Account

7 May	Sales	1,039.88		18 May	Sales returns	81.96
21 May	Sales	851.17		31 May	Balance c/d	1,809.09
		1,891.05				1,891.05
1 Jun	Balance b/d	1,809.09				

Nominal Ledger

Sales Account – Quilts

				31 May	Total S D B	1,979.40

Sales Account – Pillows

				31 May	Total S D B	1,914.50

Sales returns Account – Quilts

31 May	Total S R D B	67.15				

Sales returns Account – Pillows

31 May	Total S R D B	122.45

Value Added Tax Account

31 May	Total S R D B	33.18	31 May	Total S D B	681.44

14.2 Shandley Group

Sales Day Book

Date 20-6	Details	Paint	Wallpaper	VAT	Total
2 Nov	Nulooks Stores	274.82	396.50	117.48	788.80
3 Nov	Foyle & Barker	590.76		103.38	694.14
8 Nov	Creative Designs	350.96	407.20	132.68	890.84
14 Nov	Nulooks Stores	207.38	524.62	128.10	860.10
26 Nov	Foyle & Barker		319.78	55.96	375.74
30 Nov		1,423.92	1,648.10	537.60	3,609.62

Sales Returns Day Book

Date 20-6	Details	Paint	Wallpaper	VAT	Total
12 Nov	Foyle & Barker	46.74		8.18	54.92
18 Nov	Creative Designs	38.54	56.30	16.60	111.44
28 Nov	Nulooks Stores	37.84	29.50	11.78	79.12
30 Nov		123.12	85.80	36.56	245.48

Sales Ledger

Nulooks Stores Account

2 Nov	Sales	788.80	28 Nov	Sales returns	79.12
14 Nov	Sales	860.10	30 Nov	Balance c/d	1,569.78
		1,648.90			1,648.90
1 Dec	Balance b/d	1,569.78			

Foyle & Barker Account

3 Nov	Sales	694.14	12 Nov	Sales returns	54.92
26 Nov	Sales	375.74	30 Nov	Balance c/d	1,014.96
		1,069.88			1,069.88
1 Dec	Balance b/d	1,014.96			

Creative Designs Account

8 Nov	Sales	890.84	18 Nov	Sales returns	111.44
			30 Nov	Balance c/d	779.40
		890.84			890.84
1 Dec	Balance b/d	779.40			

Nominal Ledger

Sales Account – Paint

			30 Nov	Total S D B	1,423.92

Sales Account – Wallpaper

			30 Nov	Total S D B	1,648.10

Sales returns Account – Paint

30 Nov	Total S R D B	123.12			

Sales returns Account – Wallpaper

30 Nov	Total S R D B	85.80			

Value Added Tax Account

30 Nov	Total S R D B	36.56	30 Nov	Total S D B	537.60

14.3 Speedy Supplies

Sales Day Book

Date 20-7	Details	Handles	Hinges	VAT	Total
2 Feb	Keywise Centre	270.58	42.50	54.79	367.87
5 Feb	Sureguard Solutions	304.50	56.20	63.12	423.82
9 Feb	James Moss Ltd	398.76		69.78	468.54
18 Feb	James Moss Ltd	507.20	90.24	104.55	701.99
24 Feb	Keywise Centre		80.70	14.12	94.82
28 Feb		1,481.04	269.64	306.36	2,057.04

Sales Returns Day Book

Date 20-7	Details	Handles	Hinges	VAT	Total
14 Feb	Keywise Centre	24.58	9.50	5.96	40.04
20 Feb	Sureguard Solutions	45.92	16.36	10.90	73.18
26 Feb	James Moss Ltd	52.48		9.18	61.66
28 Feb		122.98	25.86	26.04	174.88

14.4 Colorcraft Ltd

Sales Day Book

Date 20-7	Details	Blinds	Curtains	VAT	Total
1 May	Abbeygales Ltd	217.64	490.58	123.94	832.16
3 May	Thomas Fannelli		576.92	100.96	677.88
6 May	Style Interiors	409.60	286.42	121.80	817.82
14 May	Thomas Fannelli	305.20	418.76	126.69	850.65
22 May	Abbeygales Ltd	148.50	294.30	77.49	520.29
31 May		1,080.94	2,066.98	550.88	3,698.80

Sales Returns Day Book

Date 20-7	Details	Blinds	Curtains	VAT	Total
10 May	Abbeygales Ltd	27.98	52.50	14.08	94.56
18 May	Style Interiors	72.80		12.74	85.54
27 May	Thomas Fannelli	36.24	40.62	13.45	90.31
31 May		137.02	93.12	40.27	270.41

14.5 Avenger Sportswear

Sales Day Book

Date 20-7	Details	Shirts	Shorts	VAT	Total
2 Nov	Sport & Leisure Ltd	295.90	120.68	72.90	489.48
4 Nov	K. Pointers	307.50	91.39	69.81	468.70
12 Nov	D. McKenzie Ltd	362.28	309.26	117.52	789.06
18 Nov	Sport & Leisure Ltd	394.72	162.75	97.56	655.03
24 Nov	D. McKenzie Ltd	405.36	113.52	90.80	609.68
30 Nov		1,765.76	797.60	448.59	3,011.95

Sales Returns Day Book

Date 20-7	Details	Shirts	Shorts	VAT	Total
10 Nov	Sport & Leisure Ltd	38.92	26.50	11.45	76.87
15 Nov	K. Pointers	47.36		8.29	55.65
20 Nov	D. McKenzie Ltd	25.70	50.28	13.30	89.28
30 Nov		111.98	76.78	33.04	221.80

Unit 15

15.1 Sandra Ramsden

Trading and Profit and Loss Account for the year ended 31 December 20-6

Purchases	15,269	Sales	20,662
Less closing stock	2,868		
Cost of goods sold	12,401		
Gross profit c/d	8,261		
	20,662		20,662
Rent	650	Gross profit b/d	8,261
Insurance	155		
Motor expenses	545		
Wages	2,568		
Net profit	4,343		
	8,261		8,261

Balance Sheet as at 31 December 20-6

Fixed Assets			Capital at start	6,000	
Equipment	2,850		Add net profit	4,343	
Motor vehicle	1,100	3,950		10,343	
			Less drawings	925	9,418
Current Assets			**Current Liabilities**		
Stock	2,868		Creditors		1,682
Debtors	2,350				
Bank	1,864				
Cash	68	7,150			
		11,100			11,100

15.2 Michael Seymour

Trading, profit and loss account for the year ended 31 December 20-7

Purchases	14,650	Sales	18,874
Less closing stock	3,235		
Cost of goods sold	11,415		
Gross profit c/d	7,459		
	18,874		18,874
Rates	720	Gross profit b/d	7,459
General expenses	490		
Wages & salaries	3,105		
Motor expenses	382		
Insurance	220		
Net profit	2,542		
	7,459		7,459

Balance Sheet as at 31 December 20-7

Fixed Assets			Capital at start	18,000	
Premises	7,700		Add net profit	2,542	
Fixtures & fittings	1,750			20,542	
Motor vehicles	3,900	13,350	Less drawings	1,250	19,292
Current Assets			**Current Liabilities**		
Stock	3,235		Creditors		1,926
Debtors	2,865				
Bank	1,646				
Cash	122	7,868			
		21,218			21,218

15.3 Gross profit 8,319   Net profit 3,197
    Fixed assets 9,250   Current assets 14,273
    Current liabilities 2,018

15.4 Gross profit 6,738   Net loss 1,071
    Fixed assets 29,400   Current assets 10,229
    Long term liabilities 6,000   Current liabilities 6,450

15.5 Gross profit 15,781   Net profit 8,224
    Fixed assets 19,000   Current assets 44,788
    Long term liabilities 5,000   Current liabilities 13,864

15.6 (a) Fixed assets 25,950   Current assets 14,325
      Current liabilities 1,025

(b)

Drawings Account

31 Mar	Bank	1,250	31 Dec	Capital	5,000
30 Jun	Bank	1,250			
30 Sep	Bank	1,250			
31 Dec	Bank	1,250			
		5,000			5,000

Capital Account

31 Dec	Drawings	5,000	1 Jan	Balance b/d	25,750
31 Dec	Balance c/d	39,250	31 Dec	Net profit	18,500
		44,250			44,250
			1 Jan	Balance b/d	39,250

15.7 (a) Fixed assets 68,250   Current assets 10,250
      Long term liabilities 5,000   Current liabilities 5,530

(b)

Drawings Account

31 Aug	Bank	1,750	31 May	Capital	7,000
30 Nov	Bank	1,750			
28 Feb	Bank	1,750			
31 May	Bank	1,750			
		7,000			7,000

Capital Account

31 May	Drawings	7,000	1 Jun	Balance b/d	45,250
31 May	Balance c/d	67,970	31 May	Net profit	29,720
		74,970			74,970
			1 Jun	Balance b/d	67,970

Unit 16

16.1   **Trading and Profit and Loss Account for the year ended 31 December 19-7**

Opening stock	21,190	Sales	98,650
Add purchases	76,990	Less sales returns	562
	98,180		98,088
Less purchase returns	415		
	97,765		
Add carriage inwards	204		
	97,969		
Less closing stock	22,560		
Cost of goods sold	75,409		
Gross profit c/d	22,679		
	98,088		98,088
Rent	1,855	Gross profit b/d	22,679
Wages & salaries	9,890		
Carriage outwards	251		
Insurance	365		
Motor expenses	932		
General expenses	428		
Net profit	8,958		
	22,679		22,679

Balance Sheet as at 31 December 20 7

Fixed Assets			Capital	30,200		
Furniture & fittings	4,420		Add net profit	8,958		
Motor vehicle	5,500	9,920		39,158		
			Less drawings	2,330	36,828	
			Long term liabilities			
			Loan – D. Conway		5,000	
Current Assets			*Current Liabilities*			
Closing Stock	22,560		Creditors		10,735	
Debtors	14,950					
Bank	4,620					
Cash	513	42,643				
		52,563			52,563	

16.2 Trading and Profit and Loss Account for the year ended 30 September 20-7

Opening stock	9,842	Sales	69,480
Add purchases	45,612	Less sales returns	872
	55,454		68,608
Less purchase returns	684		
	54,770		
Add carriage inwards	485		
	55,255		
Less closing stock	8,975		
Cost of goods sold	46,280		
Gross profit c/d	22,328		
	68,608		68,608
Salaries & wages	7,838	Gross profit b/d	22,328
Insurance	556	Discount received	452
Rent and rates	740		
Carriage outwards	414		
Motor expenses	526		
Discount allowed	322		
Net profit	12,384		
	22,780		22,780

Balance Sheet as at 30 September 20-7

Fixed Assets			Capital	16,900	
Fixtures & fittings	2,900		Add net profit	12,384	
Motor vehicles	7,500	10,400		29,284	
			Less drawings	2,500	26,784
Current Assets			Current Liabilities		
Closing Stock	8,975		Creditors		8,984
Debtors	10,765				
Bank	5,628	25,368			
		35,768			35,768

16.3 Gross profit 17,880   Net profit 7,080
     Fixed assets 25,900   Current assets 9,880
     Long term liabilities 3,000   Current liabilities 6,060
16.4 Gross profit 10,970   Net profit 3,592
     Fixed assets 9,700   Current assets 20,162
     Current liabilities 5,980
16.5 Gross profit 10,455   Net loss 728
     Fixed assets 17,900   Current assets 15,800
     Long term liabilities 5,000   Current liabilities 8,540
16.6 Gross profit 24,117   Net profit 12,320
     Fixed assets 28,500   Current assets 18,660
     Current liabilities 4,950

Unit 17

17.1 Cost $20,000 - 5,000 = 15,000$ divided by $5 = 3,000$
     $20,000 - 3,000 = 17,000 - 3,000 = 14,000 - 3,000 =$
     $11,000 - 3,000 = 8,000 - 3,000 = 5,000$
17.2 Cost $8,000 - 2,400 = 5,600 - 1,680 = 3,920 - 1,176 = 2,744$
17.3 (a) Straight line: Cost $10,500 - 2,520 = 7,980$ divided by $4 = 1,995$
        $10,500 - 1,995 = 8,505 - 1,995 = 6,510 - 1,995 = 4,515 - 1,995 = 2,520$
    (b) Reducing balance: Cost $10,500 - 3,150 = 7,350 - 2,205 =$
        $5,145 - 1,544 = 3,601 - 1,080 = 2,521$
17.4 (a) Straight line: Cost $3,000 - 712 = 2,288$ divided by $5 = 458$
        $3,000 - 458 = 2,542 - 458 = 2,084 - 458 = 1,626 - 458 =$
        $1,168 - 458 = 710$
    (b) Reducing balance: $3,000 - 750 = 2,250 - 563 = 1,687 - 422 =$
        $1,265 - 316 = 949 - 237 = 712$
17.5 Cost $6,500 - 1,300 = 5,200 - 1,040 = 4,160 - 832 = 3,328$
     Cost $7,500 - 1,125 = 6,375 - 1,275 = 5,100$

17.6　Machine 'M'　Cost $3,000 - 825 = 2,175 - 653 = 1,522 - 457 = 1,065$
　　　Machine 'D'　Cost $4,000 - 600 = 3,400 - 1,020 = 2,380 - 714 = 1,666$
　　　Machine 'W'　Cost $5,000 - 125 = 4,875 - 1,463 = 3,412 - 1,024 = 2,388$
　　　Machine 'B'　Cost $6,000 - 600 = 5,400 - 1,620 = 3,780$

Unit 18

18.1
Machinery Account

Apr Bank　　　　　　　　3,000

Provision for Depreciation Account

31 Dec	Balance c/d	750	31 Dec	Profit and loss	750
31 Dec	Balance c/d	1,312	1 Jan	Balance b/d	750
			31 Dec	Profit and loss	562
		1,312			1,312
31 Dec	Balance c/d	1,734	1 Jan	Balance b/d	1,312
			31 Dec	Profit and loss	422
		1,734			1,734
31 Dec	Balance c/d	2,050	1 Jan	Balance b/d	1,734
			31 Dec	Profit and loss	316
		2,050			2,050
31 Dec	Balance c/d	2,287	1 Jan	Balance b/d	2,050
			31 Dec	Profit and loss	237
		2,287			2,287
			1 Jan	Balance b/d	2,287

18.2 (a)

Vehicle Account

1 Jan	Bank	23,000

Provision for Depreciation Account

31 Dec	Balance c/d	4,000	31 Dec	Profit and loss	4,000
31 Dec	Balance c/d	8,000	1 Jan	Balance b/d	4,000
			31 Dec	Profit and loss	4,000
		8,000			8,000
31 Dec	Balance c/d	12,000	1 Jan	Balance b/d	8,000
			31 Dec	Profit and loss	4,000
		12,000			12,000
31 Dec	Balance c/d	16,000	1 Jan	Balance b/d	12,000
			31 Dec	Profit and loss	4,000
		16,000			16,000
31 Dec	Balance c/d	20,000	1 Jan	Balance b/d	16,000
			31 Dec	Profit and loss	4,000
		20,000			20,000
			1 Jan	Balance b/d	20,000

(b) Balance sheet entries at 31 December:
    20-3   Vehicle 23,000 less depreciation 4,000 = 19,000
    20-4   Vehicle 23,000 less depreciation 8,000 = 15,000
    20-5   Vehicle 23,000 less depreciation 12,000 = 11,000
    20-6   Vehicle 23,000 less depreciation 16,000 = 7,000
    20-7   Vehicle 23,000 less depreciation 20,000 = 3,000

18.3 Machinery Account 1 Oct 20-7 balance b/d 12,800

Depreciation Account

20-5 30 Sep	Machinery	5,000	20-5 30 Sep	Profit and loss	5,000
20-6 30 Sep	Machinery	4,000	20-6 30 Sep	Profit and loss	4,000
20-7 30 Sep	Machinery	3,200	20-7 30 Sep	Profit and loss	3,200

Profit and loss account entries: 20-5 Depreciation 5,000
                                      20-6 Depreciation 4,000
                                        20-7 Depreciation 3,200

Balance sheet entries: 20-5 Machinery 25,000 less 5,000 = 20,000
                               20-6 Machinery 20,000 less 4,000 = 16,000
                               20-7 Machinery 16,000 less 3,200 = 12,800

18.4 (a)

Motor van Account

1 Jun	Bank	10,800	1 Jun	Disposal	10,800

Disposal Account

1 Jun	Motor van	10,800	1 Jun	Depreciation	7,600
			1 Jun	Cash	3,000
			31 May	Profit and loss	200
		10,800			10,800

(b) *Profit and loss account entries:*   (c) *Balance sheet entries:*
   20-6 Depreciation – Motor van 3,600 Motor van 10,800 – 3,600 = 7,200
   20-7 Depreciation – Motor van 2,400 Motor van 10,800 – 6,000 = 4,800
   20-8 Depreciation – Motor van 1,600 Motor van 10,800 – 7,600 = 3,200
   20-9 Loss on sale – Motor van 200

18.5 (a)

Machinery Account

4 Jan	Bank	15,500	3 Jan	Disposal	15,500

(c)

Disposal Account

3 Jan	Machinery	15,500	3 Jan	Depreciation	12,500
31 Dec	Profit and loss	250	3 Jan	Bank	3,250
		15,750			15,750

(d)

Profit and loss account entries: Balance sheet entries:
   20-5 Depreciation – Machinery 3,125 Machinery 15,500 – 3,125 = 12,375
   20-6 Depreciation – Machinery 3,125 Machinery 15,500 – 6,250 = 9,250
   20-7 Depreciation – Machinery 3,125 Machinery 15,500 – 9,375 = 6,125
   20-8 Depreciation – Machinery 3,125 Machinery 15,500 – 12,500 = 3,000
   20-9 Profit on sale – Machinery 250

18.6

Motor Lorries Account

1 Jan	Bank	4,800	1 Jan	Disposal	4,800
1 Jan	Bank	4,800	31 Dec	Balance c/d	9,600
1 Jan	Bank	4,800			
		14,400			14,400
1 Jan	Balance b/d	9,600			

Disposal Account

1 Jan	Motor lorries	4,800	1 Jan	Depreciation	1,800
			1 Jan	Bank	2,500
			31 Dec	Profit and loss	500
		4,800			4,800

Provision for Depreciation account – 1 January 20-9 Balance b/d 5,400

18.7

AB 101 T   500 per annum   CD 202 V   600 per annum
EF 303 W   400 per annum   GH 404 X   700 per annum

Profit and loss entries:
19-9 Depreciation – Motor van 500
20-0 Depreciation – Motor vans 1,100
20-1 Depreciation – Motor vans 1,000 Loss on sale of van 500
20-2 Depreciation – Motor vans 1,100 Profit on sale of van 200

Balance sheet entries:
19-9 Motor van 2,500 – 500 = 2,000
20-0 Motor vans 5,500 – 1,600 = 3,900
20-1 Motor vans 5,000 – 1,600 = 3,400
20-2 Motor vans 5,500 – 1,500 = 4,000

Unit 19

19.1

D. Nelson Account

1 Mar	Balance b/d	76.50	30 Mar	Bad debts	76.50

Bad Debts Account

30 Mar	D Nelson	76.50

19.2

Alan Senior Account

1 Nov	Balance b/d	350.00	30 Nov	Bank	175.00
			30 Nov	Bad debts	175.00
		350.00			350.00

Bad Debts Account

30 Nov	Alan Senior	175.00

19.3

A. Baxter Account

1 Apr	Balance b/d	175.00	15 Apr	Cash	78.75
			15 Apr	Bad debts	96.25
		175.00			175.00

Bad Debts Account

15 Apr	A Baxter	96.25

19.4

Bank Account

3 Aug	Bad debt (J London)	220.00

Bad Debts Account

3 Aug	Bank (J London)	220.00

19.5 (a) A new customer may be required to supply trade references or a bankers reference.
(b) Cash only basis or pro-forma invoice.

19.6
Bad Debts Account

30 Jun	A. Noble	160.00	1 Dec	Bank (P. Jones)	6.00
31 Aug	P. Jones	120.00	31 Dec	Profit and loss	654.00
31 Oct	R. Scott	250.00			
30 Nov	L. Skirrow	130.00			
		660.00			660.00

19.7
Bad Debts Account

31 Jul	J. Brown	220.40	31 Mar	Profit and loss	615.20
30 Sep	K. Lawson	157.50			
31 Dec	B. Nicholas	114.30			
28 Feb	M. Swan	123.00			
		615.20			615.20

19.8
Provision for Bad Debts Account

31 Dec	Balance c/d	450.00	31 Dec	Profit and loss	450.00
31 Dec	Balance c/d	500.00	1 Jan	Balance b/d	450.00
			31 Dec	Profit and loss	50.00
		500.00			500.00
			1 Jan	Balance b/d	500.00

Profit and loss entries:

20-5 Provision for bad debts 450

20-6 Provision for bad debts 50

Balance sheet entries:

Debtors 9,000 less 450 = 8,550

Debtors 10,000 less 500 = 9,500

19.9 (a)
Bad debts Account

20-1			20-1		
31 Dec	Sundry debtors	750.00	31 Dec	Profit and loss	750.00
20-2			20-2		
31 Dec	Sundry debtors	4,085.00	31 Dec	Profit and loss	4,085.00
20-3			20-3		
31 Dec	Sundry debtors	2,900.00	31 Dec	Profit and loss	2,900.00

(b)
Provision for Bad Debts Account

31 Dec 20-1	Balance c/d	700.00	1 Jan	Balance b/d	500.00
			31 Dec	Profit and loss	200.00
		700.00			700.00
31 Dec 20-2	Balance c/d	1,000.00	1 Jan	Balance b/d	700.00
			31 Dec	Profit and loss	300.00
		1,000.00			1,000.00
31 Dec	Profit and loss	250.00	1 Jan	Balance b/d	1,000.00

31 Dec	Balance c/d	750.00			
		1,000.00			1,000.00
			1 Jan	Balance b/d	750.00

(c) **Balance sheet entries:**
    20-1 Debtors 14,000 less provision 700 = 13,300
    20-2 Debtors 10,000 less provision 1,000 = 9,000
    20-3 Debtors 15,000 less provision 750 = 14,250

19.10   **Provision for Bad Debts Account**

30 Sep	Balance c/d	1,186.00	30 Sep	Profit and loss	1,186.00
30 Sep	Profit and loss	186.00	1 Oct	Balance b/d	1,186.00
30 Sep	Balance c/d	1,000.00			
		1,186.00			1,186.00
			1 Oct	Balance b/d	1,000.00

(b) **Profit and loss entries:**
  20-7 Bad debts 140
        Provision for bad debts 1,186
  20-8 Decrease provision 186
(c) Balance sheet entries:
      Debtors 11,860 less 1,186 = 10,674
      Debtors 10,000 less 1,000 = 9,000

19.11
(a) A debt that is considered irrecoverable is written off as a bad debt. A provision for doubtful debts is created to provide a reserve fund to guard against the possibility of some debtors failing to pay their debts.
(b) To be prepared for any future bad debts.
    A balance sheet should always present a true and fair view of the total debtors.
(c) A bad debt written off that is recovered at a later date. The amount recovered would be transferred to the credit side of the profit and loss account.

(d) (i)   **Provision for Bad Debts Account**

31 Dec	Profit and loss	100.00	1 Jan	Balance b/d	500.00
31 Dec	Balance c/d	400.00			
		500.00			500.00
31 Dec	Balance c/d	550.00	1 Jan	Balance b/d	400.00
			31 Dec	Profit and loss	150.00
		550.00			550.00
			1 Jan	Balance b/d	550.00

Profit and loss account entries:

20-4   Decrease provision 100   20-6   Increase provision 150

Unit 20

20.1   **Sales Ledger Control Account**

1 May	Balance b/d	4,760	31 May	Sales returns	423
31 May	Sales	5,912	31 May	Bank	3,969
			31 May	Discount allowed	179
			31 May	Bad debts	57
			31 May	Balance c/d	6,044
		10,672			10,672
1 Jun	Balance b/d	6,044			

20.2   **Purchase Ledger Control Account**

31 May	Purchase returns	324	1 May	Balance b/d	8,904
31 May	Bank	6,604	31 May	Purchases	7,038
31 May	Discount received	272			
31 May	Balance c/d	8,742			
		15,942			15,942
			1 Jun	Balance b/d	8,742

20.3 Totals: 19,750   Debit Balance b/d 6,950

20.4 Totals: 31,175   Credit Balance b/d 18,082

20.5 Sales ledger control account: Totals: 215,557
        Debit Balance b/d 8,224
        Purchase ledger control account: Totals: 150,293
        Credit Balance b/d 1,845

20.6 Totals: 24,368   Debit Balance b/d 6,736

20.7 Creditors' balances:
        A. Butler   693.65
        W. Dyson   446.19
        L. Grainger   835.24
                            1,975.08 = balance on purchase ledger control account

20.8 Debtors' balances:

    G. Anderson   1,103.30
    V. Ellis   727.46
    M. Hariman   1,090.42
                 2,921.18 = balance on sales ledger control account

Unit 21

21.1

Rent Account

4 Jan	Bank	500.00	1 Jan	Accrued b/d	500.00
3 Apr	Bank	500.00	31 Dec	Profit and loss	2,000.00
5 Jul	Bank	500.00			
8 Oct	Bank	500.00			
31 Dec	Accrued c/d	500.00			
		2,500.00			2,500.00
			1 Jan	Accrued b/d	500.00

21.2

Rates Account

4 Jan	Prepaid b/d	525.00	31 Dec	Profit and loss	2,250.00
30 Apr	Bank	1,150.00	31 Dec	Prepaid c/d	575.00
5 Oct	Bank	1,150.00			
		2,825.00			2,825.00
1 Jan	Prepaid b/d	575.00			

21.3 Totals: 2,090   Profit and loss 1,803

21.4 Totals: 1,625   Profit and loss 1,045

21.5 Totals: 2,466   Profit and loss 1,678

21.6 Totals: Rent 2,700   Profit and loss 2,700
       Totals: Rent received 675   Profit and loss 600

21.7 Totals: Rent 10,200   Profit and loss 10,200
       Totals: Rent received 2,704 Profit and loss 2,496
       Totals: Electricity 1,536   Profit and loss 1,262

21.8 Totals: Rent 5,712   Profit and loss 5,712
       Totals: Sundry expenses 2,854 Profit and loss 2,356
       Totals: Rates 3,678   Profit and loss 2,528
       Totals: Rent received 2,976 Profit and loss 2,480

Unit 22

22.1   Richard Martin Trading, profit and loss account for the year ended 31 December 20-5

	£	£	£
Sales			81,250
Less sales returns			509
			80,741
Less cost of goods sold:			
Stock		3,870	
Purchases	35,420		
Less purchase returns	724		
		34,696	
		38,566	
Less closing stock		6,094	
			32,472
Gross profit			48,269
Discount received			1,648
			49,917
Less expenses:			
Motor van depreciation (25,600 – 14,800 × 25%)		2,700	
Salaries		19,135	
Discount allowed		782	
Insurances (946 – 136)		810	
Telephone (584 + 230)		814	
Rates		1,650	
			25,891
Net profit			24,026

Balance sheet as at 31 December 20-5

	£	£	£
Fixed Assets			
Land and buildings			98,000
Fixtures and fittings			11,800
Motor vehicle		25,600	
Less depreciation (14,800 + 2,700)		17,500	8,100
			117,900
Current Assets			
Stock		6,094	
Debtors		6,290	
Insurance prepaid		136	
Bank		5,092	
Cash		758	
		18,370	
Less Current Liabilities			
Creditors	2,016		
Telephone accrued	230	2,246	
			16,124
			134,024
Financed by:			
Capital at 01.01.20-5			116,148
Add Net profit			24,026
			140,174
Less drawings			6,150
			134,024

22.2 Marcus Kline Profit and loss account for the year ended 31 July 20-6

	£	£
Commissions received		28,624
Rent received (3,960 + 792)		4,752
		33,376
Less expenses:		
Advertising	2,196	
General expense (1,538 + 104 − 260)	1,382	
Wages	11,824	
Loan interest	760	
Motor expenses (592 + 128)	720	
Depreciation: Equipment (6,280 × 15%)	942	
		17,824
Net Profit		15,552

Balance Sheet as at 31 July 20-6

Fixed Assets		
Premises		92,750
Office equipment	6,280	
Less depreciation (1,884 + 942)	2,826	
		3,454
Motor vehicle		8,500
		104,704
Current Assets		
Debtors	1,830	
Prepayment	260	
Accrued Revenue	792	
Bank	1,862	
Cash	570	
	5,314	
Less Current Liabilities		
Accruals (104 + 128)	232	
		5,082
		109,786

Financed by:

Capital at 01.08.20-5	94,804
Net profit	15,552
	110,356
Less drawings	10,070
	100,286

Long term liabilities

Loan	9,500
	109,786

22.3 Kate Devlin

Gross profit 33,063 Net profit 6,104
Fixed Assets 28,598 Current Assets 20,616
Current Liabilities 7,606

22.4 Tobias Ainsworth

Gross profit 39,161 Net loss 9,930
Fixed Assets 33,182 Current Assets 40,760
Current Liabilities 5,976 Long term liabilities 12,700

22.5 Helen Robinson

Gross profit 70,920 Net profit 34,221
Fixed Assets 181,025 Current Assets 37,656
Current Liabilities 15,706 Long term liabilities 10,800

22.6 David Towers

Gross profit 67,704 Net profit 31,394
Fixed Assets 141,273 Current Assets 39,634
Current Liabilities 7,313 Long term liabilities 10,250

22.7 Douglas Van Owen

Gross profit 67,195 Net profit 32,027
Fixed Assets 158,505 Current Assets 36,042
Current Liabilities 10,004 Long term liabilities 8,200

22.8 William McKay

Gross profit 63,754 Net profit 35,022
Fixed Assets 156,324 Current Assets 31,574
Current Liabilities 10,652 Long term liabilities 9,600

Unit 23

23.1 A. Teagle

Date	Journal Entries	Dr	Cr
4 Feb	Shop fittings Arthur Blake *Purchase on credit of new shop fittings.*	8,600	8,600
15 Feb	Peter Payne Shop fittings *Sale on credit of old shop fittings payable on 1 April 20-3.*	400	400
18 Feb	Bad debts Simon Bates *Irrecoverable debt written off*	51	51
29 Feb	Harry Albert Jones Henry Jones *Correction of error in posting*	210	210

23.2 Elaine Patterson

Date	Journal Entries	Dr	Cr
3 Jun	Office furniture Crescent Furniture Ltd *Purchase on credit of office furniture*	4,500	4,500
7 Jun	Bad debts Phillip Richards *Irrecoverable debt written off*	470	470
9 Jun	John Belling John Bell *Correction of error in posting*	150	150
10 Jun	Car Trader Motor van *Sale on credit of old motor van*	70	70

23.3 Percy Green

Opening Journal entry:

Assets 46,089   Liabilities 11,565   Capital 34,524

6 May	Dr	Fixtures	950	Cr	Micawber & Sons	950
8 May	Dr	Micawber & Sons	60	Cr	Fixtures	60
12 May	Dr	Bad debts	64	Cr	A. Baker	64
22 May	Dr	Gatt & Co	90	Cr	Fixtures	90
29 May	Dr	T. Davies	130	Cr	T. Davis	130

23.4 George Jones

7 May	Dr	Rent	40	Cr	Rates	40
16 May	Dr	Motor van	2,400	Cr	Purchases	2,400
18 May	Dr	Tom Boon	250	Cr	John Boon	250
22 May	Dr	Sales	45	Cr	Cash	45

23.5 David Robson

Opening Journal entry:

Assets 39,820   Liabilities 6,190   Capital 33,630

		Dr		Cr		
(i)	Dr	T. Marsden	350	Cr	T. Marsland	350
(ii)	Dr	Bank	95	Cr	F. Ryder	95
	Dr	Bad debts	380	Cr	F. Ryder	380
(iii)	Dr	Drawings	326	Cr	Purchases	176
				Cr	Cash	150
(iv)	Dr	B. Clifton	65	Cr	Discount allowed	65
(v)	Dr	D. Anderson	790	Cr	Bank	790

23.6 Tony Simms

Opening Journal entry:

Assets 146,970   Liabilities 14,050   Capital 132,920

		Dr		Cr		
7 May	Dr	Motor van	14,750	Cr	Cash	2,000
				Cr	Better Motors	12,750
14 May	Dr	A. Baker	250	Cr	Fixtures & fittings	250
18 May	Dr	Bad debts	194	Cr	J. Smith	194
21 May	Dr	Sales	125			
	Dr	Purchases	125	Cr	T. Murphy	250

23.7 John Jennings

		Dr		Cr		
3 Oct	Dr	Office equipment	6,265.00	Cr	Bank	1,566.25
				Cr	Mega Systems	4,698.75
10 Oct	Dr	Bank	120.70			
	Dr	Bad debts	482.80	Cr	I. Hardrup	603.50
15 Oct	Dr	Bank	650.00			
	Dr	R. Groves	1,300.00	Cr	Delivery van	1,950.00
31 Oct	Dr	Cash	198.00	Cr	M. Dyson	198.00
31 Oct	Dr	J. Clarkson	390.00	Cr	T. Clark	390.00

31 Oct	Dr	Profit and loss	2,074.00	Cr	General exps	2,074.00
31 Oct	Dr	Trading account	652.00	Cr	Carriage inwards	652.00
31 Oct	Dr	Profit and loss	890.00	Cr	Dis allowed	890.00

Unit 24

24.1
> (a) A trial balance has limitations. There are six types of errors which can occur that will not be revealed by taking out a trial balance.
> (b) Original error: Error of omission.   Compensating error.

24.2
> (a) A trial balance is a first sight indication of accuracy. It is a test only of the arithmetical accuracy of the postings.
> > (i) Debit column would be understated by the amount of the opening stock.
> > (ii) No effect – closing stock is not included in trial balance.
> (b) Recheck totals. Check location of balances, ie: debit balances incorrectly entered in credit column and vice versa.

24.3 **Terry Dennis**
> Trial balance totals: 57,634   Capital 25,486

24.4 **Andrew Scott**
Trial balance totals: 98,260

15 Jun	Dr	D. Smith	200	Cr	D. Smithson	200
13 Aug	Dr	Purchases	340	Cr	R. Wallis & Co.	340
24 Sep	Dr	Motor expenses	500	Cr	Motor vehicles	500
30 Oct	Dr	Drawings	200	Cr	Motor expenses	200

24.5 **Nicholas Davidson**
> Trial balance totals: 76,250   Capital 58,500

(i)	Dr	Drawings	162	Cr	General expenses	162
(ii)	Dr	Bank	36			
	Dr	Bad debts	204	Cr	A. Slowman	240
(iii)	Dr	Purchases	158	Cr	M. Ramsden	158
(iv)	Dr	T. Greenfield	350	Cr	F. Greenwood	350

24.6 **Moortown Enterprises**
Trial balance totals: 116,900   Capital 87,250

(i)	Dr	Rates	850	Cr	Bank	850
(ii)	Dr	Bank	72			
	Dr	Bad debts	408	Cr	D. Myers	480
(iii)	Dr	K Williamson	578	Cr	K. Williams	578
(iv)	Dr	Purchases	202	Cr	A. Oldridge	202
(v)	Dr	Drawings	253	Cr	Sundry expenses	253

24.7 **Weetwood Enterprises**
Trial balance totals: 62,740   Capital 41,630

(i)	Dr	R. Foxwood	76	Cr	Purchase returns	76
(ii)	Dr	M. Keller	485	Cr	M. Kellerman	485
(iii)	Dr	Bank	54			
	Dr	Bad debts	306	Cr	C. Gulliver	360
(iv)	Dr	Drawings	105	Cr	General expenses	105
(v)	Dr	G. Sanderson	18	Cr	Discount allowed	18

Unit 25

25.1

Ruth Sampson

Trial Balance as at 30 June 20-6

	Dr	Cr
Rent and rates	5,740	
Motor vehicles	12,390	
Purchases	24,058	
Bank loan		12,750
Drawings	6,925	
Bad debts	185	
Sales		63,294
Bank	1,736	
Cash	282	
Purchase returns		856
Wages	25,018	
Sales returns	604	
Loan interest	1,020	
Sundry expenses	2,596	
Capital		14,350
Discount allowed	218	
Fixtures and fittings	2,094	
Creditors		2,638
Debtors	7,024	
Discount received		742
Equipment	3,620	
	93,510	94,630
Suspense account	1,120	
	94,630	94,630

	Journal Entries	Dr	Cr
(i)	Rates Suspense *Direct debit for Rates omitted from nominal account.*	210	210
(ii)	Suspense S. Hanif *Credit note posted to personal account twice.*	98	98
(iii)	D. Cooper Suspense *Balance on D Cooper's account of £895 brought forward as £89.*	806	806
(iv)	Discount Allowed Suspense *Cash book total omitted from nominal account.*	202	202

Suspense Account

20-5		£	20-5		£
31 Mar	Trial Balance difference	1,120	31 Mar	Rates	210
31 Mar	S. Hanif	98	31 Mar	D. Cooper	806
			31 Mar	Discount allowed	202
		1,218			1,218

Revised Trial Balance as at 30 June 20-6

	Dr	Cr
Rent and rates (5,740 + 210)	5,950	
Motor vehicles	12,390	
Purchases	24,058	
Bank loan		12,750
Drawings	6,925	
Bad debts	185	
Sales		63,294
Bank	1,736	
Cash	282	
Purchase returns		856
Wages	25,018	
Sales returns	604	
Loan interest	1,020	
Sundry expenses	2,596	
Capital		14,350
Discount allowed (218 + 202)	420	
Fixtures and fittings	2,094	
Creditors (2,638 + 98)		2,736
Debtors (7,024 + 806)	7,830	
Discount received		742
Equipment	3,620	
	94,728	94,728

Richard Vincento

Trial Balance as at 31 May 20-5

	Dr	Cr
Equipment	15,780	
Debtors	6,847	
Salaries	27,506	
Creditors		1,216
Motor vehicles	14,394	
Purchases	21,072	
Rent and rates	6,530	
Bank loan		15,000
Commission received		1,750
General expenses	3,854	
Purchase returns		613
Loan interest	1,200	
Bad debts	192	
Sales		65,613
Drawings	9,296	
Bank	2,104	
Capital		24,450
Sales returns	726	
Discount allowed	208	
Discount received		590
Cash	436	
	110,145	109,232
Suspense		913
	110,145	110,145

	Journal Entries	Dr	Cr
(i)	Suspense Tee Jays *Correction of balance b/d on account.*	612	612
(ii)	Drawings General expenses *Repairs to owner's private car incorrectly posted to general expenses.*	204	204
(iii)	M. King Suspense *Sale omitted from personal account.*	105	105
(iv)	Suspense Purchase returns *PRD Book incorrectly totalled as £209 instead of £290.*	81	81
(v)	Suspense Sales *Sales invoice omitted in SDB*	325	325

Suspense Account

20-5		£	20-5		£
31 May	Tee Jays	612	31 May	Trial Balance	913
31 May	Purchase returns	81	31 May	M. King	105
31 May	Sales	325			
		1,018			1,018

Revised Trial Balance as at 31 May 20-5

	Dr	Cr
Equipment	15,780	
Debtors (6,847 + 105)	6,952	
Salaries	27,506	
Creditors (1,216 + 612)		1,828
Motor vehicles	14,394	
Purchases	21,072	
Rent and rates	6,530	
Bank loan		15,000
Commission received		1,750
General expenses (3,854 − 204)	3,650	
Purchase returns (613 + 81)		694
Loan interest	1,200	
Bad debts	192	
Sales (65,613 + 325)		65,938
Drawings (9,296 + 204)	9,500	
Bank	2,104	
Capital		24,450
Sales returns	726	
Discount allowed	208	
Discount received		590
Cash	436	
	110,250	110,250

25.3 Andrew Montague

Trial Balance	Dr	Cr
Totals	190,238.12	192,255.92
Suspense	2,017.80	

(i)	Dr Purchases	1,685.34	Cr Suspense	1,685.34
(ii)	Dr Bank	450.00	Cr Rent received	450.00
(iii)	Dr Suspense	174.68	Cr Creditors	174.68
(iv)	Dr General exps	196.20	Cr Insurance	19.62
			Cr Suspense	176.58
(v)	Dr Suspense	10.00	Cr Discount allowed	10.00
(vi)	Dr Aspin Bros	340.56	Cr Suspense	340.56

Revised Trial Balance	Dr	Cr
Totals	192,430.60	192,430.60

25.4 William Winrose

Trial Balance	Dr	Cr
Totals	186,713.40	185,174.14
Suspense		1,539.26

(i)	Dr	Suspense	531.72	Cr	J. Mills	531.72
(ii)	Dr	Sales returns	42.50	Cr	Suspense	42.50
(iii)	Dr	Suspense	359.28	Cr	Sales	359.28
(iv)	Dr	Electricity	74.60	Cr	Bank	74.60
(v)	Dr	Suspense	690.76	Cr	Creditors	690.76

Revised Trial Balance	Dr	Cr
Totals	186,830.50	186,830.50

25.5 Nicholas Barraclough

Trial Balance	Dr	Cr
Totals	161,404.12	162,177.22
Suspense	773.10	

(i)	Dr	Suspense	250.96	Cr	Debtors	250.96
(ii)	Dr	D. Stanley	140.72	Cr	Suspense	140.72
(iii)	Dr	Drawings	428.74	Cr	Sundry expenses	428.74
(iv)	Dr	Sales	950.00	Cr	Suspense	950.00
(v)	Dr	Carriage in	92.60	Cr	Sundry expenses	9.26
				Cr	Suspense	83.34
(vi)	Dr	Suspense	150.00	Cr	Commission rec'd	150.00

Revised Trial Balance	Dr	Cr
Totals	161,236.50	161,236.50

Unit 26

26.1 (a) Capital (b) Revenue (c) Capital (d) Revenue
(e) Revenue (f) Revenue

26.2 (a) Capital (b) Revenue (c) Revenue (d) Capital
(e) Revenue (f) Revenue (g) Capital (h) Revenue (i) Revenue

26.3 (a) Revenue expenditure (b) Capital expenditure
(c) Revenue receipt (d) Revenue receipt
(e) Revenue expenditure (f) Capital expenditure
(g) Capital expenditure (h) Revenue expenditure
(i) Capital receipt

26.4 (a) Capital (b) Revenue (c) Revenue (d) Revenue
(e) Capital (f) Revenue (g) Revenue (h) Revenue

26.5 (a) Revenue (b) Capital (c) Revenue (d) Revenue
(e) Capital (f) Revenue (g) Capital (h) Revenue

26.6 **Capital expenditure**   **Revenue expenditure**
Van   Road tax
Seat belts   Insurance
Delivery charges   Redecorate shop front
Number plates
Erect shelves in stockroom

26.7 (a) Capital (b) Revenue (c) Revenue (d) Capital
(e) Capital (f) Capital (g) Capital (h) Revenue
(i) Revenue

26.8 (i)   Revenue expenditure   Trading account
(ii) Capital expenditure   Balance sheet
(iii) Revenue expenditure   Profit and loss account
(iv) Capital expenditure   Balance sheet

26.9 (i)   Revenue expenditure   Profit and loss account
(ii) Capital expenditure   Balance sheet
(iii) Capital expenditure   Balance sheet
(iv) Revenue expenditure   Trading account
(v)   Capital expenditure   Balance sheet
(vi) Revenue expenditure   Profit and loss account

Unit 27

27.1

Oakdale Youth Club

(a) **Receipts and payments account for the year ended
31 December 20-4**

1 Jan	Balance b/d	460		Electricity	905
	Subscriptions	1,704		Repairs to equipment	138
	Annual fete	852		Motor expenses	496
				New equipment	420
				Postage & stationery	184
				Insurance	375
				General expenses	118
			31 Dec	Balance c/d	380
		3,016			3,016

(b) **Income and expenditure account for the year ended
31 December 20-4**

Electricity (905 + 107)	1,012	Subscriptions	1,704
Repairs to equipment	138	Annual fete	852
Motor expenses	496		
Postage & stationery	184		
Insurance (375 – 115)	260		
General expenses	118		
Surplus	348		
	2,556		2,556

(c) Accumulated fund at 1 January 20-4 – £7,600

(d)   **Balance sheet as at 31 December 20-4**

Fixed Assets			Accumulated fund		
Furn & fittings	1,500		at 1 Jan 20–4	7,600	
Games equipment	1,060		Add surplus	348	7,948
Motor van	5,000	7,560			
Current Assets			Current Liabilities		
Insurance prepaid	115		Electricity accrued		107
Bank	380	495			
		8,055			8,055

27.2 (a) ***Northside Sports Club*** – bank balance at 31 May 20-9 – £3,970

(b) **Bar trading account for the year ended 31 May 20-9**

	£	£
Sales		2,836
Stock	708	
Purchases	1,574	
	2,282	
Less closing stock	692	1,590
Profit on bar to income and expenditure		1,246

(c) **Income and Expenditure account for the year ended 31 May 20-9**

	£	£
Profit on bar		1,246
Subscriptions		3,750
Annual dance		974
Locker rents		548
Competition fees		396
		6,914
Less expenses:		
Expenses of annual dance	432	
Rent (1,595 + 145)	1,740	
Prizes for competitions	158	
Sundry expenses (612 – 76)	536	
Insurance (495 – 78)	417	
		3,283
Surplus		3,631

(d) Accumulated fund at 1 June 20-8 – £3,994

(e) **[Balance Sheet as at 31 May 20-9]**

	£	£
Fixed Assets		
Sports equipment		1,580
Furniture (1,090 + 360)		1,450
		3,030
Current Assets		
Stock	692	
Insurance prepaid	78	
Bank	3,970	
	4,740	
Less Current Liabilities		
Rent accrued	145	
		4,595
		7,625
Financed by:		
Accumulated fund at 01.06.08		3,994
Add Surplus		3,631
		7,625

27.3 Ambrose Cricket Club
    (a) Receipts and payments account: balance at 31 May 20-5: 8,702
    (b) Income and expenditure account: surplus 3,086
    (c) Accumulated fund at 1 June 20-4 – 84,815
    (d) Fixed assets 79,195   Current assets 8,755   Current liabilities 49

27.4 Adelmead Tennis Club
    (a) Receipts and payments account: balance at 31 December 20-2: 2,437
    (b) Income and expenditure account: surplus 1,795
    (c) Fixed assets 9,411   Current assets 2,544   Current liabilities 85

27.5 Woodside Sports Club
    (i)   Receipts and payments account: balance at 31 May 20-7: 5,735
    (ii) Income and expenditure account: surplus 3,872
    (iii) Fixed assets 1,140   Current assets 5,770   Current liabilities 800

27.6 Lawnswood Tennis Club
    (a) Bar trading account: profit on bar: 2,764
    (b) Receipts and payments account: balance at 31 October 20-7: 18,624
    (c) Income and expenditure account: surplus 21,763

Unit 28

28.1 Tony Simms
Gross profit ratio: 50.48

28.2 Ruth Sampson
(i)   Net profit ratio: 26.23
(ii)   Rent and rates expense ratio: 16.14
(iii)   Salaries ratio: 26.93

28.3 John King
(i)   Gross profit ratio: 59.16
(ii)   Net profit ratio: 24.61
(iii)   Advertising expense ratio: 2.61
(iv)   Heat and light expense ratio: 3.84

28.4 Richard Martin
(i)   Gross profit ratio: 59.78
(ii)   Rate of stock turnover: 6.52
(iii)   Net profit ratio: 29.76
(iv)   Expense ratio – salaries: 23.70
(v)   Return on Capital Employed ratio: 17.93
(vi)   Current ratio: 8.18
(vii)   Acid test ratio: 5.47
(viii) Debtors' collection period in days: 28 days
(ix)   Creditors' payment period in days: 21 days

28.5 Kate Devlin
(i)   Gross profit ratio: 56.09
(ii)   Rate of stock turnover: 5.21
(iii)   Net profit ratio: 10.36
(iv)   Expense ratio – rent and rates: 12.16
(v)   Return on Capital Employed ratio: 14.67
(vi)   Current ratio: 2.71
(vii)   Acid test ratio: 2.02
(viii) Debtors' collection period in days: 84 days
(ix)   Creditors' payment period in days: 62 days

28.6 Helen Robinson
(i)   Gross profit ratio: 72.41
(ii)   Rate of stock turnover: 2.57
(iii)   Net profit ratio: 34.94
(iv)   Return on Capital Employed ratio: 16.86
(v)   Current ratio: 2.40
(vi)   Acid test ratio: 1.63
(vii)   Debtors' collection period in days: 96 days
(viii) Creditors' payment period in days: 115 days

28.7 David Towers
    (i)   Gross profit ratio: 69.54
    (ii)   Rate of stock turnover: 2.80
    (iii)   Net profit ratio: 32.25
    (iv)   Return on Capital Employed ratio: 18.08
    (v)   Current ratio: 5.42
    (vi)   Acid test ratio: 3.98
    (vii) Debtors' collection period in days: 93 days
    (viii) Creditors' payment period in days: 93 days

28.8 Douglas Van Owen
    (i)   Gross profit ratio: 68.59
    (ii)   Rate of stock turnover: 3.09
    (iii)   Net profit ratio: 32.69
    (iv)   Return on Capital Employed ratio: 17.35
    (v)   Current ratio: 3.60
    (vi)   Acid test ratio: 2.63
    (vii) Debtors' collection period in days: 96 days
    (viii) Creditors' payment period in days: 92 days

28.9 William McKay
    (i)   Gross profit ratio: 67.59
    (ii)   Rate of stock turnover: 4.05
    (iii)   Net profit ratio: 37.13
    (iv)   Return on Capital Employed ratio: 19.76
    (v)   Current ratio: 2.96
    (vi)   Acid test ratio: 2.31
    (vii) Debtors' collection period in days: 88 days
    (viii) Creditors' payment period in days: 130 days

■ Ⅳ Index